ROUTLEDGE LIBRARY EDITIONS:
HISTORIOGRAPHY

Volume 1

FOUNDATIONS OF MODERN HISTORICAL THOUGHT

FOUNDATIONS OF MODERN HISTORICAL THOUGHT
From Machiavelli to Vico

PAUL AVIS

LONDON AND NEW YORK

First published in 1986 by Croom Helm

This edition first published in 2016
by Routledge
4 Park Square, Milton Park, Abingdon, Oxon OX14 4RN
605 Third Avenue, New York, NY 10017

Routledge is an imprint of the Taylor & Francis Group, an informa business

© 1986 Paul Avis

All rights reserved. No part of this book may be reprinted or reproduced or utilised in any form or by any electronic, mechanical, or other means, now known or hereafter invented, including photocopying and recording, or in any information storage or retrieval system, without permission in writing from the publishers.

Trademark notice: Product or corporate names may be trademarks or registered trademarks, and are used only for identification and explanation without intent to infringe.

British Library Cataloguing in Publication Data
A catalogue record for this book is available from the British Library

ISBN: 978-1-138-99958-9 (Set)
ISBN: 978-1-315-63745-7 (Set) (ebk)
ISBN: 978-1-138-18960-7 (Volume 1) (hbk)
ISBN: 978-1-138-18961-4 (Volume 1) (pbk)
ISBN: 978-1-315-64151-5 (Volume 1) (ebk)

Publisher's Note
The publisher has gone to great lengths to ensure the quality of this reprint but points out that some imperfections in the original copies may be apparent.

Disclaimer
The publisher has made every effort to trace copyright holders and would welcome correspondence from those they have been unable to trace.

Foundations of Modern Historical Thought
FROM MACHIAVELLI TO VICO

PAUL AVIS

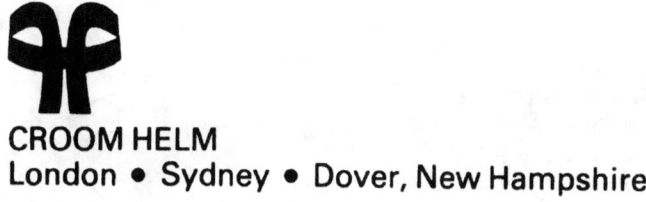

CROOM HELM
London • Sydney • Dover, New Hampshire

© Paul Avis 1986
Croom Helm Ltd, Provident House, Burrell Row,
Beckenham, Kent BR3 1AT
Croom Helm Australia Pty Ltd, Suite 4, 6th Floor,
64-76 Kippax Street, Surry Hills, NSW 2010 Australia

British Library Cataloguing in Publication Data
Avis, Paul D. L.
  Foundations of modern historical thought:
  from Machiavelli to Vico.
  1. History — Philosophy 2. Authors, European
  — Early modern, 1500-1700
  I. Title
  901   D16.9
ISBN 0-7099-0581-5

Croom Helm, 51 Washington Street, Dover,
New Hampshire 03820, USA

Library of Congress Cataloging in Publication Data applied for

Filmset in English Times
by Patrick and Anne Murphy,
Walkford, Christchurch, Dorset.

Printed and bound in Great Britain
by Billing & Sons Limited, Worcester.

CONTENTS

Preface

Introduction: Medieval and Renaissance Harbingers of History   1

  1   Machiavelli: History and Power   30

  2   Bodin and Montaigne: Speculation and Introspection   52

  3   Bacon: Towards a Science of Man   61

  4   Hobbes: History and Reason   81

  5   History and Philosophy on the Eve of the Enlightenment   104

  6   Vico: The Harvest of Pre-Enlightenment History   132

Postscript   162

Bibliography   168

  Primary Texts   168

  Secondary Studies   170

Subject Index   181

Index of Names   183

PREFACE

This book offers an introduction in depth to the major historical thinkers — their philosophies of history, society and man — from the Renaissance to the eve of the Enlightenment. In combining detailed documentary study with critical comment and an overall perspective, it operates at the level of a 'sophisicated textbook'.

The discerning prospective reader will already be asking what is meant by the phrases 'historical thought' and 'historical thinkers'. These refer to the various aspects of the historical movement that this volume studies in its remoter origins. The historical movement includes the rise of historical consciousness — the sense of the past — side by side with a new awareness of the need for scientific research of the evidence. It involves a growing recognition of the diversity of human nature and forms of civilisation, resulting in the jettisoning of the ahistorical uniformitarian approach. It represents a broadening of the historian's perspective to include social, cultural and economic factors as well as the political and military ones that had been virtually the sole concern of medieval historians. Finally, the historical movement, especially in its Romantic phase, saw a new openness to, and fascination with, the more primitive and irrational springs of human behaviour. It entails thoughout a view of man and society and thus constitutes a broad segment of the history of modern thought.

In other words, this book deals with historical ideas, with the history of thinking about history, with the philosophy of history in the context of modern culture. It is not directly concerned with historical writing, historiography, and this comes into the picture only where, as in the case of Machiavelli and Guicciardini, historical narrative exemplifies underlying principles.

I have not attempted — at least in this volume — to offer a critique of the assumptions of the historical movement. This would be, no doubt, a very desirable exercise, but one that properly belongs to the philosopher of history rather than to the historian of ideas. The extent to which the broad principles of the historical movement have now become unquestioned assumptions for most of us is obvious from the way in which, when we want to understand a particular phenomenon, we automatically ask how it came

Preface

about. This evolutionary, genetic approach is axiomatic in modern thought.

The perspective of this book is, therefore, unashamedly retrospective. It attempts to chart the growth of the historical movement and the accompanying rise of historical consciousness and — except for purposes of contrast and context — does not dwell on lost causes or almost forgotten 'footnotes of history'. To say this is simply to make explicit what must be implicit in any historical enterprise. The way things turned out determines both our initial interest and our interpretation of the course of development. The history of ideas cannot be other than retrospective. There is something to be said, therefore, for reading the book backwards beginning with the Postscript, where the issues come into their clearest focus, and then at least glancing at the Vico chapter, the point at which the conflicting or converging material of earlier chapters reaches its resolution.

The substance of this book consists in the major set-piece accounts of such figures as Machiavelli, Bodin, Bacon, Hobbes, Locke and Vico where my method consists largely in exposition of the primary sources. But in order to give an overall perspective it was necessary to provide an introductory background chapter giving a synopsis of the main developments in medieval and Renaissance historical thought. Here my indebtedness to secondary studies will be apparent. Those familiar with this area and its secondary literature would be well advised to skip the first chapter and start at Machiavelli.

There are a great many specialised monographs and articles relating to the philosophy of history in this period and most of the primary texts are available in an English translation, but no other survey covers the ground at a comparable length and level, as far as I know.

Feuter's history of modern historiography appeared at the beginning of the century. It was translated from the original German into French, but not into English. Though a pioneering work, its detailed conclusions have been challenged so often by subsequent scholarship that it has acquired a reputation for tendentiousness. Feuter, of course, deals with historical writing rather than historical philosophy. Denys Hay's little book *Annalists and Historians* falls into the same category of historiography. While comprehensive — it covers a thousand years of historical writing — it is inevitably sketchy. I am not competing with Feuter or Hay, or indeed with the various American works claiming to offer 'the history of history'. On the other hand, the recent introduction to historical thought by B. A. Haddock can be thoroughly recommended. But it too is not on the same scale as my own project, covering as it does the whole field of historical thought from the Renaissance to the present in one modest-sized volume.

From Machiavelli to Vico has an intended sequel, provisionally entitled, *Enlightenment and History*, which will begin with the makers of the Enlightenment's philosophy of history (Fontenelle, Bolingbroke, Montesquieu), continue with the giants of Enlightenment history (Voltaire, Robertson, Hume and Gibbon), and conclude with those thinkers who seem to have one foot in the Enlightenment and another in Romanticism (Rousseau, Herder, Burke, Scott and Macaulay).

I have tried to pitch this book at level that will both commend it to students beginning the study of historical thought (by dividing up the material under subheadings, giving dates of the thinkers discussed, using translations of the primary texts, and not assuming a great deal of background knowledge), and at the same time extend its usefulness to those who wish to pursue the subject further (by close reference to the central texts rather than potted summaries, detailed analysis of the arguments and generous reference to more specialised treatments). The themes and thinkers covered form the essential background to issues in the philosophy of history that are very much alive today.

The bibliography is an essential part of the book. All references are incorporated in the text. Authors are cited simply by name, full details being given in the bibliography. In the case of authors of more than one book used, a short title or code title is given. The bibliography is divided into two parts: primary texts and secondary studies. If any reader is not certain to which category a given name belongs, he should start with a simpler introduction! The references that litter the text are no doubt untidy, but not as inconvenient as other methods. They should be regarded not only as authorities for my statements but as pointers to further reading.

I would like to think that I have tried to do for history what Basil Willey did so successfully for literature in his celebrated 'Background' books. How far I have succeeded in this aim is for others to judge.

Paul Avis
Stoke Canon Vicarage, Exeter

Preface to the re-issue of 2016

When I was approached, out of the blue, by the publishers about a re-issue of *Foundations of Modern Historical Thought*, I responded with rather mixed feelings. On the one hand, it is heartening to know that the publishers believe that, as a 'sophisticated textbook', it could still be useful to students and general readers around the world. I hope that many readers will share the fascination and enthusiasm that I felt, when I worked on it as a young scholar, for the thinkers and problems that it covers, *From Machiavelli to Vico*, an enthusiasm and fascination that is undiminished in my mind today.

On the other hand, in the more than thirty years since I finished writing the book, a vast amount of literature has been published in this area, in both primary sources and secondary studies, and a simple re-issue of a title does not allow me to correct, revise or expand my text. Besides supplementing the text and bibliography from more recent literature, I am sure that I would have had second thoughts about some of my judgements and ways of putting things. For example, I have come to a very different view of Thomas Hobbes' stance vis à vis Christianity and the Church of England in my recent work *In Search of Authority: Anglican Theological Method from the Reformation to the Enlightenment* (Bloomsbury T&T Clark, 2014).

However, I have in fact been able to add a short section to the chapter on Giambattista Vico, entitled 'Vico's Theology of History', with a small supplement of additional titles to the bibliography. Without this section my exposition of Vico would have remained incomplete and in one respect misleading. It was all the more necessary to do this because some recent writers, mentioned in that new section, have mistakenly cast Vico as a secular thinker of the radical Enlightenment. He was, I believe, a Catholic thinker and a Christian apologist. His great work, the *New Science*, expounds a theology of history.

In my original Preface I mention my hopes for writing a sequel to the present volume, covering the development of historical thought in the Enlightenment. Alas, I have not yet written that book. Instead, I have moved more deeply and consistently into Christian theology, producing a number of books and articles in the fields of Anglican and Reformation historical theology, and ecumenical and philosophical theology, over the past thirty years. However,

In Search of Authority engages with the Enlightenment, providing a reassessment by distinguishing between what I call 'the Christian Enlightenment', which took place mainly in England and Germany, and the secular, anti-clerical, deistic or atheistic Enlightenment of the French *Philosophes*. In that recent work I cover several figures from the Enlightenment period, including Edmund Burke, and touch on their perspectives on history. I am working on a sequel to that volume. It begins with the influence of the Romantic movement, particularly Sir Walter Scott and William Wordsworth, on Anglican thought in the early nineteenth century, and continues with detailed expositions of such Anglican thinkers of the period as Samuel Taylor Coleridge, Frederick Denison Maurice and John Henry Newman, bringing out the significance of historical research and the philosophy of history for their theological methodology and their contribution to modern thought generally.

Paul Avis
22 September 2015

INTRODUCTION: MEDIEVAL AND RENAISSANCE HARBINGERS OF HISTORY

Intimations of Modernity

To put the historical movement in perspective, you first have to define your perspective. In the history of ideas everything is related to everything else, but to keep his exercise within manageable bounds the historian has to set some limits. Take, for example, the idea of individuality. The sense of the significance of the individual in history is particularly characteristic of the Romantic movement of the early nineteenth century, reaching its extreme form in the cult of the hero as we find it in the thought of Fichte or Carlyle. But we can trace the concept of individuality back, in both secular and religious forms, to its remote origins — through, for example, Montaigne's amiable egocentrism and the Renaissance quest for completeness of individual culture, on the one hand, and the protestant stress on personal faith and Luther's notion of the *Wundermann*, God's instrument to change the world, on the other. From the powerful egotism of Abelard and the intense subjectivity of Augustine, we can push the idea of individuality back to the New Testament's concern for the individual who must work out his own salvation. But why stop there? To complete the picture, one would need to look also at the classical antecedents of the Renaissance and the Old Testament background of the New.

In a similar way, the grasp of pattern and purpose in history that belongs to the fully fledged historicism of, shall we say, Ranke in the nineteenth century, surely stems ultimately from the Old Testament's prophetic sense of God's dealings with the nations of the world (Butterfield, *Origins*). A complete genealogy of the idea of purpose in history would be nothing less than a history of Christian philosophy of history.

If the ramifications of any one idea in history are so extensive, arbitrary limits have to be set. For our purposes, the Renaissance provides a suitable point of departure.

The effect of recent research into the development of historical thought has been to push the origins of modern historical consciousness further and further back into the past — from nineteenth-century historicism to the Enlightenment, from the

Enlightenment to the seventeenth century, from the seventeenth century to the Renaissance (Kelley, *Foundations*; Franklin, *Bodin*; Huppert, *Idea*). As George Nadel has argued, the originality of eighteenth-century achievements in this field has been exaggerated:

> Even scholars like Ernst Cassirer and Friedrich Meinecke cited as new and revolutionary certain ideas put forward by men like Bayle and Hume which, in fact, were merely paraphrases or quotations from the classics, drearily familiar to any educated person living between the Renaissance and the nineteenth century. (p. 292)

But the process cannot stop at the Renaissance. The Renaissance itself must be seen as the last and greatest flowering of a movement of cultural and political renewal that emerges from deep in the medieval past, from the twelfth century and before (Ullmann, *Individual* and *Foundations*; Bolgar; Southern, *Medieval Humanism*; Morris; Knowles, *Historian*; Haskins).

Here our concern is strictly limited to the medieval antecedents of the Renaissance sense of history. The thinkers of the Renaissance drew, consciously and unconsciously, on their medieval heritage, sometimes intensifying it to create a new focus, sometimes transcending it altogether. Even where they reacted against it to the point of rejection, as Petrarch did when he labelled the medieval period the 'dark ages' of ignorance and barbarity, it was no doubt some congenial and suggestive strand in the rich harvest of medieval thought that empowered them to do so. At the risk of crude oversimplification, let us briefly summarise the legacy of medieval thought to the emergent sense of history at the Renaissance.

Individualism

In the evolution of historical thought, the discovery (or rediscovery) of the values of individuality was an obvious prerequisite for appreciation of the significance of human life in this world in all its particularity. While we tend to think of the Renaissance as the first great flourishing of individualism — the second being the Romantic movement — we are compelled to recognise that in this respect, as in others, the fifteenth century was anticipated by the twelfth — and the twelfth century was the beneficiary of feudalism which, on account of its system of reciprocal rights and duties, provided a seed-bed for the idea of individual citizenship (Ullmann, *Individual*, Ch. 2). In the high middle ages it was the challenge of social change that precipitated an upsurge of individual self-consciousness. In a Christian society, that inevitably found expression in a concern for right motivation (in Christian terms, 'intention') leading to a stronger insistence on the practice of confession (Morris, p. 73).

Significantly, autobiographical writings begin to appear in the twelfth century. In the *City of God* (pp. 498ff) Augustine had taken the unique destiny of the individual human life as a paradigm of the unique particularity of the course of history in arguing against cyclical theories of history. Now in the shadow of the intense subjectivity of Augustine's *Confessions*, certain individuals caught up in the movement of monastic renewal and the call to a new life gave expression to their strong sense of individual vocation and made a written record of their inner struggles. As Morris has remarked, as early as the tenth century the monastic reformers, in offering to young men of the nobility an alternative way of life and system of values, caused some of outstanding gifts to find themselves as individuals (p. 32). From Odo of Cluny, Otloh of St Emmeram and Hermann of Cologne to the better-known example of Abelard's 'Historia Calamitatem' (*Letters*), we witness a widespread tendency among the intelligentsia to examine and publish one's personal experiences.

In the field of biography too, the eleventh and twelfth centuries saw a move away from stylised portraits of the saints — largely exercises in typology — to a greater recognition of the variety and individuality of human nature. In the middle ages, biography — or more accurately, hagiography — was a means of exhibiting the dominant ecclesiological framework of medieval life by portraying the subject as a baptismally reborn creature, his natural humanity being but faintly visible. As the attention to robes and regalia in medieval portraiture reveals, the subject was significant for his office and function in society, not for anything as anachronistic as personality (Ullmann, *Individual*, p. 44). But a new interest in individual humanity — presaged by Peter Damian's life of Romuald and William of Malmesbury's biographical exercises, for example — would bring about a flourishing of the biographical form and the convention of preserving the unique characteristics of near-contemporaries such as Dante or Petrarch (Ullmann, *Foundations*, pp. 69f; Morris, pp. 32, 79ff). The extent of the shift of interest that had taken place by the time we reach the early fifteenth century is signalled by the spate of translations of Plutarch's *Lives* into Latin among the Italian humanists, followed a century later by translation into the vernacular, French and English, by Jacques Amyot (1559) and Sir Thomas North (1579) respectively.

Secularism

One legacy of Augustine and patristic Christianity to the middle ages was a dualism of the earthly and the heavenly, the natural and the spiritual, the earthly city and the city of God. Man's true end was redemption from the earthly city and membership of the city of God. But Augustine had not condemned the earthly, natural sphere in which even the elect were called to live out their temporal existence, as the sectarian movements from Montanism to Donatism had. He had neutralised it and left it weak and ripe for occupation. In absorbing imperial and prophetic hopes during the middle ages, it was strengthened and freed from dependence on the spiritual — in other words, secularised (cf. Pocock, *Moment*, pp. 42ff; Markus).

One aspect of this secularisation process drew its initial impulse from a reaction against the attempted sacralisation of society in the Carolingian renaissance, which was an attempt to achieve a baptismal regeneration of society, to create an ecclesiological empire. Where ecclesiastical dominance had been strongest — that is, in the sphere of government and administration — a reaction began that sought its inspiration, not in the Bible or canon law, but in the models of antiquity and Roman law. It was a movement to recognise the validity of a purely human 'unregenerate' society, freed from ecclesiological constraints. Gaining confidence from the study of classical literature, it began to fill the vacuum created by the church's dualism of earthly and heavenly. Here we detect the beginnings of civic humanism, a movement not in essence antichristian but certainly anti-scholastic and fundamentally opposed to the hierarchical character of medieval sacral society. Against the holistic worldview that drew the whole of human life to one transcendent focus, it affirmed the validity and inherent worth of the natural (*naturalia*), the human (*humana*) and the this-wordly (*mundana*). This assertion of the autonomy of the natural order is of the essence of medieval humanism (Southern, *Medieval Humanism*, p. 57).

But it is significant that it was within the Christian cosmos that the thinkers of the central middle ages made a place for these things, reasserting the immanence of God in the world and redressing the balance between nature and grace. It was none other than St Thomas Aquinas who gave theological articulation to this reassessment of the natural, following on here from the interest that his master, Albert the Great, had evinced in natural phenomena, in physiology and psychology. As Walter Ullmann has remarked, 'Precisely because Thomas rehabilitated natural man, his doctrines can be said without fear of gainsaying to constitute the opening bars of Renaissance humanism' (*Foundations*, p. 100). Aquinas serves to remind us that a positive attitude towards civic life was not the sole prerogative of the humanists; scholastic philosophers and theologians also contributed to the growth of a civic mentality (Seigel, p. 241).

The inspiration of antiquity focused on the figures of Aristotle and Cicero. The rediscovery of Aristotle's political thought in the first half of the thirteenth century provided a complete secular theory, a *pièce justificative* for humanism with its twin pillars of the natural ends of man and the secular foundations of society. Together with Aristotle, Cicero was the greatest influence on civic thought, providing not only a theoretical expression of the humanist ideal, but also embodying in himself what it meant to live the unadulterated life of the natural man in his *vita activa* as citizen.

Relativism

The worldview presupposed by both Platonism and Aristotelianism was static, timeless and permanent. But in fact both streams of thought contained the seeds of change. Platonism provided a vision of life that made scholastic systematising uncongenial. As 'a moral meditation on life shot through with hope', and impinging more on mythology than on logic, Platonism lent itself to creative exploratory thinking and became the focal point for dissatisfaction with a closed, ordered and static world (Garin, p. 10). Aristotelianism too, as we have just noted, fostered interest in the political, civic dimension of man's life in the world. As a political animal, he was responsible for his social environment and had the making of his earthly destiny.

Once we admit the possibility of change we thereby relativise the world familiar to us and set our own age and the ages that preceded it in an historical perspective. In the late middle ages this process was intensified by travel outside Christendom and by the rise of vernacular literature. Reports by missionaries, explorers, merchants and ambassadors to the East (as later to the New World) were avidly devoured — one of the most celebrated examples being the *Travels* of Marco Polo. What their readers wanted was a description of 'unadorned existence' (Ullmann, *Foundations*, p. 79), the purely natural, this-worldy phenomena of civic, cultural and economic life. The increasing volume of vernacular writings, together with translation from one vernacular into another, inevitably helped to sharpen men's awareness of the differences of customs, habits and outlooks between neighbouring peoples, thus reflecting and simultaneously intensifying a nascent sense of national identity, of nationhood (Ullmann, *Foundations*, p. 75).

At the same time, the critical mentality of early Renaissance humanism enabled scholars to detach themselves from currently unquestioned assumptions, as, for example, Lorenzo Valla did when he finally announced that he had had enough of commenting on Aristotle, refining and polishing the logic of the Philosopher, as though there were no alternative. Aristotle's logic was only one way among many: he had done with it. Just as in this way Valla relativised Aristotle, Pico della Mirandola relativised astrology (Kristeller; Cassirer, 'Pico'). By showing how the science of astrology had originated, developed and become what it then was, he evacuated it of its mystique. Comparisons across cultures or across time had the same effect: the scholar who relativised was acting as the harbinger of history.

The Character of Medieval History

With a few outstanding exceptions, educated men in the middle ages did not construe their existence historically. Their world was structured not temporally but hierarchically, in terms of being rather than becoming. The medieval historian or chronicler recorded the doings of his world *sub specie aeternitatis*. He celebrated an ordered cosmos and took his place alongside philosophers, churchmen, poets and kings as one more exponent of universal harmony. Critical use of evidence, sensitivity to anachronism and a sense of causation in history were all in their infancy.

Evidence

Although it is not difficult to point to exceptions, such as the methodical research of Bede or of the post-Conquest monastic scholars in England who sought to validate the independence of their houses by historical proofs (Southern, *Medieval Humanism*, pp. 160f; 'Aspects', IV, pp. 246f), it is broadly true to say that medieval history was untroubled by the constraints of methodical research. Where documentary material was inserted in the narrative, following the model of Eusebius, it was employed in a non-critical way as an authority to which deference was due. For the medieval scholar with his textual concept of truth, appeal to authority held the place occupied in later historical method by demonstration of evidence. Or, to put the same point another way, the evidence to which the medieval historian appealed was the evidence of accumulated authorities — the Bible, the Fathers, Aristotle (latterly) and the Schoolmen. No clear distinction could be made between fact and myth, authentic and forged documents. Deeply indebted as it was to the rhetorical tradition of classical thought, medieval history assimilated what seemed appropriate and was guided by a sense of what was fitting.

Anachronism

Medieval history lacked a sense of historical perspective; it was not conscious of anachronism. Both historical monuments (ruins, for example) and historical documents (the Bible, laws) were accepted as, so to speak, contemporaneous with the present. Ruins were simply there and always had been. There was no call to enquire how they got there or to wonder what sort of people had once inhabited them. The Bible was invariably interpreted allegorically, reducing it to a function of medieval man's spiritual and moral requirements, eliminating its historical particularity. Law codes were not recognised as the product of circumstance, but regarded as almost outside time, to be manipulated to give answers to contemporary questions by tearing precedents out of their original context (cf. Peter Burke, *Renaissance*, pp. 1ff; Haskins, pp. 224–77). Everything is on the same temporal level. As Beryl Smalley has remarked,

> The student of medieval historiography gets used to living in an intellectual world in which he can converse with Adam and Eve or Julius Caesar or Charlemagne as though they were neighbours. As soon as we know our historian, we know how he will imagine the past; it will look like the present.

Not until the fourteenth century, she adds, did this sense of continuity snap (pp. 192f).

R. W. Southern has pointed to the impressive historical endeavours of the monastic houses in England after the Norman Conquest as exhibiting an authentic sense of the past — the work of William of Malmesbury being a celebrated example. Social upheaval at the Conquest, generating feelings of outrage, resentment and nostalgia, produced a powerful sense of a lost heritage — but one that historical study could restore, thereby strengthening the threatened integrity of the community. The prime object of this great effort of historical research, writes Southern, was to connect the community with its past by making its physical being — buildings, monuments, inscriptions, documents — 'a vehicle for the remembrance of a great army of benefactors, craftsmen, saints and enemies. The aim was a total recall of the past in order to give the community its identity in the present' ('Aspects', IV, pp. 246f, esp. p. 256). While accepting Southern's argument that this movement constituted a remarkable anticipation of the reconstructive history that came to fruition in post-Romantic historicism, I would point out that all the emphasis here falls on the continuities of history — the sense of temporal distance that gives rise to the concept of anachronism is minimal.

Causation

The medieval historians were not concerned to penetrate behind the providential or prophetic pattern of the events they were recording to exhibit secondary causes in human motivation or external circumstances. The sense of causation — like the discriminating use of sources and the concept of anachronism — was a casualty of the rigorous subordination of historical method to a pervasive didactic motive.

In his *Chronicle into History*, Louis Green has captured a sense of the limitations and also of the sterling achievement of the medieval chronicler:

> Unpretentiously, the chroniclers, apologetic for their lack of erudition and literary sophistication, claimed to do no more than set down the facts that had come to their notice in the strict order of their occurrence. They wrote in the vernacular for an audience of men like themselves, trained for a business career and experienced in the ways of the world, but outside the ambit of learning. (pp. 3f)

Green detects, at least as far as fifteenth-century Florentine chroniclers are concerned, a gradual and largely unconscious drift towards a more objective approach and a shift in standpoint from immersion in history to contemplation of it (p. 7). Steady refinement of the chronicler's method thus brought him to the verge of historical consciousness in the modern sense. But until he was prepared to exchange his transcendental theological interpretation for an immanental rational one, the chronicler could advance no further. It was precisely humanism's appreciation of the natural and the secular that would trigger off a breakthrough in historical study.

Humanist History

The humanists did not yet part company with the chroniclers in the matter of historical accuracy — they still sat fairly lightly to the discipline of research into sources — or over the didactic purpose of historical writing — humanist historiography remained a branch of rhetoric. But they broke with the providential concept of history and accepted a new secular framework which included an alternative periodisation based on the fall of the Roman empire and the rise of the city states, in place of the biblical chronology projected into the Christian era by means of the Four Monarchies of Daniel. As the new urban laymen they were not primarily interested in supernatural explanations, and their sympathy for the ages of faith was limited. The middle ages — the era of saints and miracles — were glossed over: what fired the humanist historians was the continuity between classical culture and their own age of cultural rebirth (Gilbert, *MG*.; W. Ferguson, pp. 3f; Wilcox, Ch. 1).

The study of antiquity had begun in the twelfth century in the search for guidance as to how a purely human ('unregenerate') society might be ordered and governed, as part of the reaction among intellectuals to the attempted sacralisation of society that had, as Ullman puts it, washed away the natural order in the waters of baptism (*Foundations*, pp. 10, 107, 113f). While the writings of antiquity had of course been available during the middle ages, it was only when they were scrutinised with a view to making a direct comparison between the classical world and the Christian empire that the sense of historical distance began to be acutely felt. The original civic and political motive behind humanist scholarship gave way in due course to more strictly aesthetic motives — admiration for the literary achievements of antiquity leading to the desire to experience them in their full integrity. The result, however, was the same: the broadly applied humanist method of setting a given text in its original context had the effect of deepening a nascent awareness of historical perspective and awakening a new sensitivity to anachronism. From this basic feeling for the pastness of the past, a principle of historical relativism would eventually emerge.

Furthermore, the Renaissance ideal of the cultured and accomplished individual brought historical studies into the forefront of required reading. History seemed to unite the interests of the life of action with those of the life of letters — and Renaissance man aspired to both. History was a political and moral education. 'A complete familiarity with universal history was now regarded as a fundamental obligation of the educated man' (Franklin, *Bodin*, p. 3).

As the dominantly educational purpose of history in the Renaissance suggests, the humanists perpetuated the view of history as moral *exempla* that the ancients had bequeathed to the middle ages. Cicero was quoted to the effect that 'history is full of precedents [*exempla*] in so far as it relates to commonly experienced life', and the wisdom of Seneca was retailed that life should be taught by examples, for 'long is the way if one follows exhortations, but short and efficacious if one follows patterns'. Knowledge of the past (*scientia rerum gestarum*), asserted Salutati, the humanist statesman of fifteenth-century Florence, shows how one should conduct oneself as a citizen and should therefore form part of a citizen's education (Ullmann, *Foundations*, pp. 161f). For the humanists, as for the chroniclers, history was still not an end in itself.

Nevertheless, the spirit of humanism, with its passion for recovering the remote past and making it live again, was pervaded by a sense of the pastness of the past. In *The Renaissance Discovery of Time*, Ricardo Quinones has reminded us of the heroic character of humanism as it battled against the ravages of time. When the sense of historical perspective was matched with adequate critical tools for reconstructing the past, the moment was ripe for the emergence of historical science. It was in Florence that the two streams of Renaissance thought, the creative and the critical, converged, equipping her to become 'the home of historical representation in the modern sense of the phrase' (Burckhardt).

While humanist history was undergoing a process of refinement, particularly in narrative technique and style, a tendency was gathering momentum which would eventually undermine the whole enterprise of humanist historiography and bring about an alternative approach.

While the contribution of rhetoric to fostering historical insight through its distinctive disciplines, skills and mental habits should not be overlooked (as Nancy Struever has argued), it is true to say that as long as history was regarded merely as a branch of rhetoric, modelled on Cicero's *De Oratore*, historical understanding would be ultimately frustrated. Events could be simplified and their presentation stylised without scruple simply because the historian saw himself as the servant, not primarily of historical reality, but of moral philosophy whose truths must be inculcated as persuasively as possible. What Wilcox says of Leonardo Bruni in his study of fifteenth-century Florentine history is significant for our understanding of the humanist approach in general:

> The fifteenth century considered Bruni accurate not because he had cogently refuted the traditional misconceptions and falsehoods about the course of Florentine history, but because accuracy is a virtue of ideal humanist history. Praise of Bruni as an historian proceeds as a deduction from the assumption that he has written a model history and not as an induction from the *Historiae* themselves. (p. 14)

In this respect at least (as Burckhardt points out: pp. 145ff) the highly stylised approach of the humanists represents a declension from the standards of historical realism set by the chroniclers.

This stylising of historical representation reflected the broader Renaissance preoccupation with structure, proportion and symmetry — 'the geometric spirit' of the Renaissance. As Hans Baron has written:

> In every field — the visual arts, literature and historiography — the Florence of the first years of the Quattrocento shows the same turning away from an indiscriminate interest in an abundance of insignificant details — the same effort to seize upon the large structural traits — the same delight in what is rational, symmetrical, and open to mathematical calculation. (*Crisis*, p. 170)

This late development of the humanist ideal began to come under attack in the late fifteenth and early sixteenth centuries, with obvious application to the way that history was conceived. Cortesi argued that the true aim of the historian was not perfection of narrative technique or even higher standards of accuracy, but the creation of a new historical form by the marriage of technique with principles of historical science drawn not from the theorising of Cicero but from the practice of Livy, Tacitus and Sallust (Wilcox, p. 20). The humanist approach to history was profoundly modified by Machiavelli, who injected a high dosage of political realism and a strong element of sensuousness and colour. Finally, the humanist model was transcended by Guicciardini, the friend and critic of Machiavelli, with his masterly control of narrative subservient to the recognised complexities of the historical process.

An Emergent sense of History: Four Humanists

Petrarch

Among the great Italian humanists, two particularly stand out as having made a special contribution to the advancement of historical understanding, Petrarch and Valla. In these matters, as Peter Burke and others have remarked, it is difficult not to begin with Petrarch (b. 1304). In the hackneyed but almost inevitable phrase, he was 'the first modern man'.

It takes a rash scholar to claim dogmatically to have discovered a 'first' in history — it only invites others to burrow more deeply into unfamiliar territory where some kind of precedent is sure to turn up sooner or later. In the case of Petrarch, such antecedents are to be found in medieval Italian rhetoric (Seigal, pp. 224f). But his startling originality is not disputed. His extraordinary confessional dialogue, the *Secretum*, discovered after his death, in which Saint Augustine, in the role of confessor, helps him to explore his character, motives and sins, has been described as the first example of introspective self-analysis since Augustine himself (though we have already noted the wave of self-examination and autobiographical confession generated by the movement of monastic renewal in twelfth-century France). Petrarch's *Letter to Posterity* is one of the first autobiographies, properly speaking. He is also claimed as the first to climb a mountain just for the view, and although the element of idealisation with benefit of hindsight is not to be overlooked in Petrarch's account of his ascent of Mount Ventoux, the historical core of the story seems secure (Baron, *Petrarch* and 'Petrarch'). His reading of Augustine's *Confessions* (whether or not on the actual mountain top) with their fearless exploration of the heights and depths of the human psyche, seemed to rebuke him for his mere sight-seeing curiosity. 'I looked at the peak and by comparison with the profound depths of human contemplation it seemed to be no higher than three feet.' (We have to wait for Coleridge and the romantics before we find again this sense of exhilaration in mountain walking as a sort of symbolic expression of a free-ranging exploration of the imagination, opening up unkown countries of the mind.)

Petrarch's view of nature was an ambivalent one. The first, so it is claimed, to establish the love of wild nature as a literary convention, he can be found questioning the value of natural knowledge: what is the use of it 'if one has no interest in discovering the nature of man, whence man comes, where he goes and why he is born?' Of contemporary knowledge of the world — part legendary, part mythological — he remarks: 'Most of these things are not even true; but even if they were true they would be of no consequence as far as beatitude is concerned.'

Petrarch sets the trend for later humanism in his intense consciousness of the passage of time and frenzied sense of the shortness of life. Dating all his activities to the hour, his unremitting labour is an attempt to cheat death and leave a worthy legacy to posterity. A dedicated antiquarian, Petrarch was a pioneer in the exploration of ancient ruins and had a real sense of what they signified. He reveals his sense of history in the *Familiares*, epistolary conversations with the literary giants of antiquity, revered as men, not magi, with its longing to cross the vast distances of time and counterbalancing sense of the irreversibility of history:

> While I am writing, I eagerly converse with our predecessors in the only way I can; and I gladly dismiss from my mind the men with whom I am forced by an unkind fate to live. I exert all my mental powers to flee contemporaries and seek out men of the past. As the sight of the former offends me, so the remembrance of the latter and their magnificent deeds and glorious names fill me with unthinkable, unspeakable joy. If this were generally known, many would be stunned to learn that I am happier with the dead than with the living. (Quinones, p. 117)

As Burckhardt remarks, Petrarch was 'a kind of living representative of antiquity' (p. 122; see also Kristeller, Ch. 1).

Valla

From the next century Lorenzo Valla (b. 1407) has emerged from recent research into the origins of historical science as the one outstanding individual thinker whose work marks the transition from mere critical study of ancient texts to a mature historical understanding (Kelley, *Foundations*, pp. 45f). An all-round Renaissance scholar, Valla developed a cosmology in which nature was divine, the garment of God, and a philosophy of life in which asceticism, whether Stoic or Christian, was rejected and pleasure recognised as a good in itself. In this respect Valla invites comparison with Marsilio Ficino. Both influenced by Lucretius, they alike recognised an immanent divine principle in the world (*natura naturans*) which they held to be the self-expression of God. Both wrote treatises *De Voluptate*, but for Ficino the Platonist, the pleasure-principle stood for intellectual delight in ideal beauty, divested of all sensuousness, not, as with Valla, an acceptance of the validity of the world of sense and feeling and of the good things of life as the gift of God (Garin, pp. 88ff; Seigel, pp. 251f, 145ff; Kristeller, pp. 27–37).

In defending his history of Ferdinand of Aragon against the criticisms of Bartolomeo Facio, Valla revealed his principles of method (Janik). Facio, with the full weight of the rhetorical tradition behind him, accused Valla's history firstly of lacking *dignitas* in that it included trivialities like the court jester and made King Martin fall asleep during an audience, and secondly, of employing neologisms instead of classical approximations (to describe cannon, for example). For Facio, there would be no distinction between what an author records and what he approves; he must be ruled by his sense of what is fitting.

Valla's reply enunciates a principle of the new history that would be adopted by Machiavelli and Bacon: 'I have not recorded what people ought to think, but what they do think.' If the jester had his place in the councils and chambers of the king, he has a right to his modest place in the history. Just as cooks and horse-boys are necessary members of the royal household, they have their humble but secure place in the royal history.

What is it to me, Valla demands, if the king behaved greedily or unjustly? 'Am I writing a panegyric or relating the deeds of

Ferdinand whatever they may have been?' In history, 'everything is written with the aim of relating what happened, not of proving a point'. For Valla, events have their value in themselves, not in so far as they instantiate moral or other universal truths.

Valla still accepts the principle of *inventio* — history has not yet entirely emancipated itself from rhetoric — but it must be true to human nature (e.g. the sleeping king) not governed by the external canons of rhetoric. History is bound to the particular.

For Valla philology was more than criticism: it was the door to the perception of a particular culture and the ethos of an age. His familiarity with the theological, moral and political assumptions of the early Christian era, led him to recognise that the Apostles' Creed was not apostolic, that the writings of Dionysius the Areopagite were pseudonymous and the Donation of Constantine a forgery (though here he was following his master Nicholas Cusanus in his memorandum on this matter to the Council of Basle in 1431). To the humanism and individualism of Renaissance thought, Valla added the dimensions of diversity, relativism and awareness of development. On a strong empirical foundation, concerned with human life in its particularity in this world, he built an approach which recognised the distinctiveness of different cultural achievements, the irreversibility of the historical process and the need to allow classical sources to speak for themselves by interpreting them in their own terms.

The fact that we find it convenient to assess Valla's work by means of anachronistic concepts like relativism and development, borrowed from later historicism, underlines his remarkable achievement in his time. He seems to invite comparison with later thinkers: Eugenio Garin, for example, has pointed out that 'one could well argue that Valla's generous conception of philology as the investigation, growing awareness and education of the whole of man in the orbit of *humanitas*, anticipated Vico's conception that philology had to be transformed into history' (p. 55).

Valla forms a link between Italian and Northern humanism; his critical essay on the Vulgate of the New Testament influenced Erasmus, who published it in 1505.

Budé

Renaissance humanism was a phenomenon that transcended national boundaries and rendered its practitioners citizens of the world. Having noted the significance of Valla's work on the New

Testament as forming a bridge between the Italian and the northern Renaissances, we move now across the spectrum of humanism to take Budé and Erasmus as representatives of the deepening historical grasp of northern humanism.

Guillaume Budé, born ten years after the death of Valla, in 1468, further refined the study of the relation of a text to its cultural context. Armed with developments in philology that were not available to Valla, Budé began to apply them not merely to the problems of classical literature for which they had been originally evolved, but also to the vulgar and vernacular problems (as Kelley calls them: *Foundations*, p. 79) of medieval history. Renouncing the increasingly discredited methods of seeking to come to terms with historical phenomena by either imposing alien philosophical assumptions on them (with the glossators) or of merely adducing classical parallels (with naïve rhetorical humanism), Budé called for an intense effort of historical understanding informed by encyclopedic learning and guided by a grasp of historical relativism. The result of this approach was, as Kelley puts it, 'not only to widen the range and deepen the perspective of historical inquiry but, through the insistence on encyclopaedic preparation, to improve historical method.'

Erasmus

Budé's contemporary, Erasmus (b. 1469), has an ambivalent attitude to history. Like the medieval chroniclers, he views the course of history *sub specie aeternitatis* and finds value in it, not for its own sake, but as illustrating eternal truths. This allegorical approach was reinforced by Erasmus' conviction of the perfections of scripture — compared with which all human records were inferior and unreliable. A nomadic figure and a citizen of the world, the national significance of history meant nothing to Erasmus, and he was not enthused by the new secular schemes of periodisation then coming into vogue. As a product of the Renaissance, Erasmus had a developed sense of the possibilities of human advancement, especially in the arts. But in a son of the church these were effectively neutralised by apocalyptic forebodings of the curtailment of human history.

Nevertheless, Erasmus does evince a remarkable sense of historical perspective, an acute awareness of the vanished world of the past. Writing against those who advocated a fastidious emulation of Ciceronian Latin style, Erasmus pointed out the absurdity of trying to turn the clock back:

> But can it be maintained that the situation of the present century is at all like that in which Cicero lived? On the contrary, religion, the empire, magistrates, the government, laws, customs, ordinary pursuits and the very appearance of men have all changed . . . Wherever I turn my eyes, I see all things changed, I stand before another stage and I behold a different play, nay, even a different world. (*Ciceronianus*, 1529; Gilmore, *Humanists*, pp. 103f)

On the same grounds, Erasmus defends the great patristic speculator Origen, who had early fallen foul of orthodoxy. He should not be judged, Erasmus argues, by standards that were not those of his own time. Suppose that we had lived then and had suddenly been presented with the Aristotelianised Christianity of St Thomas Aquinas? No, the church moves through various phases: she has her infancy, youth, adulthood and perhaps (a rueful contemporary comment) old age. But some would still treat the writings of all authors as though they belonged to the present (Bietenholz, p. 31).

History and Jurisprudence

When humanist study of a text combined with the broader considerations involved in the study of law, a matrix was created in which an historical approach could develop.

Whereas in England the myth of the immemorial antiquity of the common law held up comparative jurisprudence, on the Continent the reception of Roman Law was further advanced and gave rise to intense study of an historical nature. Under the influence of the humanist ideals of classical learning, clarity and elegance, the sort of one-dimensional exegesis that concentrated on logical analysis, analogy and casuistry, and assumed the static perfection of the *Corpus Juris*, gave way to a new method that gave priority to setting a given legal text in its original context. It began to be recognised that the long process of commentary and adaptation (the *mos italicus*, definitively expounded by Bartolus) had led further and further from the original intention and meaning of the text. The new method (the *mos gallicus*) stood for a return to sources, an attempt to uncover the original context. That context was recognised to have been created first by the life and circumstances of the jurist who worked on it, then by the school in which he had trained, and finally by the age and historical setting in which it originated. The mos gallicus was thus both genetic in its concern for sources and holistic in its search for an overall perspective. Pioneered by Alciati in Italy and taught by him in France, the new method was taken up, refined and given theoretical justification by a succession of French legal thinkers, Hotman, Cujas, Baudouin and others who helped to create the climate of thought in which Bodin did his work.

These developments in the study of law not only involved a new method, but also implied a new attitude to the past. While they were certainly intended to improve on Roman law, not to discredit it, their ultimate effect was rather different: intense study of the corpus revealed unsuspected flaws. The unintentional result of this enterprise was therefore, as Franklin points out, a break with the intellectual authority of Rome (p. 2).

The challenge to authority could tend in two different directions. It could lead, as in the case of Vico, to the rejection of the myth of the matchless wisdom of the ancients and to a non-anachronistic reconstruction of history and prehistory, thus contributing to the momentum of the historical movement. On the other hand, however, this discrediting of authority could lead, as it did with Descartes, to a complete break with the past and a wholesale rejection of the historical approach as such.

Reserving Bodin himself for separate and more detailed consideration, we turn now to briefly mention several figures in the ferment of history, humanism and law in Renaissance France. Francois Baudouin (b. 1520), who combined the legal humanism of Alciati and the Christian humanism of Erasmus, published his important handbook of historical method, *De Institutione historiae*, in 1561. Baudouin's contribution to historical thought was to bring together in one integrated approach the insights of legal and of purely historical study. 'I have become aware,' he remarked, 'that law books are the product of history and that historical monuments evolve from the books of law' (Kelley, *Foundations*, p. 131).

In the work of Estienne Pasquier a significant transition is made to a form of historical work that is both secular and concerned with research. The title of his treatise, *Recherches de la France*, 1560, sums it up. A practising historian, he borrowed his method from the theoretical writings of the jurists and philologists. As Huppert remarks, instead of thinking of history as an editorial task, he sees it as a scientific task. Pasquier demonstrated in practice the new methodology that others had outlined in theory.

The significantly entitled *Vicissitudes (De la vicissitude ou variété des choses en l'univers)* of Le Roy (1575) presented a universal history of 'change from the time when civilisation began to the present'. In Le Roy's work the fact of historical relativism was elevated to a methodological principle. Eschewing with Bodin, whose treatise on historical method had antedated his by nearly a decade, the comforting illusion of a past golden age, Le Roy has an almost Vichean vision of primitive man. 'The earliest men were very simple and brutal, hardly different from the beasts. They went about in the fields and mountains eating the raw flesh of animals'. As Huppert points out, intended though perhaps it was as a textbook, the revolutionary relativism of the *Vicissitudes* rendered it a 'philosophic manifesto', the prototype of the encyclopedic works of Bayle, Voltaire and Diderot (*Perfect History*, pp. 110, 117).

Finally, we must consider La Popelinière, who, writing at the turn of the century, developed a concept of universal comparative social history that we have to wait until Montesquieu and Voltaire to find carried forward. For La Popelinière, history was 'la représentation de tout'. It must include 'the character, the mores [*moeurs*], the customs [*coutumes*] and the way of life [*façons de faire*]' of a people. But 'general' or 'universal' history was not to be defined purely by reference to its scope: it also demanded the employment of a particular method — critical, genetic, interrogative — that asked:

> What are the sources, the form, the environment, the growth and the transformations of all the good and bad features of the human condition; what, for that matter, is the origin of all the ideas about society formulated by the ancient philosophers, historians and jurists? (letter to Scaliger; Huppert, *Perfect History*. p. 150)

The sense of history and the grasp of method evinced by Baudouin, Pasquier, Le Roy and La Popelinière (among others) constitutes a remarkable anticipation of the historical movement of the Enlightenment — and one that was the product not of Lockean psychology and Newtonian science but of the humanist love of a text and the juristic flair for marshalling evidence. But among these late sixteenth-century thinkers, the most powerful in retrospect is undoubtedly Bodin.

Chroniclers and Antiquarians

The Reformation stimulated historical study both directly and indirectly. One direct consequence of the upheavals of the sixteenth century was to flood the markets of Europe with manuscripts and books from the dissolved religious houses. These eventually found their way into the libraries of individual gentlemen scholars and protestant universities. A second direct consequence of the Reformation was to generate diligent study of church history as both sides tried to exhibit an unbroken pedigree stretching back to the apostles — on the catholic side, a succession of order; on the protestant side, a succession of gospel-truth.

The longer-term, indirect effects of the Reformation use of history were twofold. In the first place, the growing sensitivity to anachronistic readings of history was consolidated by the method of Reformation polemics of comparing the church of the present with the church of the early fathers. Roman polemicists understood this to demonstrate that the Reformers had departed from the truth. The protestants, for their part, attempted to prove their continuity with the early church and the apostasy of Rome. But the effect was the same: a widening gulf between 'now' and 'then', a growing sense of historical perspective.

In the longer term, the Reformation also contributed to the secularisation of historical study. Men began to feel the futility of trying to prove theological truth by historical means. No amount of energetic marshalling of texts from the fathers could prove that Luther had been raised up by providence. Study of the contingencies of church history, however voluminous, could never demonstrate that God was on the side of the Reformers, or of the papacy, as the case may be.

There is no need to underline the irony of protestantism and the catholic Reformation contributing to the Enlightenment, of Foxe and Bellarmine preparing the way for Voltaire and Gibbon.

Just as Reformation controversies had generated a frenzied search of the records of antiquity, so too the growing resentment of the new nation-states in the sixteenth century against papal tutelage set in train strenuous efforts of research in ancient law for precedents which would support a loosening of the papal yoke. In England the Act of Appeals of 1533 asserted that

> by divers sundry old authentic histories and chronicles it is manifestly declared and expressed that this realm of England is an empire, and so hath been accepted in the world, governed by one supreme head and king having the dignity and royal estate of the imperial crown of the same.

In France the Gallican controversy had the same effect, as champions of the French church against the papacy undertook to support their claims from the study of the development of canon law. From this starting point the inquiry gradually broadened out into a general interest in secular history.

The appeal to precedent — to what had been the case time out of mind — found its strongest expression in customary law, which offered not only a defence for kings against the pope, but also for the commons against the king, for local rights against the centralising tendencies of Roman law. The effect of this emphasis on customary law was ambivalent. On the one hand, it held up development of a critical approach to medieval history and fostered the perennial myths of the origins of English society (Brutus and the Trojans, Joseph of Arimathea, Arthur, etc.) and with its stress on time immemorial minimised the reality of historical development. But on the other hand, it had the effect of highlighting the themes of 'gradual process, imperceptible change, the origin and slow growth of institutions in usage, tacit consent, prescription and adaptation' (Pocock, *Ancient Constitution*, p. 19). The roots of English romantic philosophy of history go back through Burke's notion of prescription to this study of custom in the Renaissance.

The chronicler was indeed the ancestor of the modern historian, though he clearly belongs on the far side of the great watershed in historical consciousness that takes its rise in aspects of Renaissance humanism and jurisprudence. For the chronicler, as we have noted earlier, a concern for accuracy and an awareness of the need for a critical approach to sources were outweighed by his pervasive didactic motive — which was, as often as not, to hold up a mirror to kings and princes. The result, as F. J. Levy writes, was 'a compilation, loosely organised, whose author . . . thought of the events of a hundred years before his own time as occurring in a context identical to the world in which he himself lived' (p. ix). The chronicler was concerned solely with ecclesiastical, political or military history, ignoring the great subterranean causal movements in the social dimension of customs, institutions and beliefs. Raphael Holinshed, to whom Shakespeare lent a reflected immortality, concludes the line of English chroniclers. Polydore Vergil and Ralegh mark the transition to a new concept of history.

Polydore Vergil (1470–1555), one of the most widely read and influential of sixteenth-century historians, left his mark on two streams of Tudor historical thought: political history and social anthropology (if that is not too anachronistic a term).

Vergil has been described as a typical humanist historian. For Vergil the past is static, influenced only by the occasional actions of notable monarchs. Human nature is at the mercy of chance tempered by a destiny that is half Christian Providence and half pagan Fortune: man is not yet, as he is with Machiavelli, alone with his destiny in an indifferent world. History yields moral and political lessons. Altogether, Vergil was 'conservative to the point of being medieval in his basic approach to historical questions' (Hay, *Vergil*, p. 64).

His philosophy of history may have been deficient, but he shows advances in historical method. He is 'shrewd and critical in his handling of authorities, capable of telling the story of English reigns with selectivity and continuity, and, up to a point, a rational analysis of human motive' (A. B. Ferguson, *Clio*, pp. 7f).

Vergil's socio-economic study, the *De Inventoribus Rerum*, while it is a pioneer work, is weakened by his tendency to see all inventions as springing straight from the heads of individual geniuses. This is precisely where Bacon, with his awareness of the corporate enterprise of the mechanical arts, marks a significant advance.

Sir Walter Ralegh's *History of the World*, written in the Tower of London in the early years of James I's reign, seems to make a conventional beginning, Clio the historian's muse being pictured on the frontispiece with an abacus for chronology and a trumpet for celebrating the deeds of famous men — but the work contains progressive and even radical elements. Ralegh's historical perspective is indeed overarched by a ruling providence as first cause with a static conception of nature working by law and interpreted by reason. But Ralegh tends to take that for granted (sometimes overlabouring the lip-service to dispel critics who charged him with 'atheism', i.e. naturalistic interests combined with republican leanings): his real fascination is with second causes. 'To say that God was pleased to have it so, were a true but idle answer (for his secret will is the cause of all things) . . . Wherefore we may boldly look into the second causes' (Hill, p. 181). For example, while God led men to see the need for kingship, which he had ordained by his eternal providence, 'speaking humanly', we can account for 'the beginning of empire' by reference to reason and political necessity. As Christopher Hill has commented, Ralegh secularised history, not by challenging the traditional providential first-cause scheme, but 'by concentrating his vision on secondary causes and insisting that they are sufficient in themselves for historical explanation' (p. 181).

If Ralegh has a place in the secularising tendency of the historical movement stemming from the Renaissance, he also contributed to its relativising effect. He could make first-hand comparisons between the patriarchal narratives of Genesis and what he had witnessed of primitive peoples in the New World. His significance lies in the fact that he could apply this secular, relativist and comparative approach to a period of world history that was also (apparently) covered in biblical history.

Ralegh followed Machiavelli and anticipated Hobbes in his realistic view of the origins of human society and of the frail crust of civilisation that was liable to crumble before an irruption of selfish passions in times of civil strife. He was not alone among the English humanists in accepting a Promethean myth of man as a creature struggling upwards from primitive, almost bestial beginnings and in the face of the hostility of nature. This meant that, with Bodin, he was rejecting the rival myth of an idyllic Golden Age. Human affairs are ruled by expediency and conflict of interests. In civil wars,

> all former compacts and agreements for securing of liberty and property are dissolved, and become void: for flying to arms is a state of war, which is a mere state of nature, of men out of community, where all have an equal right to all things: and I shall enjoy my life, my subsistence, or whatever is dear to me no longer than he that has more cunning, or is stronger than I, will give me leave. (Hill, p. 150; A. B. Ferguson, *Clio*, p. 74)

Here is the sense — central to the new historical thought of Machiavelli, Bodin and Bacon — that men have the making of their history, that change could be channelled and controlled. As Hill has pointed out, secular assumptions are essential for this attitude to develop: not only do second causes have to be recognised in their own right, but politics have to be separated from morals and become a practice related to changing social and economic circumstances. Ralegh 'trembled on the edge of a science of politics which would be dominated by history' (p. 198). This dualism of sacred and secular, morals and politics, became explicit and programmatic in Bacon, who did in fact advance a science of politics drawing on history. Here Ralegh's place in the evolution of English historical thought becomes clear, as the man who provides the link between the advanced continental thought of Machiavelli, Bodin and the scepticism of Charron (Ralegh translated the sceptic Sextus Empiricus) and both streams of English historical philosophy in the seventeenth century, the empiricism of Bacon and the rationalism of Hobbes.

Sir Philip Sidney's *Apology for Poetry* (c. 1583) assisted in further undermining the didactic, exemplarist notion of history. Echoing Aristotle's teaching in the *Poetics* (1451 b 3) that 'poetry is a more philosophical and higher thing than history, for poetry tends to express the universal, history the particular', Sidney asserted (and he could only make this assertion as a result of the advances that humanist methods had achieved) that history cannot indulge in general principles, since it is bound to specific happenings, to what is actually the case ('not to what should be, but to what is'). It must not embroider or idealise. But to tell the truth in such a world as this is incompatible with exhibiting a moral ideal. 'The historian, being captivated to the truth of a foolish world, is many times a terror from well doing and an incouragement to unbridled wickedness.' Sidney took away the exemplary function that had traditionally belonged to history and gave it to poetry. Hobbes and the rationalists would take it from poetry and hand it to reason. The romantics would cut short the argument by claiming, as Carlyle did, that history is itself poetic: 'In the right interpretation of Reality and History does genuine Poetry consist'.

The antiquarian tradition constitutes an important sub-theme of the historical movement, from the early sixteenth century to the Romantic movement. The antiquarian of the sixteenth century evolved into the *érudit* or polymath who was the glory of European learning before the Enlightenment. Antiquarians preserved and organised the sort of evidence — coins, charters and inscriptions — that the chronicler tended to neglect, and gave to historical study a social and cultural dimension in the study of customs, institutions, art and religion, that fell outside the scope of political history.

Antiquarianism was particularly exposed to the dangers of undisciplined amateurism, to obsessiveness and myth-mongering. 'The voice of the antiquary could still be like a siren's call, likely only too often to lure the incorrigible romantic on to the rocks of legend' (A. B. Ferguson, *Clio*, p. 104). But in collecting and shifting evidence he did a valuable job. As Momigliano has remarked: 'The antiquary was a connoisseur and an enthusiast... his ideal was the collection. Whether he was a dilettante or a professor, he lived to clarify' (*Studies*, p. 25). He was not attempting to write history; he lacked both an overall perspective and an organising principle and this constituted his decisive limitation. 'The philological context in which his skills had been wrought left him without a theoretical language commensurate with his technical achievement' (Haddock, *Introduction*, p. 59).

In England, the Society of Antiquaries was found in 1584–6, but this later withered under the disapproval of James I, who suspected its members of dabbling in civil history that might have a bearing on current state afffairs. Antiquarian research flourished again after the Civil War and the new Society of Antiquaries was founded in 1707, the Anglican clergy being strongly represented, giving rise to the saying *Stupor Mundi Clerus Britannicus*.

John Leland devised grand projects in Elizabeth's day that were destined to come to fruition in the late seventeenth century in the philological, archeological and topographical work of Hickes, Wanley, Hearne and others, 'the best sustained and the most prolific movement of historical scholarship' ever undertaken in England (Douglas). William Camden pioneered both social history in his *Britannia* and civil history in his *Annals*. Though, as with Polydore Vergil, the two approaches went on side by side and were not integrated, Camden revealed new possibilities. Along with the French historian de Thou, Camden followed Bodin in rejecting both humanist literary history with its fictitious rhetoric and moral exampla and the ecclesiastical framework of medieval history which saw it as decreed by God, revealed by prophecy, guided by providence.

In the course of the seventeenth century, the distinction between the pure antiquary and the historian became blurred. The tasks to which the antiquarian had devoted himself were absorbed into historical study, as part of the historian's stock in trade. Antiquarian, historian or polymath, the érudit of the seventeenth century saw himself simply as a scholar, recognised no hard and fast boundaries within the world of scholarship, and stood for the unity of all learning. Imperceptibly, the antiquary evolved into the historian, and antiquities themselves came to be regarded not so much as prizes for a man's collection but simply as the raw material of historical study (Fussner, p. 114). This process fulfilled one of the conditions for the emergence of post-Romantic reconstructive history in the nineteenth century.

In its passionate love of learning and scrupulous attention to detailed evidence, antiquarianism — mediated and transfigured by Sir Walter Scott — provided a model for such great nineteenth-century historians as Niebuhr and Ranke. But before romantic history could appear, the static world of the antiquary had to be infused with the dynamism of historical change. The sources of this transformation can be detected in the pioneering work of the Tudor historians with their dawning awareness of the movement of social and economic realities. They set the tone of historical study until the next major developments in the Enlightenment.

Advances in Critical History

Commenting on the achievement of Renaissance historians, Peter Burke claims that the new awareness of the constraints of historical evidence constitutes 'one of the greatest intellectual achievements of Renaissance Europe' — the real 'historical revolution', comparable to the scientific revolution. But he is obliged to add that 'what was developed was a sense of the importance of primary sources and a capacity for detecting sources which were not primary, although they claimed to be'. For it was not until the eighteenth and nineteenth centuries that Western historians developed 'the art of doubting what is in the primary sources, and of extracting from them information that their authors would not have known that they possessed' (*Renaissance Sense of the Past*, p. 76).

Between these two phases of historical study there occurred a remarkable flourishing of corporate historical enterprises in two of the religious houses of Europe, the Bollandists and the Maurists. They further refined the critical evaluation of sources and came close to anticipating the sort of hermeneutical interrogation of the text associated with later developments.

In the course of the seventeenth century, a succession of Belgian Jesuit scholars — Rosweyde, Bolland, Henskens and Papenbroch — undertook the reform of catholic hagiography, establishing a tradition of research into the lives of the saints that has continued until the present — interrupted only by the temporary dissolution of the Jesuits between 1794 and 1837. They could hardly have chosen a more difficult field for modern historical method to cut its teeth on. As David Knowles has written:

> The hagiographer is plunged at once into the nightmare of early medieval diplomatic and forgery, into all the tangled chronological difficulties of the *fasti* of half the sees of Europe, into the labyrinthine ways of martyrologies, necrologies and calendars, into the linguistic, social and psychological varieties of Christian sentiment — Greek, Persian, Egyptian, Syrian, Slav and Oriental — into the magical mists and colours of the Celtic woodland, and into the changes and translations that lapse of centuries and popular devotion can bring about in a matter that is of its nature peculiarly dependent upon personal knowledge and popular acclaim. (*Great Historical Enterprises*, p. 9)

Not to mention all the problems involved in coming to terms with the halo of alleged supernatural claims and paranormal effects that surrounded the saints in tradition!

Bolland himself, in his celebrated preface to the *Acta Sanctorum*, discriminates between his sources: excepting those 'who derive their material from on high, either by direct inspiration of God, or by dictation or instruction through an angel or other heavenly agent' (this shows the limitations of Bolland's modernity: he has no inkling of biblical criticism which would radically modify the notion of inspiration; even Papenbroch took the prophecies of Joachim of Fiore seriously), those 'who write after the manner of mortals' can be divided thus:

> To the first and highest category of historical writing ... the leading class, belong those who commit to writing events at

which they were present and which they saw enacted . . . They hold the second place who have not themselves seen what they relate, but have received it from men who viewed it with their own eyes . . . The third class is composed of those who relate not what they have received from the eyewitnesses themselves, but from those to whom the eyewitnesses related it. In the fourth class must be placed those who have collected their facts from historians who belong to one of the classes enumerated, or from reliable remains of donations, wills, agreements, or from other accounts.

'All these', he comments, 'assuredly deserve credence' (Collis, pp. 298f). But as for the producers of hagiographical fiction, how dare they trifle with the deeds of holy men! 'A falsehood should never be used as an incentive to piety. God is Truth' (ibid., p. 301).

Always mentioned in the same breath as the Bollandists are the Maurists, the Benedictine community of Saint Maur that boasted among a succession of outstanding scholars the illustrious names of Mabillon (d. 1707), author of *De Re Diplomatica* (1681), which pioneered the science of criticising manuscript charters, official letters and documents of all kinds, establishing a standard valid until modern times (though it should not be overlooked that the *Monasticon* of Dodsworth and Dugdale in England preceded Mabillon's book by a decade), and Montfaucon (d. 1741), whose interests embraced not only the Greek fathers but history as well.

Mabillon — 'one of the world's greatest scholar-historians' (Knowles, 'Mabillon') — is distinguished among his contemporaries in a scholarly age by his outstanding critical and creative powers. While others were laying down principles for mathematics and natural science, Mabillon was the first to create a method for the study of diplomatic and liturgy. In comprehensive critical power, Mabillon ranks with the moderns; Renaissance humanism is left well behind.

When he takes up a problem, great or small, he shakes it out and holds it up and then applies to it tests of every kind from every angle. Whether it is Augustine's teaching on grace, the meaning of a word in the Rule, the eucharistic practice of the early church, the order of succession of bishops and abbots, or the date of a charter, Mabillon brings to bear upon it the same acuteness of observation, the same sanity of judgement, the same lucidity of exposition. When he has done with it, the matter is, in four cases out of five, settled for good. (Knowles, 'Mabillon', p. 233)

1 MACHIAVELLI: HISTORY AND POWER

Machiavelli: Private Passion and Political Crisis

Though regarded as a poor historian, even by the standards of some of his contemporaries such as Francesco Guicciardini, Machiavelli (1469–1527) is a highly significant figure in the evolution of historical consciousness. The writings of this extraordinary man helped to crystallise the movements of secularism, empiricism and (indirectly) relativism that modern historical thought derives from the Renaissance through the Enlightenment. As far as his own historical writings are concerned, Machiavelli was hampered by the humanist framework that he knew best in its literary or rhetorical, rather than in its new critical form, but he claims a place in any account of historical thinking in three respects.

Firstly, Machiavelli tried to look at politics and history in the light of experience and not in the light of faith. He contemplated human existence in its stark reality, objectively, and not in a moral or religious perspective. There is no intimation in Machiavelli that men are answerable for their actions to God; the note of judgement, so pervasive in medieval thought, is conspicuous by its absence. His method is (or purports to be) descriptive not prescriptive. Bacon praised Machiavelli for showing man as he is rather than as he ought to be. He thus helped to free the study of politics and history from moral and religious constraints so that they could eventually become sciences in their own right.

Secondly, Machiavelli contributed fresh insight into the nature of the historical process in his recognition of the superhuman power-structures (for which he used the time-honoured classical and medieval name *fortuna*) that sway the course of events. As Acton remarks, Machiavelli put his finger on 'the law of the modern world, that power tends to expand indefinitely and will transcend all barriers . . . until met by superior forces'. This dynamic of power, Acton continues, 'produces the rhythmic movement of history' (Acton, p. 60).

Thirdly, Machiavelli penetrated beneath the surface of events to the deep human needs and passions that drive men on, for which he used the term *necessità*. His clear, unwavering, unillusioned gaze rests upon the struggle of human existence in history, illuminating the grip of circumstances and the fundamental inward drives that determine human destiny.

Machiavelli's own life and thought highlight this conjunction of inward and outward factors, that, reacting upon each other, go to the making of history. Machiavellianism (to use an admittedly anachronistic but convenient term) was the product of the abrupt convergence of the cultural flowering of the Italian Renaissance and the catastrophic political crisis of 1494 when Charles VIII of France invaded Italy (Meinecke, *Machiavellianism*, p. 29). The presence of French armies in occupation of Italian soil opened the eyes of Machiavelli and his contemporaries to the vulnerability of the Italian city-states to the movements of world history. The little lagoon of peninsular politics and Renaissance culture was suddenly awash with the tidal waters of power-politics on a continental scale.

Machiavelli brought to the crisis a mind dominated by two great passions. The first was his passion for politics — a passion that Machiavelli, unlike his compatriot Dante who also wrote in the bitterness of exile from Florentine civic life, was unable to sublimate into a religious or moral vision. Federico Chabod has spoken of Machiavelli's 'hunger' for political experience, his insatiable political curiosity (Chabod, p. 10). This passion was fired, not by commitment to an ideal state, a utopia (though there are, as we shall see, strong utopian or eschatological elements in Machiavelli's thought), but by the actuality of political life in early sixteenth-century Florence — seen, not through the mists of time which might lend enchantment, but by a participant, from day to day.

In *The Prince* Machiavelli remarks that many other writers have held forth on how a ruler should govern his subjects, but he aims to do something different and unprecedented and says:

> I have thought it proper to represent things as they are in real truth, rather than as they are imagined. Many have dreamed up republics and principalities which have never in truth been known to exist; the gulf between how one should live and how one does live is so wide that a man who neglects what is actually done for what should be done learns the way to self-destruction rather than self-preservation. (pp. 90f)

It is this total commitment to realism that leads Machiavelli to eschew the sort of high-sounding generalities that political theorists from Aristotle onwards had customarily indulged in and to plunge, from the very first sentence of *The Prince*, into the actualities of the political world: all kinds of states, he begins, can be divided into republics or principalities.

This striking feature of Machiavelli's thought explains why several commentators have seen him as, so to speak, the first positivist — 'a cold technician, ethically and politically uncommitted, an objective analyst of politics, a morally neutral scientist' who applied inductive methods to social and historical material (cf. Berlin, *AC*, pp. 29f). Nothing could, in fact, be further from the truth than the suggestion that Machiavelli was morally and politically uncommitted: his commitment was — body and soul — to the state, and his ethics were those of civic virtue (*virtù*) that put the survival and well-being of the state first. But those who detect an incipient positivism in Machiavelli have at least drawn attention to the fundamentally empirical thrust of his approach. He himself felt that this was what gave his work its originality. 'I have determined,' he announces at the beginning of the *Discourses*, 'to enter upon a path not yet trodden by anyone' (p. 190).

But it is sometimes the case that a first-class theoretician of a science makes a poor showing when it comes to putting his principles into practice: Machiavelli is a case in point. A teacher of the art of duplicity, Machiavelli was a ham-fisted diplomat and negotiator. As Garrett Mattingly has pointed out, 'in his dealings both with his own government and with foreign potentates, he was usually inept at concealing his fealings, likely to show his hand, and, in negotiation, blunt to the point of tactlessness'. And as an observer of the political scene, he was not particularly acute, discriminating, or even accurate (p. 62). Though he had special responsibility for military affairs and wrote a treatise on the art of war, his judgement was distorted by the exaggerated respect he had for the ancients: if they had prosecuted war successfully without either gunpowder or fortresses, sixteenth-century states should learn from them to trust to virtù not technology. But this brings us to the second of Machiavelli's great passions — antiquity.

The flame of Renaissance humanism which took antiquity as its model of perfection, burned fiercely and consumingly in Machiavelli, though he stands apart from his contemporaries in two respects. Firstly, he reserves his greatest admiration not for Greece, but for Rome. And secondly, for him, the genius of the ancient world was not primarily literary or artistic, but political. Federico Chabod has commented on Machiavelli's 'passionate devotion to the Roman world, which is not merely envisaged, but is glorified and idealised in virtue of its stupendous political genius' (p. 11).

In the *Discourses* and *The Prince*, illustrations from antiquity are brought together with examples from European, and specifically Italian, modern history to substantiate Machiavelli's principles for the conduct of political life. As Felix Gilbert has remarked, for Machiavelli and his contemporaries, 'the image of the past comprises the programme of the future' (*MG*, p. 181).

The broad assumption behind this approach was that the world had declined from its former glory and that only by emulating antiquity could society be revitalised. Machiavelli shared this assumption, but in him it was tinged with eschatological expectation. Good times would come again. A nation could be reborn by returning to its origins. And there were some respects in which life in the sixteenth century marked an advance. In one passage in the *Discourses* Machiavelli remarks that, though it is human nature to compare the present unfavourably with the past (he himself was constantly doing this, castigating contemporary leaders for their failures, pointing them to the illustrious examples of antiquity), it may in fact be superior — not, needless to say, in the matter of the arts, but in the lives and habits of men. Taking it all in all, the world has always been much the same. 'When I meditate on how these things move, I judge that the world has always gone on in the same way and that there has been as much good as bad' (pp. 321ff).

The external catalyst that brought about the formation of a new historical consciousness was the series of decisive interventions in Italian territorial affairs that began with the French invasion of 1494 and continued until the critical years 1525–30, culminating in the fall of the Florentine republic and the sack of Rome by the armies of the Emperor Charles V. As Burckhardt remarks, France and Spain had begun to resemble the centralised Italian states, and indeed to copy them, only on a gigantic scale (p. 59). Machiavelli's works were written before the final débâcle, but he had grasped the implications of the new state of affairs long before. He was compelled to acknowledge the limitations that had to be set to the humanist commonplace that man is the maker of history. Events seemed to have revealed man's powerlessness in the face of the uncontrollable forces of world history. The pride of Renaissance Italy was humbled; Fortuna was mistress of the world. Return to the past was closed. It was no longer a question of making a few diplomatic or tactical adjustments to restore stability and the balance of power as it had been in the days of Lorenzo the Magnificent. New developments were continually unfolding; the tide of history was sweeping all before it.

The new situation had an immediate effect on both historical science and political ethics.

(a) Felix Gilbert has pointed out the significance of the sequence of events that began to unfold in 1494 for the growth of historical understanding.

> As long as it was believed that man could exert a formative influence on events, the search for rules of political conduct and for perfect political institutions was of paramount importance; but when man appeared to be unable to create lasting institutions that would withstand the forces of fortuna, the chase after the laws of politics became futile. Explanations of how things came about seemed more relevant than prescriptions for what ought to be done. (*MG*, p. 270)

Considered in the perspective of the whole historical movement, Machiavelli was writing in a time of transition, tempering the humanist heritage of literary and didactic history with his hard-won political realism and anticipating the power-consciousness and world-historical grasp of later historicism with his notions of necessità and fortuna. Plunged violently with all his generation into a world of power-politics that were secular, relativistic and pragmatic, Machiavelli was making a desperate effort to grasp the logic of the new political reality, to understand the rules of the game.

(b) In humanist thought, as we find it in Alberti, for example, virtù was understood in a moral sense and had the power to overcome adversity: goodness (virtù) was greater than fortuna (Garin, pp. 62f). Machiavelli regards this as naïve, and attempts to overturn the tradition of (Christian) humanism.

In the realm of political ethics, the survival of the state became the overriding concern, displacing all personal moral scruples. The existence of the state became an end in itself, a moral absolute. Christian ethics were admirable in a man's private walk of life, but disastrous if introduced into public affairs, and in the *Discourses* Machiavelli asserts:

> When it is absolutely a question of the safety of one's country, there must be no consideration of just or unjust, of merciful or cruel, of praiseworthy or disgraceful; instead, setting aside every scruple, one must follow to the utmost any plan that will save her life and keep her liberty. (p. 519)

To take a practical example, 'a prudent ruler cannot, and should not honour his word when it places him at a disadvantage and when the reasons for which he made his promise no longer exist'. Possibly in an attempt to clarify his ethic in the light of Christian and Platonic ethical traditions, Machiavelli adds: 'If all men were good, this precept would not be good; but because men are wretched creatures who would not keep their word to you, you need not keep your word to them.' Traditional ethics are fine in the abstract but unrealistic in practice.

> Everyone realises how praiseworthy it is for a prince to honour his word and to be straightforward rather than crafty in his dealings; nonetheless contemporary experience shows that princes who have achieved great things have been those who have given their word lightly, who have known how to trick men with their cunning and who, in the end, have overcome those abiding by honest principles. (*The Prince*, pp. 99f)

Machiavelli was the theoretician of the modern secular state — in Acton's words, 'the state that suffers neither limit nor equality and is bound by no duty to nations or to men, that thrives on destruction and sanctifies whatever things contributed to increase of power' (pp. 59). The political crisis thus brought about in the mind of Machiavelli a crystallisation of an alternative political ethic. We shall pick up the implications of this for the concept of historical relativism later, but we can appreciate already at this stage the force of Felix Gilbert's claim that the conjunction of Renaissance humanism and political catastrophe had brought about 'the existence of a new historical consciousness' (*MG*, pp. 253f).

Machiavelli on Man and History

Machiavelli's outlook on man and history is one of broad, though not unrelieved cynicism. Human nature, which is in all ages essentially the same, is fundamentally evil. Men will only do good for some ulterior motive, or when necessità compels.

> One can make this generalisation about men, they are ungrateful, fickle, liars and deceivers, they shun danger and are greedy for profit; while you treat them well, they are yours. They would shed their blood for you, risk their property, their lives, their children, so long . . . as danger is remote; but when you are in danger they turn against you. (*The Prince*, pp. 96f)

It is useless to appeal to men's better natures: they respond only to threats.

> Men worry less about doing an injury to one who makes himself loved than to one who makes himself feared. The bond of love is one which men, wretched creatures that they are, break when it is to their advantage to do so; fear is strengthened by a dread of punishment which is always effective. (Ibid.)

Take Hannibal as an example: although he led vast armies, composed of men of many races, on gruelling campaigns, including the crossing of the Alps, dissension in the ranks was unknown, and for this — Machiavelli concludes with breathtaking matter-of-factness — 'his inhuman cruelty was wholly responsible'. Recognition of this fact would have made the chroniclers of his campaigns better historians, for inhibited by religious or moral scruples, they 'on the one hand admire what Hannibal achieved, and on the other condemn what made his achievements possible' (pp. 96ff). It costs the historian nothing to take this short-sighted and sanguine view of human nature — he is not usually writing to save his skin — but for a ruler to overlook the harsh realities of power is, literally, fatal. He has to assume 'that all men are evil and that they are always going to act according to the wickedness of their spirits whenever they have free scope.' Even when all is quiet and his rule apparently unchallenged, the prince has to remind himself that human wickedness is always latent, waiting for a suitable moment to erupt (*Disc.*, p. 201).

Machiavelli believes that he has exposed for the first time in Christian civilisation the real driving forces behind all human exertion. (Though Dati, writing 1407–8, has a strong sense of the elemental determinants of men's actions, will and passion: Baron, *Crisis*, p. 159). What drives men on is necessità. Men will never do anything good unless they have to. They will be idle until spurred on by hunger and poverty. They will only be law abiding by compulsion. Their actions are motivated by hunger, poverty, fear, ambition ('love of power') and avarice ('love of substance' (*roba*)). Though a few great men, redemptive figures, will be activated purely by virtù and concern for the well-being of the state, they should quickly rid themselves of the illusion that other men are motivated by the same high ideals that inspire them — if they want to survive (*Disc.*, pp. 201, 272).

Human nature, Machiavelli assumes, is in all times and places the same. This belief undergirds Machiavelli's entire historical worldview, whose central tenet is that history repeats itself, and that one can learn from the past. History teaches lessons and these lessons can be — though they seldom are — learned. 'I have heard it said,' writes Machiavelli (and 'I have heard it said' is the sort of discreet circumlocution for 'in my opinion' that Machiavelli had learned to use early in his career as a writer of diplomatic dispatches, to protect himself in case his advice backfired or got into the wrong hands, another stock phrase being 'sound men here are of the opinion') — 'I have heard it said that history is the teacher who determines our actions, and above all our principles, and that the world has been inhabited in all ages alike by men who have always been subject to the same passions' (Chabod, p. 132).

The cyclical character of history deriving from the uniformity of human nature, enables one to predict future developments; and Machiavelli writes in *Discourses*:

> He who considers present affairs and ancient ones, readily understands that all cities and all peoples have the same desires and the same traits and that they always have had them. He who diligently examines past events easily foresees future ones in every country and can apply to them the remedies used by the ancients, or, not finding any that have been used, can devise new ones because of the similarity of the events.

The facile way in which Machiavelli presented his doctrine of historical analogies based on the uniformity of human nature and the cyclical character of the historical process laid him open to the scathing criticisms of his contemporary Francesco Guicciardini. The sort of remark that provoked Guicciardini was this:

> He who wishes to see what is to come should observe what has already happened, because all the affairs of the world in every age have their individual counterparts in ancient times . . . Since they are carried on by men who have always had the same passions, of necessity the same results appear . . . Future things are also easily known from past ones if a nation has for a long time kept the same habits, being either continuously avaricious or continuously unreliable, or having some other similar vice or virtue. (*Disc.*, pp. 278, 521)

It is clear that Machiavelli does not espouse the traditional Christian scheme of a linear unfolding of a divine plan that moves forward from its beginning in creation to its predestined end in the judgement of the world. But neither does he betray any leaning towards the Enlightenment's notion of progress, or Romanticism's concept of organic development. For Machiavelli, historical change is kaleidoscopic, a limited number of patterns arranging themselves into a limited number of configurations. As Herbert Butterfield has commented:

> Human passions, being constant, move men at all periods to the same kinds of action, driving the story to the same crises and conjunctures; so that history tends to fall into repeating patterns, instead of progressing to an unforeseeable future that is pregnant with hidden shapes. (*Statecraft*, p. 30)

But it would be quite misleading to create the impression that Machiavelli's historical worldview, cyclical though it is, is that of a dispassionate, cynical and world-weary observer of history, resigned to endless and pointless repetition. There is a note of hope and expectation in Machiavelli. Society could be reborn. It could return to the source and well-spring of its life under the leadership of a good, wise and firm prince, just as St Francis (the example is Machiavelli's) had revitalised and reformed his order, and just as the Reformers sought to renew the face of the church by a return to the doctrine and practice of the fathers (this example, though not

Machiavelli's, brings home the extent of common assumptions among intellectuals in the early sixteenth century; Guicciardini, incidentally, does give Luther favourable mention). For Machiavelli, as for all who were influenced by the humanist vision, renewal came not through development into a new and unprecedented stage of society, but through a return to origins, a repristinisation (*Disc.*, pp. 419ff).

The major works of Machiavelli — *The Prince*, the *Discourses* and the *History of Florence* — have a redemptive theme running through them. The theological term 'redemption' is not accidental, for there is a biblical, eschatological quality about Machiavelli's longing for the political messiah who will save his country. He longs for the day when 'Italy, after so long a time, may behold its saviour', and becomes ecstatic at the thought of the welcoming hosannas of the liberated people.

> I cannot express with what love he would be welcomed in all those provinces which have suffered from these foreign inundations, with what thirst for vengeance, with what resolute loyalty, with what devotion and tears. What doors would be closed to him? What people would deny him their obedience? What envy would stand in his way? What Italian would refuse him allegiance?

But biblical overtones notwithstanding, Machiavelli is consistent to the end. It is not the Christian virtues that will accomplish this, for Christianity has become passive, indolent and feeble when it could have been vigorous and militant, but the pagan virtù of the ancients, *l'antico valore* of which Petrarch had sung (*The Prince*, p. 138; *Disc.*, p. 331).

Machiavelli's contribution to historical understanding is beginning clearly to emerge: recognition of the determinants of history in external circumstances (fortuna) and inward drives (necessità), and the need therefore for men on the stage of history to be 'in harmony with the times' (*Disc.*, pp. 450ff); the beginnings of a 'world-historical' grasp following the events of 1494; and finally, the moral realism that accepts that political decisions are a choice of evils and that 'men do not rule states with paternosters in their hands' (as Machiavelli makes Cosimo the Old say in the *History of Florence*).

It is this last element in Machiavelli that led Croce to claim that, by his discovery of the autonomy of politics, which are 'beyond good and evil', determined by the inexorable laws of political necessity, and which cannot be exorcised from this world with holy water, Machiavelli had laid the foundations of the science of politics. Chabod has commented on this that 'by a single stroke of the pen, Croce reversed the age-long denunciation of Machiavelli's "immorality"' (Chabod, p. xii).

Interpreters differ as to whether this was in fact Machiavelli's meaning and as to the nature of Machiavelli's ethical dualism. Was it simply a dualism between public and private morality (for which there is ample support in the Christian tradition of exegesis of the Sermon on the Mount), or was it, as Isaiah Berlin claims (*AC*, pp. 45ff), a dualism of Christian ethics of personal holiness on the one hand and classical pagan ethics of civic virtù on the other? Or was it, as Croce intimates, a much more radical attempt to isolate politics from moral considerations altogether? There is a world of difference between asserting that politics are, *ipso facto*, amoral, beyond good and evil, and claiming that politics operate in the realm where every choice is a choice between relative evils. If this was all Machiavelli had done, he could without much difficulty have been assimilated into the Christian tradition of political realism that runs from Augustine through the medieval canonists and casuists, through Aquinas, Luther and Cromwell, to Temple, Bonhoeffer and Reinhold Neibuhr. But Machiavelli goes much further than this: his political realism is more sinister — and indeed more tragic — than anything in Christian theology. The survival and safety of the state are indeed his aims, but to survive you have to become the aggressor. Attack is not just the best, but the only means of defence. There is no *status quo*: political reality is like a swift-flowing, turbulent and piranha-infested river; you must eat or be eaten. Machiavelli enunciated a sort of political Darwinism based on the principle of the survival of the fittest, and produced the same shock waves among his contemporaries in the sixteenth century as Darwin did in the nineteenth.

There is a profound element of tragedy in Machiavellianism. Evil is inevitable; quixotic idealism is fatal. The man of clean hands and a pure heart who brings high ideals to public life must quickly be prepared to dip his hands in blood. Here is the making of a tragic view of life: good men compelled by circumstances to embrace evil. But Machiavelli is not, in the last analysis, the creator of a great tragic vision of human life. He is not on that scale. He remains the intriguer, the schemer, the manipulator of local power-politics. His symbol is the stiletto, not the cross. When we begin to project his little world onto the larger canvas of twentieth-century history, the results are horrifying. If fratricide, why not genocide; if the poisoned chalice, why not germ warfare? Yet, in the last analysis, one cannot subscribe to the thesis of the total depravity of Machiavelli's thought. One is haunted by the vocabulary of high ideals into which he is betrayed when he contemplates Italy's saviour: the vocabulary of love, loyalty, devotion and sacrifice.

Machiavelli as Historian

Machiavelli imitated the formal elegance of his humanist predecessors and, like them, sat lightly to factual accuracy. He criticised them for their lack of interest in domestic affairs, their preoccupation with wars and treaties, and explained this bias in the prologue to his *History* as due to both reasons of principle and reasons of expediency: 'I think that they did this either because these matters seemed so insignificant that they did not consider them worthy to be written up' — a recognition of the humanist vocation to perpetuate in letters only those things worthy of honour — 'or because they feared offending the descendants of those who would be attacked in narrating these things'.

Machiavelli's casual attitude to matters of historical accuracy can be attributed to three factors, each of which is significant of his place in the evolution of historical thought. Firstly, he was the heir of the humanists — a dyed-in-the-wool humanist himself, indeed — for whom aesthetic considerations would always outweigh scientific ones. Secondly, as the *Discourses* reveal, he was acutely conscious of the difficulty of getting at the facts, of the inaccessibility of the past. Thirdly, his approach was essentially deductive, not inductive. His ultimate aim was not scientific but didactic. From the assembled facts he would proceed to make far-reaching deductions. The historical analysis was merely the vehicle of the synthesis. It is precisely this approach that makes Machiavelli's thought so compelling: he is concerned with the present, not the past. As Federico Chabod comments, 'The historical fact is not swallowed up in its immediate context: instead it is developed as a creative force' (p. 6). Herbert Butterfield has called Machiavelli 'doctrinaire' and labelled him a dreamer. Altogether Machiavelli reminds us of some nineteenth-century theoretician of world revolution, dreaming of power in the bitter isolation of exile, brooding over the blueprint of a new order that would one day be brought to birth regardless of the cost in human suffering.

In technique, then, Machiavelli was behind the times. He was out of sympathy with the new critical philology, the *mos gallicus* (so called because, though pioneered by the Italian scholar Alciati, the method had a better reception among French, rather than Italian, humanists (Gilmore, *Humanists*, pp. 33f)). He was following humanist rhetoric rather than humanist criticism in his historical method, making rather arbitrary use of materials and stylising facts and events with a free hand. Felix Gilbert has shown how closely Machiavelli adhered to the humanist model in his *Istorie Fiorentine*: prefacing each book with general reflections, studding the narrative with carefully wrought speeches, announcing important events with celestial portents, giving painstaking attention to battle-scenes, following one author at a time and merely rewriting his account in a more elaborate style (*MG*, pp. 237, 170).

As Gilbert suggests, Machiavelli has not quite emancipated himself from the supernatural element in medieval historiography. He acknowledges that signs and portents in the heavens presage great events, though he seems bemused by the existence of these phenomena and gropes for a naturalistic explanation (*Disc.*, pp. 311f). We shall see that even Guicciardini, though in general he represents an advance on Machiavelli's historical method, has a field-day with the alleged portents that heralded the French invasion of 1494.

Machiavelli's historical vision is narrowly political as we would expect from the acknowledged originator of what later became known as *Real-politik*. But it is not only because he is himself a political animal, but also because he follows the medieval chroniclers and Renaissance humanist historians that Machiavelli recognises only the political dimension. While he transcends his predecessors by his awareness of the realities of fortuna and necessità in the historical process, he betrays no sense of the fascination that we find in, for example, Voltaire two hundred years later, for human culture in its broadest aspect, the history of civilisation. And even within the limits of political history, Machiavelli did not achieve a balanced approach, for his great passion is military tactics and here his advocacy of a militia in place of the mercenary armies that were a ubiquitous feature of fifteenth- and sixteenth-century warfare became an obsession that distorted his judgement.

There is, however, one striking feature of Machiavelli's *Istorie* that marks a radical departure from his classical and humanist models. The *raison d'être* of history in the classical mould was to hold up the shining achivements of the past for the emulation of the present. As Quentin Skinner points out, it was above all this sense of 'the panegyric quality of the historian's task' that the humanists of the Renaissance borrowed from the study of Livy, Sallust and other historians of antiquity. As Machiavelli's predecessor Poggio Bracciolini expressed it, 'the great usefulness of a really truthful history' (and here 'truthful' must mean 'conforming in every respect to the humanist ideal') lies in the fact that 'we are able to observe what can be achieved by the *virtus* of the most outstanding men', their desire for glory, for their country's liberty, for the good of their children, the gods and all humane things.' As we read, our own virtù is aroused and we are spurred on to follow their example.

Though Machiavelli apparently sets out in his *Istorie Fiorentine* to conform to the humanist model in this as in other respects, as he comes nearer to the present and to the causes of the city's disastrous decline, he makes a radical break with the humanist discipline of historiography (just as in *The Prince* and the *Discourses* he had broken with the humanist tradition of the virtuous prince, the model of probity). He finds nothing to praise and no examples worth following in the dismal record of Florentine affairs during the last century or so. 'The things done by our princes, abroad and at home, cannot, like those of the ancients, be read of with wonder because of their virtù and greatness', nor is there any story to tell 'of the bravery of soldiers or the virtù of generals or the love of citizens for their country'.

It is significant that in discarding in this way the panegyric style of historiography, Machiavelli was not enunciating a scientific, dispassionate approach, concerned for clinical objectivity. He still has an axe to grind; he writes with a polemical purpose. Instead of telling a story that 'kindles free spirits to imitation', he hopes to kindle such spirits to avoid and get rid of present abuses'. In seeking to let history serve a contemporary programme of reform and removal of abuses, Machiavelli shows himself to be, in this respect at least, a forerunner of the Enlightenment historians, and, supremely, of Voltaire (Skinner, *Machiavelli*, pp. 80ff).

It was E. Feuter's opinion in his standard account of the development of modern historiography that Machiavelli's *Istorie Fiorentine* was a landmark in historical thought. Here Feuter was no doubt influenced by Burckhardt, who commented that, in his Florentine history, Machiavelli 'represents his native city as a living organism and its development as a natural and individual process', adding, 'he is the first of the moderns who has risen to such a conception' (p. 53). But it is not primarily as an historian that Machiavelli claims a place in the evolution of philosophy of history. Machiavelli did not need to write history in order to secure this: he made history by changing men's vision of their world. Federico Chabod has claimed convincingly that it was precisely because Machiavelli was such a poor historian by the canons of modern — and even late Renaissance — historiography, that he was able to make such an impact upon western thought.

> In order to recognise fully the value and autonomy of poltical activity . . . he had first to embrace a philosophy of extremism and simplification. It was necessary for him to focus his attention exclusively on the central power, the government, which must be concentrated in a clearly specified individual . . . All the errors and defects of historical evaluation which had determined the creation and the practical effectiveness of *The Prince* thus became the chief source of its universal vitality: if Machiavelli had judged the events of his time in a truly critical spirit he would not have written his treatise . . . The serene curiosity of the man who wishes only to observe and judge had to give place to the vehement, reckless passion of the man who wishes to create something new.

In conclusion, continues Chabod, 'Had he been a shrewd and profound historian Machiavelli would merely have written a masterpiece. As it was, he was a very bad historian, and he thereby became a universal influence' (Chabod, pp. 119f).

Machiavelli contributed to the stream of historical thought powerful doses of empiricism, secularism and relativism. He saw men and events for what they are, not for what we wish them to be, or the church says they should be, or political propagandists claim they are. Not that Machiavelli himself was a notable exponent of scientific method, but as Bacon observed, this was the ideal that he held out. Secondly, he intensified, though not without meeting ferocious opposition, the trend to secularism pioneered by the humanist historians. The state was now the unit of history; the qualities that counted in the affairs of men were the pagan ones of civic virtù; the political and historical process — if not exactly 'beyond good and evil', as Croce claimed for Machiavelli — was at least a law unto itself. Its inexorable determinants were the forces of necessità, not the Ten Commandments, and its destiny decreed by the Lady Fortuna, not the providential purposes of God. But (thirdly) perhaps Isaiah Berlin is correct in claiming that western thought owes to Machiavelli primarily an intensification of its nascent relativism, when he writes:

> One of the deepest assumptions of western thought is the doctrine, scarcely questioned during its long ascendancy, that there exists some single principle which not only regulates the course of the sun and the stars, but prescribes their proper behaviour to all animate creatures.

It is the belief in a natural law or universal reason or chain of being — a single principle that holds together the physical, the intellectual and the moral in perfect harmony. There is one key to the mysteries of nature, one truth to be attained, one right way for man to live. It is an assumption as old as human nature, common to both the Hebrew and the Greek traditions, systematised in the middle ages, transposed into classical modes of thought at the Renaissance, forged anew in a synthesis of Christian and classical assumptions at the Reformation, undermined unwittingly by the Enlightenment, and renounced by the Romantics. This rock of absolutism Machiavelli split. He uncovered, as Isaiah Berlin puts it, an insoluble dilemma and planted a permanent question mark in the path of posterity. It stems from his *de facto* recognition (and it was only *de facto*, for 'there was no problem and no agony for him; he shows no trace of scepticism or relativism') that 'ends equally ultimate, equally sacred, may contradict each other, that entire systems of value may come into collision without possibility of rational arbitration' (*AC*, pp. 67, 70, 74f). Without believing in historical relativism himself, Machiavelli formulated the issues in such a way that the fatal fascination of his thought inevitably raised the problem for those who came after.

Guicciardini: Critic of Machiavelli

Born of patrician stock, Guicciardini was destined, unlike Machiavelli, to wield power, not just to observe it. Guicciardini earned the title 'the first of the Machiavellians' from his modern biographer, Ridolfi, for his non-ethical approach to political reality. But like Machiavelli, he wrote his greatest works in exile, where he developed a shrewd analytical insight into political behaviour that fed on his mood of dejected irony.

Though he moderates Machiavelli's passionate extremism by his patrician aloofness, he follows Machiavelli in holding that 'political power cannot be wielded according to the dictates of a good conscience'. For almost all forms of power have originated in violence and cannot be maintained by benevolence (*Ric.*, C48). As Phillips remarks, Guicciardini reveals an Actonesque sense of the licentiousness of power. For example, he follows Machiavelli in advocating that, in the interests of the safety of the state, the progeny of tyrants must be exterminated (*Ric.*, B149).

Nevertheless, Guicciardini makes some far-reaching criticisms of Machiavelli in the *Ricordi* and the *Considerations on the 'Discourses' of Machiavelli*. The thrust of his criticism is that Machiavelli, for all his claims to be describing what is the case, fails to do justice to empirical reality, he is not true to the facts. His approach is simplistic and lacking in discrimination. Sometimes it is just theoretical: some of Machiavelli's recommendations 'are more easily given form in books and in men's imaginations than carried into effect' (*Con.*, p. 79). Guicciardini is sceptical of Machiavelli's characteristic method of dividing to conquer — all states are either principalities or republics; armies are either mercenary forces or militia. Or as it could be parodied: all men are either fat or thin; now if your enemy is a fat man. . .! (Phillips, p. 88). Guicciardini gives a detailed example of his dissatisfaction with Machiavelli's method and of his own alternative approach in considering the strategic merits of the pre-emptive first strike. This question, Guicciardini writes, demands consideration of many more factors than have been adduced by Machiavelli:

> For it is not enough to make that one distinction: either I have armed subjects, or they are without arms, but it is necessary to think beyond that. Either my people are faithful or they are capable of rebellion; either the towns are strong or they are

weak. Either I can stand a long conflict financially even with the war on my own territory, destroying my reserves, or I cannot afford it. Further one has to consider the circumstances of the enemy, that is, what troops he has, what lands, what reserves, what resources to support war on his own ground, how he would pursue it beyond his frontiers... (*Con.*, p. 110)

The words 'but one must distinguish' run like a refrain through the *Considerations*. 'Against the vision, passion and simplification of Machiavelli, Guicciardini puts order, analysis and, above all, discrimination' (Phillips, p. 83, cf. p. 88).

Secondly, Guicciardini does not accept the uniformitarian assumptions that enable Machiavelli to extrapolate from the past in order to predict the future. It is true that Guicciardini does seem to endorse a basic uniformitarianism: 'the world has always been the same, and everything that is and will be, once was, and the same things recur' (*Ric.*, B114). But superimposed on the substratum of uniformity is a rich layer of variety that distinguishes the fundamental similarities. 'As a result of changes in arts and religion and the movements of human affairs, it is not surprising that men's customs too should vary, which often take their direction from an institution, from chance or from necessity' (*Con.*, p. 108). Theoretically, the future is predictable, but in practice it is almost impossible to take every factor into consideration — one miscalculation would throw the whole scheme out (*Ric.*, C114) — and allowances have always to be made for the uncertainties of Fortune. Altogether, Guicciardini concludes, 'the future is so deceptive and subject to so many accidents, that very often even the wisest of men is fooled when he tries to predict it' (*Ric.*, C23). It is significant that while Guicciardini pays lip-service to the uniformitarian assumptions that he shared with the whole Western tradition, what really interests him is the variety of the human scene and the elusiveness of historical reality.

Thirdly, in his view of human nature, Guicciardini tones down Machiavelli's extreme cynicism. Not that he embraces anything approaching the naïve moral optimism of Lockean psychology. Men are deceitful and not to be trusted. They are 'so false, so insidious, so deceitful and cunning in their wiles, so avid in their own interests and so oblivious of others' interests, that you cannot go wrong if you believe little and trust less' (*Ric.*, C27, C157). Though naturally inclined to good rather than evil, they are so easily led astray that 'to speak of the people,' — this is the voice of aristocratic disdain for the masses — 'is really to speak of a mad animal gorged with a thousand and one errors and confusions, devoid of taste, of pleasure, of stability' (*Ric.*, C134, C140). On balance, most men are 'either not very good or not very wise' (*Ric.*, C41) and respond better to severity than to kindness — though one should avoid a Machiavellian extremism in this matter, for Machiavelli 'was always extremely partial to extraordinary and violent methods' (*Con.*, 92).

A corollary of Guicciardini's rejection of Machiavelli's doctrinaire views of cyclical history and uniform human nature, is that he does not agree with Machiavelli that there is as much good in one age as in another. Though Machiavelli is right to insist that ancient times are not always to be preferred to the present, 'it is not true to deny that one age is sometimes more corrupt or more virtuous than others' (*Con.*, p. 108). So while continuing to acknowledge what we might call an 'ontological' uniformitarianism, Guicciardini explicity renounces ethical uniformitarianism.

Finally, Guicciardini sits much more lightly than Machiavelli to classical precedents, in particular the example of the Romans. The conditions for a direct comparison between present and former times are not present. 'How wrong it is to cite the Romans at every turn. For any comparison to be valid, it would be necessary to have a city with conditions like theirs and then to govern it according to their example' (*Ric.*, C110). On Machiavelli's low opinion of the tactical value of fortresses, Guicciardini comments: 'One should not praise antiquity so far that one condemns all modern uses which were not current with the Romans, for experience has revealed many things not thought of by the ancients' (*Con.*, p. 117).

Guicciardini asserts his independence not only of Machiavelli, but also of the humanist historiographical tradition in general. He does this in three principal respects: he discards the exemplarist notion of history, he makes a critical and comparative use of his sources, and he seeks a depth and power of rational explanation that will do justice to the complexity and scope of events.

Like Machiavelli when he comes to the period of Florence's decline, Guicciardini finds little to praise in the story he relates. But the significant departure in *The History of Italy* is that, from beginning to end, there is little trace of the conventional classical and humanist assumption that the narrative serves to provide moral examples and philosophical lessons. Montaigne said of this work that he could not find in it a single instance of a generous action. The story that Guicciardini has to tell is 'a tragedy that never becomes heroic . . . filled with petty men and wasted opportunity' (Phillips, p. 183; cf. Gilbert, *MG*, p. 282).

As far as his use of sources is concerned, Guicciardini marks a departure from the humanist method of following one writer at a time, merely polishing the narrative and perfecting the style. Early in his career Guicciardini had become accustomed to drawing on archival material from the family records; he had taken this further in the *Cose fiorentine* of his middle period; and in *The History of Italy* he evinced a grasp of all available sources and a judicious weighing of the evidence, to form a comprehensive and integrated narrative.

This comprehensive mastery of sources is matched by a power of rational explanation in which Guicciardini attempts to set down all the possible causes of an event: the turpitude of men, the precariousness of power-structures, the unpredictability of fortune. But, with one eye on Machiavelli, Guicciardini is wary of oversimplifying the picture. As a result, the tension between his scepticism and his desire for understanding 'impelled him towards the creation of the most comprehensive possible description of contingent political realities' (Phillips, p. 80). The result is a vast and complex web of narrative, with all the players on the stage at once, with causal connections extended as far as they could be to reveal their ultimate ramifications in the conflict of interests and clash of power-structures among the European powers. Guicciardini's masterpiece strains narrative history in the humanist tradition to the limits. As Phillip remarks,

> There is grandeur but not simplicity. There are too many questions and too few lessons, too many objects and not enough space, too much irony and too little certainty, too much movement and too little repose, too much strain and very little ease. (p. 182)

Guicciardini is breaking the mould of humanist historiography.

The grandeur of Guicciardini's historical vision is particularly seen in his conception of the dynamism of historical movement. This is envisaged as the interaction of the wild, uncontrolled power of fortune which renders human affairs 'a sea tossed by the winds', on the one hand, and the slow, steady determinants of history that can be charted and understood, on the other. As Gilbert points out, the assumption that events can be rationally explained and the acceptance of the domination of fortune are incompatible. But Guicciardini's power as an historian is revealed in his ability to combine the two. This power of synthesis

> engendered the distinguishing and novel features of *The History of Italy*: more intensive psychological explanations of human motivations; a larger historical framework taking into account the inter-connected nature of the European state-system; a more extensive application of critical methods. (*MG.*, pp. 290f)

Underlying Guicciardini's narrative power is his sense of the momentum of history, the forward drive of events, that distinguishes him so markedly from the medieval chroniclers. One of his most characteristic concepts is impetus (*impeto*): he sees men and structures as vehicles of energy, and the events of history as eruptions of energy under uncontrollable pressure (Phillips, pp. 168–73).

The *History of Florence* of 1510, Guicciardini's point of departure as an historian, sounds a dramatic or even apocalyptic note, as he describes the immediate effects of the French invasion of 1494:

> Now wars were sudden and violent; entire kingdoms were conquered and captured in less time than it used to take to conquer a village. Sieges were successfully carried out not in months but in days or hours. Battles were fierce and bloody. And, finally, states were maintained, ruined, given and taken away, not by plans drawn up in a study, as used to be the case, but in the field, by force of arms. (Phillips, p. 30)

In his mature work, Guicciardini gives the impression that he regards such dramatic revolutions of fortune as superficial: the deep transformation of political reality work much more slowly. 'The things of this world do not stay fixed. In fact, they always progress along the road on which they should, according to their nature, come to their end'. But they move, Guicciardini adds, harping on a favourite theme, 'more slowly than we believe' (*Ric.*, 140). Here is an awareness of historical change that is more than classical mutability — though it is not yet a fully fledged notion of development. Mark Phillips has aptly styled this Guicciardini's notion of 'glacial change'.

Finally, in order not to seem to modernise Guicciardini too much, we should take note of one aspect in which he is very much a man of his time. Guicciardini reflects the revival of apocalyptic at the end of the fifteenth century. But as Louis Green points out, the supernatural was no longer integral to a sacral world view, but detached from it, an alien power impinging on a self-contained secular system (pp. 146f). The French invasion of 1494, the great watershed in Italian history, is marked in his narrative with all due solemnity by signs and portents. 'And now, not only were preparations being made on land and sea, but the very heavens and mankind concurred in predicting the future woes of Italy'. Soothsayers predicted that 'stranger and more horrible events were about to occur than had been seen in any part of the world for many centuries'. In various parts of the country there began to appear 'things alien to the natural course of nature and the heavens'. Three suns shone in the sky, monstrous prodigies were born of men and animals, sacred images sweated with fear, and in one place 'an infinite number of armed men on enormous horses were seen for many days passing through the air with a terrible clamour of drums and trumpets' (*The History of Italy*, pp. 43f). The modern reader is inevitably struck by the incongruity of this passage in Guicciardini's portrait of a world 'come of age'.

2 BODIN AND MONTAIGNE: SPECULATION AND INTROSPECTION

Bodin

Bodin (1530–96), author of the *Methodus ad Facilem Historiarum Cognitionem* (1566), has been called the Montesquieu of the sixteenth century. Like the author of *The Spirit of the Laws*, Bodin occupies a transitional position between two different epochs of historical thought. Bodin carries forward many of the pre-critical and unhistorical assumptions of medieval thought, yet points ahead to the new world of historical consciousness. As Kelley has observed, on the one hand Bodin appears to have 'the scholastic philosopher's unhistorical and indiscriminate attitude towards his authorities and his faith that an ideal system may be assembled merely by the proper arrangement and criticism of these', while on the other, he sometimes seems to be striving to capture 'the spirit of the laws' by a sophisticated comparative method ('Bodin's Method', p. 147).

The paradox of Bodin's thought is created by his attempt to achieve a fusion of universal principles and individual particulars — of philosophy and theology on the one hand, and humanism and law on the other. In this dual commitment to the characteristically Platonist concern with the ideal and the Aristotelian interest in the empirical, Bodin stands in the company of the great post-Renaissance synthesisers — Bacon, Grotius and Vico. His method is, like theirs, a combination of deductive and inductive approaches. But in the case of Bodin the balance between the two is difficult to judge.

Franklin stresses the inductive, empirical aspect of Bodin's thought, calling it 'the first attempt to derive a general theory of law from the materials of universal history' (p. 69). Kelley, however, emphasises the speculative, rational element in Bodin's thought, arguing that he sought a conceptual rather than a temporal scheme, in which the substance of history could be subsumed under the categories of law. For while history was placed by Bodin 'above all sciences', its function was nevertheless purely to serve jurisprudence and political philosophy. Bodin's ultimate motive was not, as with Vico, historical understanding for its own sake, but utility. He wanted not so much to make history itself a science, as to extract a science from it — not to perfect history, but to transcend it. Bodin was not concerned with historical research. The *Methodus* has little to say about source-criticism or scientific methods of investigation, though Bodin's use of mythology and philology reveals that he was groping towards these methods. The utilisation, rather than the discovery of historical fact was the aim of the *Methodus* (Brown, p. 193; Kelley, 'Bodin's Method', p. 130; *Foundations*, pp. 136ff; cf. Berlin, *AC*, p. 104, n2).

The truth is that Bodin, like Vico, straddles both worlds of thought — the Platonic, speculative approach and the Aristotelian, empirical one. Comparison with Vico is illuminating, for a similar scholarly controversy has been going on in Vichean studies, as to whether Vico's method was predominantly speculative or empirical. Both Bodin and Vico were creative synthesisers: if their work could be explained in terms of one conceptual tradition, they would not have the significance or exert the fascination that they do for later thought. It is only in retrospect that the tension between the two approaches appears as inconsistency, and it would be anachronistic to label it as such.

Bodin's *Methodus* stands in the rhetorical tradition; it belongs to the genre of *ars historica*. But Bodin infuses the traditional form with strong juridical, political and economic elements. He is more concerned with facts and their significance than with elegant presentation and conforming to a received model of what a treatise on the art of reading history should be like. This departure Bodin shares with the German protestant historians with their factual, geographical and chronological emphasis forged in ecclesiastical controversy. But Bodin was no uncritical borrower. While German history was polemical (against Rome) and theocratic (against the pope), his own approach was distinctively secular. German history provoked Bodin's refutation of the notion of the Four Monarchies and his defence of biblical chronology against the radical element in German thought. It gave him his interest in the origins of peoples.

Bodin reflects the growing enthusiasm for the political realism of Tacitus and is favourably disposed towards Machiavelli for similar reasons, though he is capable of criticising him — for example, for his endorsement of the *stato misto* (mixed constitution). While Bodin's *Republic*, written ten years later, is virulently anti-Machiavellian (a tactical concession to changed public opinion which had hardened against Machiavelli in the meantime), in the *Methodus*, Machiavelli is praised as the first to revive the doctrine of the state and to develop a secular political philosophy after 1200 years of benighted ecclesiastical monopoly in this sphere. Likewise, Bodin is enthusiastic about the work of Guicciardini because of his passion for facts and discriminating use of sources.

Bodin is a man of his time in his evaluation of the purpose of history. His *Methodus*, he announces, is to enable the reader 'to cull flowers from history to gather thereof the sweetest fruits.' Correctly understood — i.e. in the light of the principles he is setting forth in the treatise — history will interpret the present and predict the future, incite to virtue and deter from vice; it will provide guidance for human life in society (pp. 1, 9). (But Bodin recognises the limits of a moralistic approach and attempts to guard against bias when he remarks, 'It is difficult for a good man, when writing of villains, to refrain from imprecation, or to avoid bestowing love and gratitude on heroes' (p. 43)).

It is astonishing to us that, while Bodin transcends the historical outlook of his time in his recognition of relativism and diversity in human institutions, he should nevertheless assert that, by virtue of that very fact, these phenomena fall outside the scope of his enquiry. Laws, religions, sacrifices, festivals and other institutions do not lend themselves to philosophical generalisation — and thence to historical study itself, let the reader understand — 'because they vary infinitely and change within a brief period through natural growth or at the will of a prince'. For the Romantic historians following Vico this is, of course, precisely what constitutes their fascination and renders them the fitting subjects of historical investigation. Bodin, however, proposes to seek his subjects 'not from the institutions of men, but from nature, which are stable and are never changed unless by great force or long training, and even if they have been altered, nevertheless eventually they return to their pristine character' (p. 85).

This passage is remarkable for its anticipation of the Vichean sense of the diversity and relativity of all human achievement, on the one hand, and of Cartesian, Lockean uniformitarianism, on the other. But here we are seeing the development of a sense of cultural relativism at a time when it had not yet been assimilated into historical method. When eventually so assimilated, in the thought of G. B. Vico, it would result in a radical transformation of the nature of history.

Bodin's thought, like that of Vico, can accommodate both relativist and uniformitarian elements (though these are not fully integrated). Man is a part of nature; his varied life is seen against the backdrop of the universe; history is a movement that stirs only the surface of the cosmos. As Beatrice Reynolds, the translator of the *Methodus*, has pointed out, Bodin linked history to man, man to his nature, and nature to the cosmic powers working through the elements. In Bodin's cosmology the universe is a hierarchy of superimposed powers, forming a world that is both transitory and unending, maintaining the type while the individual members pass through a cycle of birth, rise, decline and death (Bodin, pp. xiv, xxvi).

But Bodin did not espouse a theory of irreversible decline: he was too much a product of the Renaissance for that. Though he did not commit himself to a doctrine of progress as, for example, Bacon did, he was sufficiently optimistic about the possibilities of human advancement to reject the current interpretation of the prophecy of the book of Daniel. The suggestion that Daniel's statue with feet of clay represented the progressive decline through the Four Monarchies to man's present clayey state was unacceptable in a time, like the Renaissance, of confidence in human achievement. (Bodin opposed the Four Monarchies scheme on other grounds too, pointing out against the chauvinistic notion of the Germans that the Roman Empire had been transferred to them — *translatio imperium ad Germanos* — that the Turks, with their extensive conquests, had a better claim to be the continuators of the Holy Roman Empire.)

Bodin anticipates Montesquieu in giving a significant place to the influence of climate and geography in determining the character of a people. The diversity of political forms and laws reflects these factors. Bodin still describes this character in terms of the theory of humours, but declares that the nature of peoples is not determined by the stars and that astrology is an unreliable guide to the future — numerology being far more reliable!

As Huppert has pointed out, Bodin's indiscriminate collection of facts badly needs a principle of selectivity. Such a principle Bodin possesses in rudimentary form in his concept of civilisation, which he sees as having come about not by divine ordinance or in an attempt to impliment abstract political theories of social contract and the like — the so-called Golden Age being in reality cruel and primitive — but ultimately in response to man's primeval instinct of self-preservation. The *Methodus* was the first book to be published (though similar ideas were already circulating) to advance a theory of universal history based on a purely secular study of the growth of civilisation. As an organising principle, the idea of civilisation also determines Bodin's distinctive periodisation of history.

Bodin develops a remarkable periodisation that rests not on the unfolding of salvation-history but on the natural determinants of man's existence. Where national character is attributed to the influence of climate and geography rather than to divine ordinance or to the stars, there arises the possibility that human nature will be regarded as malleable and open to development. Bodin accordingly sees the pattern of human history unfolding in three epochs of 2,000 years each. The first is the age of the southern peoples, contemplative by nature, who developed religion and philosophy. Then followed the ascendency of the peoples of the temperate zone who excelled at politics and government. These in turn gave way to the ingenious northern peoples whose distinctive gifts were for mechanical invention and who gave themselves to the art of war. Bodin's periodisation, contrived though it is, is significant as a secular scheme based on the contributions made by different races to the growth of civilisation. It anticipates Vico's three ages — the ages of the gods, of the heroes and of men — but even more remarkable is the similarity to Hegel's division of history into oriental, Graeco-Roman and Germanic cultures (cf. Brown, pp. 96ff).

Kelley has summarised Bodin's overall achievement and limitations in a form that merits quotation:

> In an age of academic inhibition he was a boldly speculative thinker; in an age of doctrinal faction a philosophical syncretist; in an age of discriminating criticism a compulsive and rather credulous eclectic. Not satisfied merely with investigating the past, he sought to extract from it principles of universal and eternal import; not satisfied with determining rules of human behaviour, he wanted to arrange them into a coherent system; not satisfied with analysing society in rational terms, he wanted to uncover the *arcana* of nature as well as of the imperium.

Kelley's concluding words serve to place Bodin firmly where he belongs, not in modern post-Enlightenment historical science, but in an age when history merged into natural philosophy and natural philosophy into the occult: 'These overreaching philosophical ambitions,' he says, 'led him down strange and even forbidden paths and gave him an almost Faustian reputation' ('Bodin's Method', p. 124).

Montaigne

As a contemporary of the historians and historical theorists that we have already considered, Montaigne (1553–92) responds to the same cultural stimuli and intellectual challenges that they do. For example, he is fascinated by the news of peoples inhabiting the recently discovered lands. But he stands apart from the mainstream of the historical movement. His interest is that of a moralist rather than a historian. The question he puts to every new item of knowledge is, 'What does this say to us about how to live and how to die?'.

Of the various tributaries of historical understanding, Montaigne contributes nothing to method or criticism or structure. But what he does offer — and in this lies his significance in the present context — is an enhancement of the vision of humanity through self-awareness. Donald M. Frame's account of the development of Montaigne's thought is entitled, *Montaigne's Discovery of Man*: we only need to add that it was made through his discovery of himself. So Montaigne belongs in that dimension of historical understanding that we have associated with Augustine's *Confessions*, the new biographical and autobiographical genres of the twelfth century, and the self-revealing writings of Petrarch.

Montaigne was a relativist suffering from arrested development. Influenced by the relativistic metaphysic of the writings of Nicholas Cusanus, Montaigne was receptive to the tales of other lands where the customs and values of Christendom seemed to be reversed. His wide experience of travel and public affairs fostered a tolerant outlook. It has been said that Montaigne's relativism 'ranged from the smallest detail of personal relationships to the largest affairs of humanity and the cosmos' (Keller, p. 146). But this was purely a cultural or synchronic relativism. Several factors prevented its developing into an historical or diachronic relativism.

Firstly, there was Montaigne's commitment to antiquity. A passionate adherent of the high humanism that held that classical values and the wisdom of antiquity could never be surpassed, Montaigne sided with the conservatives in the argument over the respective merits of ancient and moderns. As Peter Burke remarks, his cultural relativism was overcome by his admiration for classical antiquity (*Montaigne*, p. 52).

Secondly, Montaigne's innate conservatism was reinforced by the miseries and uncertainties of the religious civil wars in France. He was deeply committed to things as they were, and may well have sensed that to delve too deeply into questions concerning the historical relativism of political institutions would get him into deep water (Keller, p. 152).

Thirdly, Montaigne's early sense of the diversity of human nature and the uncertainty of knowledge led him beyond the sceptical crisis of his middle years into his later phase characterised by a new sense of the unity of humanity, of the process of becoming and of solidarity with his fellow men — an acceptance of the whole.

Montaigne certainly lacks a developed historical sense — but he does not set out to write as a historian but as a moralist. For his purposes, as he freely admits, fabulous examples are as good as true ones, provided they are feasible.

> Whether they happened or not, in Paris or in Rome, to John or to Peter, there is always some turn of the human mind about which they give me useful information . . . There are some authors whose purpose is to relate actual events. Mine, if I could fulfil it, would be to tell what might happen. (pp. 46f)

Montaigne's pages are thick with examples from ancient and modern history, but he does not attempt to set them in historical perspective. While he uses history, it is not as history that he uses it. Caesar and Alexander could have equally well been modern worthies — their exemplary purpose would not have been affected (Keller, p. 150).

Nevertheless, Montaigne was an avid reader of historians — Tacitus, Herodotus, Caesar and Plutarch (if Plutarch can be classified as an historian) among the ancients; Machiavelli, Guicciardini, and Commines among the moderns. He favoured those who went beneath the surface of events to expose inner motivations, and observed that the historians best qualified to do this were those who themselves had been involved in public affairs, Guicciardini being a notable example. While he regards him as a careful and reliable historian, Montaigne has his reservations:

> I have also noticed that in all the many characters, actions, motives and designs that he judges, he never attributes anything to virtue, religion, or conscience; it is as if these factors were entirely extinct in the world. However noble an action may seem in itself, he always traces it to some vicious motive or to the hope of gain. (p. 172)

Tacitus exerted considerable fascination over Montaigne; he was the one author he could not put down (p. 307). Remarking 'I know of no author who introduces into a public chronicle so many reflections on the natures of private men', Montaigne evaluates Tacitus' method and merits:

> This form of history is by far the most useful . . . The *Annals* of Tacitus are an assessment rather than an historical account: they contain more precepts than stories. This is not a book to read, but one to study and learn from; it is so full of maxims that they appear in and out of season. It is a nursery of ethical and political reflections for the equipment and adornment of those who play a part in the management of the world.

A 'sick and disturbed state, such as ours is at present', reflects Montaigne, would benefit from Tacitus' diagnosis (p. 308).

Montaigne reveals that he had been pressed to write an account of his own times on the grounds that he viewed things with eyes less clouded by passion than other men, and at closer range, having had access to the leaders of the various factions of French politics. However, he was not to be persuaded:

> But they do not realise that I would not undertake the task for all the fame of Sallust; that I am a sworn foe to constraint, assiduity and perseverance; and that nothing is so foreign to my style as an extended narrative . . . Therefore I have undertaken to say only what I can say, suiting my matter to my powers. (p. 47)

That 'matter' — Montaigne's own thoughts and experiences — and those 'powers' — of unrivalled self-analysis and portrayal — created a new literary form, the essay, and exercised a powerful long-term influence on several central figures of the historical movement. Pascal created his concept of the natural man in dialogue with Montaigne (Pascal, pp. 242ff); Bayle followed him in his distrust of reason and reliance on fact and experience; Rousseau on the first page of the *Confessions* echoed the claim that Montaigne had been the first to make when he had written:

> if strangeness and novelty do not save me . . . I shall never come off with honour from this foolish enterprise. But my purpose is so fantastic, and so very different from the common custom, that this will perhaps enable it to pass . . . This is the only book in the world of its kind and its plan is both wild and extravagant. (p. 137)

3 BACON: TOWARDS A SCIENCE OF MAN

The Basis of Baconian History

Bacon's programme for the 'great instauration' — the reform, reorganisation and renewal of learning in all its departments — included measures to set history on a completely fresh footing. His contribution to historical science (the term is no longer anachronistic when we reach Bacon) was threefold. Firstly, in the realm of theory Bacon provided a methodological grounding for history as an empirical study, dealing with experience and proceeding inductively. Secondly, he offered a new rationale for historical study in which it provided the data or raw material for a science of man in society. Thirdly, in the realm of historical practice Bacon transcended the efforts of the chroniclers (and the limitations of his own system, for that matter) in his history of the reign of Henry VII, establishing himself as the first analytic or explanatory English historian (Quinton, p. 71).

(a) Bacon's approach presupposes, first, a dualism of science and religion. He both takes for granted and further intensifies the breakdown of the unified cosmos and integrated intellectual world characteristic of the middle ages. He was building on the gathering consensus that a preoccupation with providential first causes was incompatible with a scientific investigation of empirical phenomena at the level of second causes. But Bacon went further even than Machiavelli in making absolute the division of things human and things divine, science and religion, what is the case and what ought to be.

In *Cogita et Visa* (1607) Bacon attacked the synthesis of science and religion that was being attempted in the Christian Platonism of the Renaissance, labelling it a 'dangerous tendency'. 'No opinions are in such favour today', he complained,

> as those which with solemn pomp seem to celebrate a legal marriage between Theology and Natural Philosophy, that is, between Faith and the evidence of the senses, and which charm the minds of men with a pleasing variety of matter while

producing a disastrous confusion between the human and the divine...

There was more danger to science from 'this specious and ill-matched union' than from open hostility, he concluded.

Bacon's objections were grounded in the fact that such a synthesis tended to freeze existing scientific knowledge. Religion is characteristically not interested in pursuing fresh lines of enquiry, only in assimilating to an existing system what it feels it must come to terms with: 'all fresh growth, additions, improvements are excluded more strictly and obstinately than ever before. In fine, every development of philosophy, every new frontier and direction, is regarded by religion with unworthy suspicion and violent contempt' (*PFB*, p. 78).

(b) But it would be wrong to deduce from these statements that Bacon's attitude was detached, clinical and impersonal. Bacon was fired by an intense personal vision, a vision that can only be called humanistic. His aim was the glory and well-being of man. 'My purpose', he declared in the *Novum Organum*, 'is to try whether I cannot in fact lay more firmly the foundations and extend more widely the limits of the power and greatness of man' (*PW*, p. 294). Bacon reiterates that his purpose is 'to establish and extend the power and dominion of the human race itself over the universe' (ibid., p. 300).

(c) More closely defined, the thrust of Bacon's thought was utilitarian. He set out to improve the lot of man and to make science serve human needs, to put philosophy at the service of work. The divine purpose of knowledge was, in Bacon's view, 'the benefit and relief of the state of man' (*PW*, p. 188). As Bacon asserted in the *Novum Organum*, revealing himself, as Paolo Rossi has pointed out, as the beneficiary of the alchemical tradition: 'the true and lawful goal of the sciences is none other than this: that human life be endowed with new discoveries and powers' (ibid., p. 280). History, as well as natural science, was to serve a practical purpose, providing the data for the construction of a science of man.

But there is a check on ruthless exploitation of nature for practical ends. For though the whole tenor of Bacon's thought is concerned with activity, he sometimes pauses to acknowledge the intrinsic value of contemplation. As light is more beautiful to behold than all the uses to which it is put, 'so assuredly, the very contemplation of things, as they are, without superstition or imposture, error or confusion, is in itself more worthy than all the fruit of inventions' (*PW*, p. 300).

(d) Like Descartes, Hobbes and Spinoza after him, Bacon is determined to tear up the past and make a fresh start. The intellectual resources of Western philosophy have little to offer to the enterprise that Bacon has in hand. He will begin *de novo*. As early as 1603, in the *Temporis partus masculus* (Masculine Birth of Time), Bacon asserted 'It would not be a proper thing for me, who am preparing things useful for the future of the human race, to busy myself in the study of ancient literature' (*PFB*, p. 68). And in the *Novum Organum* (1620) he claimed:

> We should at once and with one blow set aside all sciences and all authors; and that too without calling in any of the ancients to our aid and support, but relying on our own strength . . . For new discoveries must be sought from the light of nature, not fetched out of the darkness of antiquity. (*PW*, p. 297)

(e) To start from scratch in this way — to demolish or brush aside received knowledge and build again from first principles — Bacon, like Descartes, needed an epistemology capable of doing the job. Whereas Descartes found a suitable instrument in introspection, Bacon employed a simple and naïve theory of perception, whereby we can have direct and undistorted knowledge of reality. 'All depends', he says in *The Great Instauration*,

> on keeping the eye steadily fixed upon the facts of nature and so receiving their images simply as they are, for God forbid that we should give out a dream of our own imagination for a pattern of the world; rather may he graciously grant to us to write an apocalypse or true vision of the footsteps of the Creator imprinted on his creatures. (*PW*, pp. 253f)

Not that Bacon naïvely assumes that most men can attain this level of perception without preparation. In the present state of learning,

> the mind of man is far from the nature of a clear and equal glass, wherein the beams of things should reflect according to their incidence; nay, it is rather like an enchanted glass, full of superstition and imposture, if it be not delivered and reduced. (*AL*, p. 132)

Under the discipline of true method, perceptions can become clear, distinct and unequivocal. The various idols that warp our understanding of reality can be demolished. Bacon's view is the antithesis of the post-Kantian romantic idea of perception, summed up, for example, in Blake's saying that we see, 'not with but through the eye'.

Another phrase of Bacon's brings comparison with Kant to mind: 'What I purpose', he declares, 'is to unite you with *things themselves* in a chaste, holy and legal wedlock' (*PFB*, p. 72 — original emphasis). Indeed, one could be forgiven for regarding Bacon's epistemology as a sort of pre-emptive strike against the views argued by Kant a century and a half later. Bacon's claims are almost a calculated provocation to later theories of knowledge: 'I am building in the human understanding a true model of the world, such as it is in fact, not such as man's own reason would have it to be' (*PW*, p. 298).

(f) Bacon's approach presupposed the unity of all science and the comprehensive applicability of his method. All empirical studies concerned with experience are forms of history: natural history on the one hand, civil (ecclesiastical and literary) history on the other. The study of nature and the study of mankind are to be conducted according to the same empirico-inductive method. Bacon is the forerunner of Descartes, Hobbes, Locke, Hume and the later positivist tradition in assuming that both the natural and human realms are amenable to the same methods of investigation. There is no hint in Bacon of the later romantic and idealist thinkers' separation of the natural sciences (*Naturwissenschaften*) from the human sciences (*Geisteswissenschaften*) — no recognition of the view that informed the great flowering of historical study in the nineteenth century, that the life of man is resistant to analytical and quantitative methods of investigation.

For Bacon, as later for Hobbes, even politics and ethics are to be pursued by the same method. The scope of his science is the measure of the universe itself.

> For the world is not to be narrowed till it will go into the understanding (which has been done hitherto) but the understanding to be expanded and opened till it can take in the image of the world, as it is in fact.

And then, Bacon concludes, 'we shall be no longer kept dancing within little rings, like persons bewitched, but our range and circuit will be as wide as the compass of the world' (*PW*, pp. 404f; cf. p. 299).

(g) One consequence of this all-embracing scope of Bacon's method marks a clear break with the classical-humanist rhetorical tradition. It was an axiom of rhetoric that one confined one's discourse to those things alone that were worthy of inclusion, the virtuous, noble and excellent. Bacon, following in the footsteps of Lorenzo Valla, challenges this assumption when he points out that nothing, however humble, distasteful or squalid can be excluded from the province of scientific knowledge.

> There are to be received into this history, first, things the most ordinary, such as it might be thought superfluous to record in writing, because they are so familiarly known; secondly, things mean, illiberal, filthy . . .; thirdly, things trifling and childish . . .; and lastly, things which seem over subtle, because they are in themselves of no use.

To the pure, he reminds conservative critics, all things are pure (*PW*, p. 406). The sunlight penetrates the sewer just as it does the palace, yet the sun 'takes no pollution'. In 'laying a foundation in the human understanding for a holy temple after the model of the world', Bacon adopts the principle that 'Whatever deserves to exist deserves also to be known, for knowledge is the image of existence; and things mean and splendid alike exist' (*PW*, pp. 295ff). The effect of this approach on traditional historical writing is not difficult to envisage.

(h) The key to Bacon's whole scheme of thought is found in his celebrated method. He believed that he had discovered a technique that, put into the hands of any competent person, would inevitably produce results. This method, he declared, 'leaves but little to the acuteness and strength of wits, but places all wits and understandings nearly on a level' (*PW*, p. 270; cf. p. 297). It was the instrument 'by means of which all things else shall be discovered with ease' (ibid., p. 300). Not that he claimed finality for his method; he envisaged it being superseded by more refined procedures. But this was not modesty on Bacon's part, for he held that his method would lead not only to innumerable useful discoveries, but also to more advanced methods of discovery. The 'art of discovery' would itself advance as discoveries advanced (*PW*, p. 301).

What was the method for which Bacon claimed so much? He himself believed that it consisted in the inductive logic operating on the endless tables of facts that he attempted to gather in every sphere of knowledge. But to make Bacon an exponent of the pure inductivism of J. S. Mill that has been exploded by twentieth-century philosophers of science such as Whitehead, Popper, Northrop and Polanyi, would be a caricature. Bacon makes it quite clear that enumerative induction is puerile (*PW*, pp. 290f; *PFB*, p. 89). It is true that he lays the emphasis on the gathering of facts but he also stresses the importance of structuring and interpreting them. The traditional division of the sciences into those that are empirical and those that are rational, creates a false dichotomy. The empirical and rational methods must be combined.

> The Empirics, like ants, gather and consume. The Rationalists, like spiders, spin webs out of themselves. The Bee adopts the middle course, drawing her material from the flowers of the garden or the field, but transforming it, by a faculty peculiar to herself. (*PFB*, p. 131; cf. *PW*, p. 288)

Experiment without method is futile:

> For experience, when it wanders in its own tracks, is . . . mere groping in the dark and confounds men rather than instructs them. But when it shall proceed in accordance with a fixed law, in regular order, and without interruption, then may better things be hoped of knowledge. (*PW*, p. 289)

Though Bacon believed that the inductive logic was his greatest contribution, his critics have pointed out that even Bacon himself never managed to use it; indeed it is far too cumbersome to be workable. Much more valuable in the long run was Bacon's broad empirical approach, his quest for objective truth and interest in the phenomena of natural and human life. These things were not the prerogative of genius, but provided a programme for the broadly based scientific movement of two centuries. In this sense Bacon was right to claim a levelling effect for his theories:

> My system and method of research is of such a nature that it tends to equalise men's wits and capacities . . . Men are very far from realising how strict and disciplined a thing is research into

truth and nature, and how little it leaves to the judgement of men. (*PFB*, pp. 118f)

(j) Bacon advocated a style of writing to match the rigour and discipline of his method. It was to be characterised by 'chastity'. Words were 'counters' and 'signs' and had an exact value. Bacon is the founder of the analytical view of language that has a long history through Descartes, Hobbes and Locke, Bentham in the nineteenth century, to the early Wittgenstein. According to this view, language reaches its full potential only when metaphors are ironed out and a virtual univocity attained, so that each word can be treated as an atomic unit, a counter of meaning, and clarity itself is supposed to give us the 'simple' truth. It is an attempt to close language up, to 'desynonymise' (a Coleridgean word). This tendency can be seen at work in Bacon's attempt to restrict metaphor to illustration and ornament, Hobbes's treatment of duty and inclination, love and lust as synonymous, and later, Bentham's view of poetry as misrepresentation.

It is worth mentioning that, while Bacon is generally regarded as the father of this school of thought, Coleridge, a close student and admirer, and leader of the alternative 'fiduciary' view of language, failed to detect this tendency in him. A contemporary scholar has also defended Bacon against this charge (Righter). Although Bacon describes words as 'counters', he also speaks of them as 'symbols' which perhaps points towards a less crude view.

However, the doctrine that each word ideally represents a single object, concept or relation, and its accompanying assumption that the penumbra of allusion, imagery and ethos needed to be stripped away, was certainly regarded as Baconian, and was prevalent among the Fellows of the Royal Society from the Restoration onwards. It has been said of Locke, for example, that 'he is forever talking as if lucidity is the same thing as simplicity; he cannot see that the truth might be so complex, or so approximate, that only a complex or approximate statement might be accurate' (Watson).

Philosophical style for Bacon was to be brief, concise and chaste, stripped of all extraneous matter:

Away with antiquities and citations or testimonies of authors; also with disputes and controversies and differing opinions; everything in short which is philological. Never cite an author except in a matter of doubtful credit; never introduce a controversy unless in a matter of great moment. And for all that concerns ornaments of speech, similitudes, treasury of eloquence, and such like emptinesses, let it be utterly dismissed. (*Parasceve ad historiam naturalem et experimentalem*, 1620; *PW*, p. 403)

As we shall see more clearly when we come to consider Hobbes, as far as history is concerned an approach is being advocated here which stands in exact antithesis to that of Vico and his successors, for whom metaphor and imaginative creations were the key to historical understanding.

Theory and Practice of History in Bacon

(a) It is a familiar paradox that the Renaissance, which had begun as an appeal to antiquity against the degenerate state of contemporary letters and learning, issued in a challenge to the assumptions and values of the classical world and the assertion of the merits of modernity. Similarly, the Reformation, which was essentially an appeal to the primitive church against the corrupt church of the time, gave rise to progressive views that sought to transcend many of the absolute assumptions of both the patristic and the medieval church.

Bacon recognised the impetus that the Reformation had given to scholarship and inquiry when he remarked in *The Advancement of Learning* that Luther, finding himself isolated, one man against Christendom, 'was enforced to awake all antiquity, and to call former times to his succours to make a party against the present time'.

> So that the ancient authors, both in divinity and humanity, which had long time slept in libraries, began generally to be read and revolved. Thus by conequence did draw on a necessity of a more exquisite travail in the languages original, wherein those authors did write, for the better understanding of those authors, and the better advantage of pressing and applying their words. (p. 23)

Others before Bacon had challenged some of the central themes that linked the ancient world with the Renaissance. Bodin, for example, had ridiculed the notions of the Golden Age, the Four Monarchies derived from the prophecy of Daniel, and the *translatio imperium ad Germanos*. But Bacon's criticism of antiquity is remarkable for its attempt to neutralise the formidable authority of the classical-medieval tradition by a process of historical relativising.

It was vital, in order to get a hearing for his radical programme, for Bacon to undermine the massive prestige of the contemplative-speculative approach of the classical tradition. He was attempting to divert attention from the authority of the ancients to the study of the world. 'Science is to be sought', he declared in 1603, 'from the light of nature, not from the darkness of antiquity. It matters not what has been done; our business is to see what can be done' (*PFB*, p. 69).

So alongside the assertion of his own principles, Bacon prepared a crushing indictment of the received philosophical tradition, accusing it of ignorance, irrelevance and aridity. It was essentially static and complacent, assuming that 'whatever has not yet been discovered is indiscoverable' (*PFB*, p. 74). It could boast not a single experiment which had had the effect of improving the lot of man (*PW*, p. 276; *PFB*, p. 85). Classical philosophy was barren, lacking a principle generative of good. It is to be compared to the boyhood of knowledge 'and has the characteristic property of boys: it can talk but it cannot generate; for it is fruitful of controversies but barren of works'. The present state of learning as a result, is like the mythological figure of Scylla 'who had the head and face of a virgin, but her womb was hung round with barking monsters' (*PW*, p. 243). The classical tradition was vitiated by the 'pernicious and inveterate habit of dwelling on abstractions' (ibid., p. 303). It was marked by 'professorial pomp' and 'sterile contentiousness' (cf. Rossi, Ch. 2).

But what else, asks Bacon, could be expected from the infancy of science, when it was 'in matter of knowledge but as the dawning or break of day' (*PW*, p. 190). We should see the limitations of the ancients in historical perspective: nations were self-contained; travel was minimal; there was no community of scholarship; men and states were motivated more by desire for self-aggrandisement than by aspirations to improve the life of man. The great philosophers of antiquity may have been colossal intellects (though Bacon is not over impressed), but their achievements were circumscribed by the conditions of the time:

> Whether then you reckon times or spaces, you see within what narrow confines the great intellects of those ages moved, or were shut in. A history worthy of the name did not extend over a thousand years. The rest was but legends and dreams. And of the wide regions of the earth how small a part they know . . . whole climates and zones, in which countless men breathe and live, were pronounced uninhabitable. The peregrinations of a Democritus, a Plato, a Pythagoras, which seemed wonderful in their eyes, were hardly more than suburban excursions. (*The Refutation of Philosophies*, 1608; *PFB*, p. 110)

This attempt to relativise the past provides the background to Bacon's assertion of the advantages of the present and the promise of the future.

(b) As Bacon surveyed the sad record of the past, it seemed to resolve itself into a cyclic pattern. Philosophers had been moving in circles, their speculative, sterile arguments. Covering the same old ground: 'carried round in a whirl of arguments', 'content to circle round and round for ever amid the darkest idols of the mind under the high sounding name of contemplation' (*PFB*, p. 82). The circle is for Bacon the image of futility (Guibbory).

The cyclical view of history is almost universal, but Bacon's position was defined by the Christian and classical tradition: he took the doctrines of the Fall of Man seriously, and believed too in a Golden Age from which man had steadily declined. In the light of these notions, his cycle of futility turned into a spiral of decay. Though there have been visitations of enlightenment and learning — the Greek, the Roman, the revival of letters — achievement in the arts and sciences has become steadily weaker. The river of time has carried down to us 'the light and windy and sunk the solid and weighty' (*PFB*, p. 68; cf. *PW*, p. 191). Whereas in the mechanical arts such as painting, artillery and sailing, progress is cumulative, in 'sciences of conceit' the process is reversed: 'the first author goeth furthest and time leeseth and corrupteth'. Philosophy was strongest at the beginning, in the work of Plato, Democritus and Hippocrates, but degenerated through tradition (ibid., *Valerius Terminus*, ? 1603).

Only one thing could break this spiral of decline and that was his own scientific method. Already the opportunities were there in the advances of Renaissance life and learning:

> When I set before me the condition of these times, in which learning hath made her third visitation or circuit, in all the qualities thereof; as the excellency and vivacity of the wits of this age; the noble helps and lights which we have by the travails of ancient writers; the art of printing . . .; the openness of the world by navigation, which hath disclosed multitudes of experiments, and a mass of natural history; the leisure wherewith these times abound . . . the present disposition of these times at this instance to peace . . . I cannot but be raised to this persuasion, that this third period of time will far surpass that of the Grecian and Roman learning. (*AL*, 208)

If Renaissance man would only grasp the instrument (*organum*) that Bacon was holding out to him, there would be no limit to what he could achieve with it.

The first requirement was confidence in man's own ability. 'You will never be sorry for trusting your own strength, if you but once make trial of it', urged Bacon in the *Refutation of Philosophies* (*PFB*, p. 114f.). The second was to trust to nature: just as no one could have predicted the invention of firearms or the discovery of the silk-worm, we should go forward in the expectation that 'there are still laid up in the womb of nature many secrets of excellent use, having no affinity or parallelism with anything that is now known' (*PW*, p. 292). The probable balance between extant knowledge and what remains to be discovered is suggested by a comparison of the Old World with the New (*PW*, p. 189).

Bacon condemned the defeatism of the view that the sciences — like all human endeavour — must inevitably follow a cycle in which they first flourish then decline and collapse. 'By far the greatest obstacle to the progress of science', he claimed,

> is the despair fostered by the assumption that in the revolution of time and of the ages of the world the sciences at one season . . . grow and flourish, at another wither and decay, yet in such sort that when they have reached a certain point and condition, they can advance no further.

It is a fatal error to imagine that in the sciences there is a fixed upper limit of attainment and that this can be reached within the life of an individual who is capable of bringing his field of study to a state of definitive and absolute perfection. On the contrary, every science grows by the patient observations of many men, one grasping one truth, one another, and handing on their contributions like a relay of torchbearers, a notion Bacon had learned from the co-operative enterprises of the guilds of artisans (*PFB*, p. 126; *De Sapientia Veterum*, 1609; *PW*; Zilsel).

Bacon anticipates the nightmare of modern science, that its enormous power might fall into the wrong hands or be perverted to evil ends. But he is sanguine, commenting that 'the same may be said of all earthly goods' — an observation that, while reasonable at the time, seems fatuously inadequate to the scale of the dilemma as it appears today. But Bacon grounds his optimism in the revealed will of God: 'only let the human race recover that right over nature which belongs to it by divine bequest, and let power be given it; the exercise thereof will be governed by sound reason and true religion' (*PW*, p. 300).

Bacon's vision of scientific progress is not the secular utopia of the later positivist tradition, but is formulated in Christian and biblical terms. He takes as his text Daniel 12:4, 'Many shall run to and fro and knowledge shall increase', which being interpreted signifies the conjunction of scientific discovery with the great voyages of exploration to the New World and the East. For

> it would be a disgrace for mankind if the expanse of the material globe, the land, the seas, the stars, was opened up and brought to light, while, in contrast with this enormous expansion, the bounds of the intellectual globe should be restricted to what was known to the ancients. (*PFB*, p. 94; cf. *PW*, 287)

Bacon sees himself explicitly as the Columbus of scientific discovery.

If the expansion of knowledge could be seen as a fulfilment of prophecy, this was one more piece of evidence that the last age of the world was at hand. Bacon's vision of a beneficent future to be brought about by technological advance strikes an apocalyptic note: by God's appointment, the tree of knowledge will bear its finest fruit 'in this autumn of the world' (*PW*, p. 188). Bacon's vision was, in theological terms, eschatological: he believed that scientific movement would usher in a new and last age, stored in the womb of time, and ready, by divine decree, to be inaugurated. The age to come would constitute, first, a restoration of man's prelapsarian state and powers, and secondly, the enjoyment of the eternal sabbath promised to the people of God.

The true end of knowledge, Bacon asserts, is 'a restitution and reinvesting (in great part) of man to the sovereignty and power . . . which he had in his first state of creation'. Just as Adam named the creatures and had dominion over them, science gives the power to call the creatures by their true names (i.e. natures) and once again command them.

> For man by the fall fell at the same time from his state of innocency and from his dominion over creation. Both of these losses however can even in this life be in some part repaired, the former by religion and faith, the latter by arts and sciences.

But in two ways the curse of the Fall cannot be reversed: firstly, 'that vanity must be the end in all human effects', and secondly, that man is destined to earn his bread by the sweat of his brow. In this interpretation of Genesis 3:19, Bacon takes the curse to refer to the labours of science and the mental effort involved (*O felix culpa!*), not to physical exertion which can be eased by inventions (*PW*, pp. 188f, *Valerius Terminus*; pp. 386f, *Novum Organum*; cf. Guibbory).

This eccentric interpretation of a biblical metaphor links up with a further theme in Bacon's great vision of a restoration of all things (*instauratio magna*): the promise of a sabbath rest for the people of God, by analogy with the seventh day of creation when God had rested from his work. The prayer that concludes the Plan of the Work says, 'if we labour in thy works with sweat of our brows thou wilt make us partakers of thy vision and thy sabbath' (*PW*, p. 254). While the image of the sabbath rest is in apparent conflict with the dominant images of ceaseless progression, advancement and discovery, it points nevertheless to a more radically eschatological dimension of Bacon's thought in which scientific control of the elements has become complete and man can enter into an ultimate state of technological bliss.

Bacon's theory of progress is one of the more original aspects of his thought. He was perhaps the first to combine the utilitarian concept of knowledge and the notion of cumulative scientific research to create a doctrine of scientific progress. It was this aspect of his thought (as well as his clear demarcation between religion and science) that commended Bacon to the Enlightenment.

(c) With the myth of the Golden Age went the myth of the

matchless wisdom of the ancients — the theory that a lost civilisation, existing before Greece and Rome, had attained a level of knowledge as great or greater than our own and had enshrined its wisdom in myths and fables to preserve it for a later age. This theory above all reveals the limitations of Bacon's historical grasp. For him human nature was always the same, essentially rational and comprehensible. The relativistic, evolutionary assumptions of later historicism were not anticipated by Bacon. The real watershed in modern historical thought comes with Vico who, in challenging Bacon, one of his masters in philosophy, was led to originate relativistic, developmental concepts that could accommodate the wild irrationality of primitive man.

In Bacon's successive publications we observe a gradual warming to the notion of the wisdom of the ancients, until it becomes integral to his final philosophical position. In the *Advancement of Learning* (1605) Bacon had recognised the role of hieroglyphics and symbolic gestures in communication among primitive peoples, and had pointed out the analogy with the sign language of the deaf and dumb (though not, as later thinkers were to do, with the first attempts at speech of little children) (*AL*, pp. 136f). But in the *Refutation of Philosophies* (1608) Bacon is openly flirting with the myth of the wisdom of the ancients. He imagines a conducted tour through a portrait gallery of the ancients: a portion of the gallery is cut off by a curtain:

> Behind that curtain lie the secrets of that antiquity which preceded the learning of the Greeks . . . well I know, if I wished to be insincere, that it would not be difficult to make men believe that among the sages of old, long before Greek times, philosophy and the sciences flourished with greater value and less noise. If I did this I could, by referring my present propositions to those ancient times, invest them with a certain solemnity. . .

But he will resist the temptation to perpetuate an 'imposture'. Nevertheless, he is persuaded that the fables are 'the sacred survivals of better times' and conjectures that scientific projects even more advanced than his own may have been known to remote antiquity. But he must stand by his oft-repeated principle that 'truth must be discovered by the light of nature, not recovered from the darkness of the past' (*PFB*, pp. 120f).

A year later Bacon came into the open with *De Sapientia*

Veterum (1609) in which he purported to reveal the hidden meaning of classical myths. There were possibly two reasons for this change of mind. Undoubtedly the idea of an occult wisdom had captured his imagination and all the more so as he became increasingly convinced that the tenets of his own philosophy had been anticipated by the ancients. He was no longer a voice in the wilderness, working, as he had complained, in complete isolation. Secondly, he no doubt had a tactical motive for espousing the theory of the matchless wisdom of the ancients. Conscious of the difficulties of getting a favourable reception for his ideas, with their outrageous attacks on tradition, Bacon had withheld publication of the three tractates *The Masculine Birth of Time* (1603), *Thoughts and Conclusions* (1607), and *Refutation of Philosophies* (1608). To comment now on the myths and fables of antiquity would be a covert way of propagating his views. Accordingly, the leading themes of *De Sapientia Veterum* were the importance of separating science and faith, the advantages of scientific naturalism, the need for method, the function of research and, finally, a defence of political realism in the tradition of Machiavelli.

In line with this went a change of mind on the question, 'Which came first, the fable or the meaning?'. In the *Advancement of Learning* Bacon confesses his belief that the fable was original and the interpretation derivative. By the time he comes to write *De Sapientia Veterum* he has reversed his opinion. While not prepared to dogmatise, he is so impressed by the close correspondence between a myth and its meaning that he 'cannot help believing such a signification to have been designed and meditated from the first, and purposely shadowed out'. Other stories are so absurd that out of respect for the ancients one has to suppose that they contain a hidden meaning. Bacon could not accept — and Vico would condemn him for this — that the myths of primitive man (and of course Bacon himself would have repudiated the notion of man ever being truly primitive) might have been spontaneous, imaginative responses to the universe brought forth by inarticulate beings under pressure of the emotions of awe, fear and appetite. It is summed up in Bacon's saying: 'As hieroglyphics came before letters, so parables came before arguments' (*PW*, pp. 822ff; cf. Rossi Ch. 3).

(d) It is paradoxical then, that Bacon does possess an almost Vichean sense of the inaccessibility of history, of the obscurity of the past and the extreme difficulty of recovering it in historical science. Bacon speaks, in a rather Carlylean phrase, of 'the deluge of time', and is startlingly modern in what he says about ransacking all available sources of information to get at a lost world.

'Uttermost antiquity', he remarks in *Valerius Terminus*, is 'like fame that muffles her head and tells tales'. But the historian must resist the temptation to imitate those cartographers who fill their ignorance with wastes and deserts (*PW*, p. 190). Time is the river that carries down to us on the surface the trivialia, the flotsam and jetsam of history, and allows things of substance to sink into its dark depths (*PFB*, p. 68). The task of the true historian is to rescue those 'remnants of history' that, like the spars of a shipwreck, tell a tale. Even though

> the memory of things be decayed and almost lost, yet acute and industrious persons, by a certain perseverance and scrupulous diligence, contrive out of genealogies, annals, titles, monuments, coins, proper names and styles, etymologies of words, proverbs, traditions, archives and instruments as well public as private, fragments of histories scattered about in books not historical — contrive, I say, from all these things or some of them, to recover somewhat from the deluge of time.

This is a labour of love for the true antiquary for it is 'joined with a kind of reverence' for the human past (*PW*, p. 433).

But the research of the antiquary is only a beginning; it must be followed by interpretation and reconstruction. In his stress on imaginative recreation and the role of historical judgement Bacon could be a nineteenth-century historian of the school of Ranke, lacking only the facility of documentary criticism. His ideal is a noble one:

> To carry the mind in writing back into the past, and bring it into sympathy with antiquity; diligently to examine, freely and faithfully to report, and by the light of words to place as it were before the eyes, the revelations of times, of characters, of persons, the fluctuations of counsels, the courses and currents of actions, the bottoms of pretences, the secrets of governments, is a task of great labour and judgement. (ibid., p. 432)

(e) In Bacon's all-embracing scheme history is the first of the three divisions of learning and corresponds to the mental faculty of memory. It is followed by poesy, corresponding to imagination and philosophy corresponding to reason. Many commentators on Bacon have been led astray by this apparently simplistic demarcation into accusing Bacon of inconsistency — for his own historical efforts obviously involve both imaginative reconstruction and rational interpretation. Stuart Clark has warned against pressing the division too far, and pointed out that in employing what was after all a commonplace of Renaissance faculty psychology, Bacon was safeguarding scientific history against imaginative inventions on the one hand and deductive generalisations on the other. But Bacon's indentification of history with the faculty of memory does have several significant consequences in his thought.

First, as we have just seen, Bacon fails to attain the Vichean understanding of myths and fables as imaginative constructions, an inarticulate response to the mystery of the universe, to be relived by the historian through the faculty of *fantasia*. This would have brought the power of imagination to the heart of Bacon's historical method.

Secondly, Bacon abandoned the rhetorical commonplace that history was philosophy teaching by examples. He transferred the aesthetic function of history to poetry and its didactic function to philosophy.

Imaginative or fictional history (*historia conficta*) serves better than factual history to delight and elevate the mind, for 'Poesy seems to bestow upon nature those things which history denies to it; and to satisfy the mind with the shadows of things when the substance cannot be obtained'.

> There is agreeable to the spirit of man a more ample greatness, a more perfect order and a more beautiful variety than it can anywhere (since the Fall) find in nature. And, therefore, since the acts and events which are the subjects of real history are not of sufficient grandeur to satisfy the human mind, Poesy is at hand to feign acts more heroical; since the successes and issues of actions related in true history are far from being agreeable to the merits of virtue and vice, Poesy corrects it, exhibiting events and fortunes as according to merit and the law of providence; since true history wearies the mind with satiety of ordinary events, one like another, Poesy refreshes it by reciting things unexpected and full of vicissitudes. So that this Poesy conduces not only to delight but also to magnanimity and morality.

Unlike reason and history which buckle and bow down the mind to the nature of things, poesy accommodates the show of things to the desires of the mind (*rerum simulacra ad animi desideria*) (*PW*, p. 440).

Philip Sidney in his *Apology for Poetry* had already made the fundamental distinction between the particular truths of history and the universal truths of poetry. But whereas Sidney's aim was to instil the glory of poetry and the nobility of imagination, Bacon's use of the dichotomy was intended to disparage and trivialise poesy, for from a rigorously empirical point of view, fiction is synonymous with falsehood. Hobbes was soon to take the argument a stage further by arguing that both empirical and imaginative truth was inferior to mathematical demonstration, thereby trivialising history as well as poetry. For Hobbes, history could only be illustrative of rational truth, and for that purpose 'typical' history will serve as well as the real thing.

By distinguishing the task of history, which was to establish an accurate record of events, from the task of philosophy, which was to draw out precepts and generalisations from the facts as a basis for a science of man in society, Bacon completed his destruction of the received view of history as philosophy teaching by examples. Just as natural history, in Bacon's system, forms a foundation for applied science or natural philosophy, so civil history forms a foundation for a science of man comprising ethics and civil philosophy (politics). These disciplines operate in an empirical and inductive way on the basis of the facts provided by history. They are thus solely concerned with 'what is' not with 'what ought to be'.

The work of the historian is essential to the philosopher but he must not trespass on the latter's territory:

> For a man who is professedly writing a Perfect History to be everywhere introducing political reflexions, and thereby interrupting the narrative, is unseasonable and wearisome. For though every wise historian is pregnant (as it were) with political precepts and warnings, yet the writer himself should not play the midwife. (*PW*, p. 437)

The philosopher himself, acting as midwife, can produce a 'Georgics of the Mind', a science of human nature, and to do this he will find that character and disposition are best studied in the histories of Livy, Tacitus, Herodian, Comines, Machiavelli and Guicciardini. Bacon has a special word of praise for Tacitus and Machiavelli. While the ethics of Plato and Aristotle are much admired, he remarks, 'the pages of Tacitus breathe a livelier and truer observation of morals and institutions'. Machiavelli too shows us man as he is, not as idealists have imagined him to be (*PW*, pp. 57f; *PFB*, pp. 71f).

There is a nice Machiavellian touch in one of Bacon's *Sacred Meditations* (perhaps inaptly named in this case). Bacon is underlining the need for a man of affairs, a reformer, to be seasoned in villainy, and remarks that 'wicked men, who have not a wholesome thought in them, naturally assume that goodness springs from a certain simplicity of moral character and ignorance and inexperience of human affairs'. They must be made to realise that 'every recess of their wicked hearts lies open to the understanding of him' (not God but the philosopher-statesman) with whom they have to do. The man who seeks to serve the public good should acquaint himself with what Scripture calls 'the deeps of Satan', for

> there are neither teeth nor stings, nor venom, nor wreaths and folds of serpents, which ought not to be all known and as far as examination doth lead, tried: neither let any man here fear infection or pollution; for the sun entereth into sinks and is not defiled. (*Works VII*, p. 245; 'Of the Innocency of the Dove and the Wisdom of the Serpent')

Like Hobbes after him, Bacon complains that moralists have held up a model of perfect moral rectitude, but have done little to help those who are struggling with actual moral decisions, involving compromise or a choice of evils. He attributes this to the disdain felt by philosophers in the classical-rhetorical tradition to soil their thoughts with what is common or mean — 'that hidden rock whereupon both this and so many other barks of knowledge have struck and foundered' (*PW*, p. 562). Bacon's programme for the reform of learning will issue in a scientific ethical system, the crown of his science of man.

(f) Bacon's *History of the Reign of Henry VII* was intended, like the *Essays*, as an exercise in Baconian psychology, Georgics of the mind, providing the raw material for the science of human nature. As Stuart Clark has pointed out, this did not necessarily involve Bacon in any detailed research or criticism of documents. He believed that 'it was historically quite valid simply to take the story that was readily available in existing accounts of the reign, purge it of its interpretative framework, and substitute one of his own'. It is not as a model of how to write history that Bacon has his place in the evolution of modern historical thought. As Clark has remarked of *Henry VII*, 'In its annalistic structure, causal analysis and use of sources it was . . . as "literary" and "unscientific" as other sixteenth-century works of its kind' ('Henry VII', p. 116). Neither does his significance lie in his celebrated inductive logic. His true importance is twofold. First, it lies in his progressive vision. In Bacon we have not yet reached a fully fledged rationalist idea of progress — that had to await Descartes' reformation of the ideal of knowledge in mathematical terms, which Pascal could then employ in a theory of the cumulative march of the scientific mind. Nevertheless, Bacon is, as Anthony Quinton has claimed, 'the most confident, explicit and influential of the first exponents of the idea of progress' (p. 29). Secondly, Bacon's significance is to have secured the integration of historical studies into the general scientific — empirico-inductive — movement (Fussner, p. 264), to have formulated for the first time a *science* of history. From Vico to Coleridge and from the *philosophes* to Macaulay and Mill, Romantics and rationalists alike, Bacon dominates historical thought — for the one a giant to be overthrown in the path of historical understanding, for the other the undisputed father of historical science.

4 HOBBES: HISTORY AND REASON

Descartes

Renaissance humanism had given a strong impetus to historical study. This had been reinforced by the comparative and inductive method advocated by Bodin and Bacon. History seemed set fair to continue its development within the new scientific movement. Between the Renaissance and the Enlightenment, however, a new movement of thought intervened that was rationalist in character and fundamentally anti-historical in its thrust. Its representatives were, on the Continent, Descartes and Malebranche, and in England, Thomas Hobbes. While they succeeded in temporarily arresting the progress of historical thought, they nevertheless contributed to its revival in the Enlightenment: Descartes through his focus on individual consciousness; Malebranche through his influence on Voltaire's scientific thought; and Hobbes through his influence on Locke.

It is a striking paradox that Descartes (1596–1650), the founder of a militantly anti-historical rationalism, and whose contempt for history is notorious, should have been singled out by such notable interpreters of the historical movement as Troeltsch and Flint for the impetus that his thought gave to historical consciousness.

It was Troeltsch's view that, by his method of systematic doubt followed by reconstruction from a subjective centre, Descartes had provided the indispensible premise of an historical outlook: he had brought human consciousness into the forefront of attention (Rubanowice, p. 85). Flint pointed out that the principle of methodical doubt challenged all traditional authorities and provided the critical independence of judgement that is a precondition of historical inquiry.

It is also clear that Descartes, like the other post-Renaissance proponents of patent methodologies, believed that his favoured method had unlimited application and could be turned to tackle all outstanding scientific and philosophical problems. With Bacon, whose *Novum Organum* appeared in the year that Descartes made his great 'discovery' (1620), Descartes gave currency and credibility to the idea of progress.

On the other hand, however, Descartes is undoubtedly the fountainhead of the rationalistic, uniformitarian idea of history that we can trace through the thought of Hobbes (where it is unadulterated), Locke (where it is moderated by his stress on experience), and aspects of the Enlightenment, to the Utilitarians and rationalists of the nineteenth century. Its central feature is the notion of clear and distinct ideas; its method is mathematical and deductive.

Before he formulated his distinctive position, Descartes already had a low view of history; his method, when espoused, merely reinforced a basically ahistorical outlook. He reflected in the *Discourse on Method*:

> I thought I had already given enough time to languages, and even also to the reading of the ancients, to their histories and fables. For to converse with those of other centuries is almost the same as to travel. It is a good thing to know something of the customs and manners of various peoples in order to judge of our own more objectively . . . But when one spends too much time travelling, one becomes eventually a stranger in one's own country; and when one is too interested in what went on in past centuries, one usually remains extremely ignorant of what is happening in this century. (pp. 30f)

We find Malebranche, half a century later, drawing the same analogy.

On that memorable day in 1620, shut up with (or in) a stove, Descartes began to examine his thoughts. His first meditation is particularly significant for our purposes. It concerns the principle of development, a notion that Descartes found highly questionable (p. 35). He began by observing that often less perfection could be discerned in composite works produced by several hands: 'So it is that one sees that buildings undertaken and completed by a single architect are usually more beautiful and better ordered than those that several architects have tried to put into shape'. Ancient towns with their layers of development, winding streets and asymmetrical layout are inferior to the planned orderly creations of a single mind.

Similarly, with regard to society, those peoples who emerged gradually from semi-savagery, making their laws piecemeal as they went along in response to crimes and quarrels, 'could not be so well organised as those who, from the moment at which they came together in association, observed the basic laws of some wise legislator'. (It still remained, of course, for a Vico to demythologise the great law-givers of antiquity and, in doing so, to turn Descartes's view of tradition on its head, reversing his values and finding the real springs of human society, law and culture ultimately in the obscure and irrational products of primitive imagination.)

It was only a short step for Descartes from the infancy of society to the childhood of the individual. Just as society had emerged, thanks to clear and articulate reasoning *de novo*, from the thralldom of instinct and the tutelage of tradition, into the ordered, rational states devised by the great legislators of antiquity, so children, ruled by their appetites and led astray by incompetent tutors, have their powers of reasoning permanently impaired. If only we had had the full use of our reasoning faculties from the moment of birth and had never been guided by anything else! (p. 36).

There is a striking contrast once again between Descartes's attitude to childhood and that of the Romantics, exemplified in Wordsworth's Immortality Ode, just as there is between the Cartesian and the Vichean views of society (cf. Willey, p. 87). As Maritain asserted in his essay on Descartes: 'If Cartesianism showed itself so savage a ravager of the past in the intelligible order, it is because it began by disowning in the individual himself the essential intrinsic dependence of our present knowledge on our past' (p. 62).

Since the remainder of this book will deal either with the elaboration of Descartes's principles, as in the case of Hobbes, or with views worked out in opposition to them, as with Vico, it will be worth our while to acquaint ourselves with them, even if their relevance to historical philosophy is not immediately obvious.

Descartes's proposals involve, first of all, a stripping away of the accumulated prejudices of a lifetime — the 'tradition', as it were, of the individual mind — by a process of methodical doubt. But having attempted to doubt all that he already believes, Descartes finds one idea in his mind that is unassailable — the notion that he is actually doubting. *Cogito ergo sum*, 'I think therefore I am', is a clear, distinct and indubitable concept. Now if Descartes can find other ideas that are equally clear and distinct, he can begin the process of reconstruction.

For Descartes, as for Plato and a long tradition of Western philosophy, that includes Cusanus, Leonardo da Vinci, Galileo, Kepler and Spinoza, mathematics is the model of certain knowledge; its terms are clear, distinct and self-contained. All the problems of natural knowledge could be solved by applying the method of pure logical reasoning. Whereas Descartes retains an interest in empirical, experimental inquiry, Spinoza pushed the method to its ultimate conclusion. It is true to say of Spinoza that 'no other philosopher has ever insisted more uncompromisingly that all problems, whether metaphysical, moral or scientific, must be formulated and solved as purely intellectual problems, as if they were theorems in geometry' (Hampshire, p. 24) — not even Hobbes.

With regard to Descartes himself there are several qualifications that need to be made. First of all, while Descartes stakes all on the criteria of clarity and distinctness, a certain lack of these two attributes can be detected in the principles themselves. The Cogito is his model, but the clarity and distinctness here involves a movement of thought — instantaneous though it be — from premise to conclusion: Cogito *ergo* sum. But in the *Meditations* Descartes employs his canons of clarity and distinctness more generally: not only to ideas that involve a train of reasoning, however implicit, but also to perceptions (his own example is a piece of wax).

Secondly, in the Cogito the premise 'I think' is obviously drawn from experience, not from logic. This makes the Cognito a synthetic *a posteriori* statement (to put it in the received philosophical jargon). Here we may contrast the method of Spinoza who does not rely on experience at all; his statements are all *a priori*.

Thirdly, Descartes does not hold that either clear and distinct ideas (the Cogito) or clear and distinct perceptions (the piece of wax) in themselves constitute objective knowledge of reality. The canons of clarity and distinctness prove that objects (which may be physical or mental) are present to the mind, not that they correspond to the actual state of affairs 'outside' the mind, in the 'real' world — for, as Descartes so ingenuously says, it might all be a dream. To guarantee the veridical status of both our ideas and our perceptions, Descartes has to introduce the notion of clear and distinct judgements — and underlying these, the existence of God (proved by the clear and distinct reasoning of the ontological argument) — a God who would not permit his creatures to be fundamentally and permanently deceived (Keeling, pp. 173f). For

Spinoza, on the other hand, clear and distinct ideas, in and of themselves, provide a knowledge of reality. For according to Spinoza, thought is itself one of the two knowable attributes (out of an infinite number) of ultimate reality or God — the other being extension.

When looked at in this way, the philosophical ideal based on clear and distinct ideas seems somewhat lacking in clarity and distinctness itself. In its origins complex and enmeshed with abstract metaphysical speculation, this model of philosophical discourse was destined to enjoy a long history and to exert considerable influence on historical thinking either by way of development or reaction. One recurrent theme of this long-running controversy concerns the nature of language.

In the philosophical tradition that stems from Descartes, the notion of clear and distinct ideas carries the corollary of a rationalistic, analytical view of language. We find in Descartes himself a radical distinction between the cries of animals which are the product of nature (instinct) and the first articulate speech of men which is solely the creation of reason (p. 75). 'One should not confuse words', he asserts, 'with the natural movements which bear witness to the passions'. It follows 'not only that animals have less reason than men, but that they have none at all' (!). Here again, Descartes's view contrasts markedly with the later theory of Vico, worked out in explicit antithesis to Cartesianism, that there is a line of continuity between animal cries and the inarticulate expressions of primitive man.

Nicholas Malebranche (1638–1715) experienced a sudden and total conversion to Descartes's philosophy as a young Oratorian, and devoted his life to forging a synthesis of Christian theology and Cartesian philosophy. Impressed above all by Descartes's concentration on method, Malebranche's *De la recherche de la vérité* (1674–5) is a cumulative metaphysical argument for a method that is fully revealed only at the end of this hefty treatise. But Malebranche's method is not indebted only to Descartes's rationalism — he is critical of the arbitrary aprioristic approach of the later Descartes — but also to Bacon's empiricism. Malebranche's concept of truth rests on the twin pillars of rational and empirical demonstration and is overarched by a Christian moral purpose. It is applicable to every department of knowledge (Rome).

History cuts a poor figure in the light of Malebranche's rigorous conditions of truth. It was neither capable of rational demonstration nor susceptible of experimental proof. Its moral and religious import was often hard to detect. Taking up Descartes's remark that those who become absorbed in the history of other ages lose touch with the times in which they live, Malebranche pours scorn on the antiquarian mentality. Chronology, genealogy, study of the way of life and the languages of the ancients is all lost labour, *recherches inutiles* (pp. 62f, 200f). Malebranche's sustained polemic against pure historical research forms a bridge between Descartes's principles, inimical to history, and the philosophes' suspicion of 'pedantry'.

Hobbes in Context

Hobbes (1588–1679), like Descartes, presents us with the intriguing case of a thinker, militantly anti-historical in his mature thought, yet whose significance in the evolution of modern historical consciousness is unquestionable.

Hobbes's most fascinating intellectual relationships are with Machiavelli, Bacon, Descartes and (posthumously) Vico. In his pessimistic estimate of human nature and grasp of the dynamics both of the individual's drive for power and of social transformation, Hobbes has strong affinities with Machiavelli, though he does not mention him. Machiavelli's naked rationalism lives again in Hobbes. As D. G. James has remarked of Hobbes: 'He, more than any other great writer of the seventeenth and eighteenth centuries, preached the power and scope of human reason' (p. ix). Hobbes's ethical realism or (as we would describe it today) relativism, link him with both Machiavelli and Bacon.

More than a mere amenuensis, Hobbes was Bacon's companion and the confidant of his philosophising. As Aubrey tells us: 'The Lord Chancellour Bacon loved to converse with him . . . His Lordship would often say that he better liked Mr. Hobbe's taking his thoughts, than any of the other, because he understood what he wrote' (p. 308f).

In his mature work Hobbes hailed Copernicus, Galileo and William Harvey as founders of the new natural science, but conspicuously failed to mention Bacon. He did not attempt to conceal his contempt for the experimentation of the Royal Society along Baconian lines (*EW*, IV, p. 437). And while Bacon weakened his case by not taking sufficient account of the role of mathematics in scientific procedure, Hobbes went to the opposite extreme, excluding as unscientific and therefore irrelevant anything that could not be pressed somehow into a mathematical mould (history being a prime casualty). But the common ground between Bacon and Hobbes is significant and lies in the presuppositions rather than the content of their philosophies.

First, they are both — along with other outstanding thinkers of the time — obsessed by method. As Hobbes remarks, 'Most men wander out of the way and fall into error for want of method' (*EW*, I, p. 1). Not only was method a reliable (even infallible) guide; it was also a short cut. As Hobbes puts it: 'Method, therefore, in the study of philosophy, is the *shortest way* of finding out effects by their known causes or of causes by their known effects' (ibid., p. 66, emphasis altered). As this statement suggests, methods may be deductive or inductive — Hobbes strongly favouring the former, Bacon the latter. Both believed that their preferred methods would bring about a scientific reconstruction of the knowledge of man in society, i.e. of the sciences of ethics and politics.

While Hobbes does not necessarily owe his passionate interest in method to Bacon (as a philosophical issue it goes back to Aristotle; and Descartes was a more recent exponent of method), they stand together as the two most outstanding methodologists of the seventeenth century before Newton.

Secondly, Bacon and Hobbes share the analytical view of language that has subsequently become a salient feature of the English positivist tradition. They both refer to words as 'counters', fight shy of metaphor, and seek a one-to-one correspondence between a word and its meaning. I defer consideration of this aspect of Hobbes's thought in order to take it in conjunction with his view of history which it illuminates.

Thirdly, Bacon and Hobbes share a concern to ameliorate the lot of man by the application of science to industry. For them both, knowledge is not virtue (as for Plato) or salvation (as for Christianity), but power. 'The end or scope of philosophy', Hobbes claims, consists in use and application, 'as far as matter, strength and industry will permit, for the commodity of human life'. Purely intellectual triumphs are hollow victories and not worth the effort. The only philosophical game worth the candle is the one that presupposes that 'the end of knowledge is power' (*EW*, I, p. 7). All the commodities of civilised life are produced by those arts such as measurement, movement, construction, navigation, calculation, etc., that are created when philosophy is put to work — 'By which sciences', comments Hobbes, the would-be benefactor of mankind, 'how great benefits men receive is more easily understood than expressed' (ibid.).

Bacon had initiated a revolution in the method of the sciences: Hobbes himself stood for a counter-revolution. Bacon's empirical approach — pruned of its extravagancies — was prophetic of modern scientific and technological achievement. The men of the Enlightenment looked on Bacon — along with Locke and Newton — as a founding father. Hobbes, on the other hand — along with Descartes and Spinoza — represents a mathematical, *a priori*, deductive approach that, as a method, has been less central to modern thought, but in its conclusions has been immensely influential. This distinction of method and content raises the question, touched on by Strauss and others, whether Hobbes's purported geometrical method was not largely incidental to a philosophical vision that was primarily the creation of imagination tempered by incisive observation of human nature. In any event, Hobbes's eccentric method was no handicap to the influence of his ideas which were fundamentally rationalist, secularist and relativist in their import, and on those grounds alone claim a place in any survey of historical thought. Of Hobbes's influence, G. P. Gooch wrote: 'To a far greater degree than Bacon, he was the author of the atmospheric change which substituted the secular for the theological standpoint throughout the boundless realms of thought and speculation' (p. 57).

The link with Descartes is, if somewhat paradoxical, at least relatively straightforward. While adopting and radicalising Descartes's mathematico-deductive method, Hobbes uses it to establish opposite conclusions: for Descartes reality is essentially thought; for Hobbes it is basically material (James, p. 15). In common with Machiavelli and Bacon, Descartes is not mentioned in Hobbes's writings.

If it is appropriate to look back to Machiavelli to draw comparisons with the thought of Hobbes, it is also appropriate to look ahead to Vico. But surely Hobbes and Vico stand at opposite ends of the spectrum of historical thought — the one militantly rationalist, temperamentally averse to the contingencies of the historical process, distrustful of the conjectures and uncertainties of historical study; the other the originator of the method of imaginative reconstruction of the past, plunging with relish into the dark and difficult recesses of history? Adducing precedents in the history of thought is always exposed to the charge of special pleading; in this case it would appear to be bordering on the absurd.

In fact, however, what Hobbes and Vico do have in common is a fundamental methodological principle — that we can truly know only what we have made ourselves, expressed by Vico in the formula *verum factum convertantur* or *verum ipsum factum*, the true and the made are convertible. This is axiomatic for both philosophers, but they draw opposite conclusions from it. Both apply it to mathematics, principally geometry, but whereas Hobbes concludes that all the sciences must be made to conform to geometrical method in order to give assured results, Vico asserts that the much vaunted self-evidencing character of geometry constitutes it as a vacuous science that can tell us nothing about the world of men, nothing that we really want to know. Again, while Hobbes bases his claim to have discovered an infallible science of ethics and politics on the grounds that we create the commonwealth ourselves, it does not occur to him that the same principle provides a foundation for historical science. For Vico, however, the verum factum principle constitutes the basis of historical understanding, for the creations of history are not arbitrary mental constructs, like geometrical figures, but leave their tracks in time and can therefore be studied empirically. However, the extent of Vico's indebtedness to Hobbes on this matter is open to conjecture (Cotroneo).

Hobbes's System

Hobbes's thought falls into two broad phases, the first being the humanist phase in which his fundamental assessment of human nature was formed and which culminated in his translation of Thucydides in 1629. The second, the rationalist phase, stemmed from his discovery of Euclid in 1630, and led to the attempted science of man in society on a geometrical model. Interpretation of Hobbes's development is a minefield for the unwary. In taking the view that the outline of Hobbes's view of human nature was formed before his conversion to mathematics, I am in agreement with Leo Strauss, among others (cf. also Oakeshott, pp. 136–44). But it would be unrealistic to assume that his beloved mathematical method had no influence on the content of his political ideas. So I would agree with Watkins in seeing further major developments of Hobbes's specifically political thought after 1630.

In 1630 Hobbes made the discovery that revolutionised his thinking and determined his mature system. He had already (if our interpretation is correct) adopted the fundamentally materialistic and somewhat Machiavellian principles of his view of life, but he still lacked a method which would unify and mobilise those principles, turning them into a powerful political philosophy.

As is well known, Hobbes discovered his method on the occasion when, happening to catch sight of an open copy of the *Elements* of Euclid in a gentleman's library, he was fascinated to find that the proposition that seemed quite impossible was simply the inevitable outcome of a series of logical steps based on indubitable axioms (Aubrey, p. 309). But Hobbes was a philosopher not a mathematician (in spite of — or perhaps one should say with some of his long-suffering contemporaries, because of — his claims to have squared the circle!), and philosophy, though it may borrow methodological insights from geometry, requires a content that is specifically its own. Hobbes found this content in the notions of motion and generation.

He owes these two fundamental concepts primarily to Galileo and to William Harvey, the discoverer of the circulation of the blood. In the *De Corpore* Hobbes reveals his debt: 'Galileus in our time . . . was the first that opened to us the gate of natural philosophy universal, which is the knowledge of the nature of motion' (p. viii). And Harvey, adding to the category of motion (as in *The Motion of the Blood*), the category of generation (as in *The Generation of Living Creatures*), gave a genetic twist to the new method with his concept of recapitulation (ibid.). We should note, however, that Hobbes did not take this genetic interest, as he might have done, in an historical sense, but in a logical sense. He was concerned solely with logical sequence understood in a quasi-mathematical sense as *computation*. Reasoning, or more accurately, *ratiocination*, was a question of adding or subtracting definitions. As Hobbes put it in *Leviathan*: 'In sum, in what matter soever there is place for *addition* and *subtraction*, there is also a place for *reason*; and where these have no place, there *reason* has nothing at all to do' (*Lev.*, p. 82 — original emphasis).

Harvey had studied at Padua, the centre of Renaissance methodology, and no doubt Hobbes was influenced by Paduan thought through him. Paduan methodology focused on the time-honoured process of analysis and synthesis (there termed resolution and composition). But Galileo had introduced a refinement, a sort of middle term, in which the elements of analysis were idealised into quasi-mathematical formulae before being brought together again in a new synthesis. As Hobbes asserts in the *De Corpore*: 'There is, therefore, no method, by which we find out the causes of things, but is either *compositive* or *resolutive*, or *partly compositive* and *partly resolutive*. And the resolutive is commonly called *analytical* method, as the compositive is called *synthetical*' (p. 66 — original emphasis; Watkins, Chs 3 and 4).

Corresponding to this distinction in Hobbes's thought was the fundamental division of knowledge into rational and empirical sciences. Rational, deductive science proceeds synthetically, following the motions (sic) of men's minds; it operates in the realm of hypothetical (or 'conditional' as Hobbes calls it) knowledge and its judgements are infallible (*Lev*., p. 87).

Empirical, inductive, science proceeds analytically following the deliverances of sense; it operates in the realm of categorical (or as Hobbes says, 'absolute') knowledge and its findings are conjectural (*Lev*., p. 111; *De Corp*., pp. 73f; Peters, pp. 50f).

In Hobbes's system everything is ultimately reduced to motion. Just as there are motions of bodies, so there are also motions of minds. Bringing together in a phrase the two concepts of motion and generation that we have identified as fundamental to his scheme, Hobbes speaks of 'generated motions' (*De Corp*., p. 73). Physical motions in the natural world are generated by nature; they are external, so to speak, to us, and we can have only indirect, conjectural, empirical knowledge of them.

The motions of the lines of geometrical figures are generated by the reason of men; they are the creations of the human mind and can therefore be known with demonstrable certainty.

The motions of political bodies or commonwealths, would seem, according to Hobbes, to be in an intermediate position. They have a physical reality and are therefore susceptible of being studied inductively and empirically (*De Corp*., pp. 73f). But on the other hand, they are pre-eminently generated by human reason and will ('made by the wills and agreement of men', *De Corp*., p. 11). In this respect, geometry and the commonwealth come into the same category. They are our own creations: we can know their causes, generation and construction. 'Geometry therefore is demonstrable, for the lines and figures from which we reason are drawn and described by ourselves; and civil philosophy is demonstrable, because we make the commonwealth ourselves' (*EW*, VII, p. 184). No need, therefore, to resort to the painstaking empirical study of society: the nature of the commonwealth may be discovered by any man 'that will but examine his own mind' (*De Corp.*, p. 74). Hobbes believed that on this basis he could construct rational, deductive sciences of politics and ethics (*Lev.*, p. 111).

The *De Homine* (1658) provides one of Hobbes's most explicit statements of this this claim. Geometry, on the one hand, and politics and ethics on the other, are on the same footing as products of the human mind. Geometry is obviously a demonstrable science because we ourselves create the figures ('the generation (sic) of the figures depends on our will'). Similarly:

> politics and ethics (that is, the sciences of *just* and *unjust*, of *equity* and *inequity*) can be demonstrated *a priori* because we ourselves make the principles — that is the causes of justice (namely laws and covenants) — whereby it is known what *justice* and *equity*, and their opposites *injustice* and *inequity* are. (*De Hom.* — original emphasis)

The grounds for this assertion are found in Hobbes's view of the state of nature that will concern us shortly: 'For before covenants and laws were drawn up, neither justice nor injustice, neither public good nor public evil, was natural among men any more than it was among beasts' (*De Hom.*, pp. 41ff).

In *Leviathan*, Hobbes asserts that 'the skill of making and maintaining commonwealths' is a matter of following certain rules of procedure, as in arithmetic or geometry, not a matter of practice or skill, as in playing tennis, — 'which rules, neither poor men have the leisure, nor men that have had the leisure, have hitherto had the curiosity, or the method to find out' (p. 203). In other words, Hobbes himself is revealing them to the world for the first time, thanks to his infallible method. (As Hobbes himself claimed, 'Natural Philosophy is . . . but young, but Civil Philosophy yet much younger, as being no older . . . than my own book *De Cive*' (*EW*, I, p. ix).) A similar point is made in the *De Corpore*, in which Hobbes reverts to the familiar bugbear, civil war: civil war arises because men are ignorant of the scientific causes of war and peace:

> there being but few in the world that have learned those duties

which unite and keep men in peace, that is to say, that have learned the rules of civil life sufficiently. Now the knowledge of these rules is moral philosophy. But why have they not learned them, unless for this reason, that none hitherto have taught them in a clear and exact method. (p. 8)

Here we are at the heart of Hobbes's extraordinary system. While today we would probably be prepared to accept a strong *a priori* element in ethics, we would certainly regard political science as being an essentially inductive study and closely related to history. Not so for Hobbes. While he concedes the theoretical possibility of an inductive approach to politics, moving from the interpretation of sense-data to the invention of principles (*De Corp.*, p. 74), his whole emphasis is on the deductive, *a priori* approach. It is possible to attain, he affirms in the *De Corpore*, 'the knowledge of the passions and perturbations of the mind, by the *synthetical method*, and from the very first principles of philosophy' (p. 73 — original emphasis), and then to project one's findings on to the commonwealth itself, which, after all, is but an artificial man (*Lev.*, p. 59), and so, 'proceeding in the same way, come to the causes and necessity of constituting commonwealths, and . . . knowledge of what is natural right and what are civil duties'. In a word, 'the principles of the politics consists in the knowledge of the motions of the mind' (ibid., p. 74).

It would be anachronistic to look in Hobbes for a modern concept of historical relativism. But there is undoubtedly a strong relativistic principle in his thought. It is a principle of moral relativism couched in historical or quasi-historical language. As we have already noted in passing, for Hobbes the state of nature precludes moral distinctions with the sole exception of the overriding imperative to secure one's survival by whatever means are necessary. To protect oneself is the most basic moral duty, and even in a civilised society no social contract or voluntary renunciation can undermine that right. It is an interesting side-light on contemporary discussion that Hobbes had no place for pacifism or non-resistance: 'A covenant not to defend myself from force, by force, is always void. For . . . no man can transfer or lay down his right to save himself from death, wounds and imprisonment' (*Lev.*, p. 153, cf. p. 146).

In the state of nature 'the notions of right and wrong, justice and injustice, have . . . no place. Where there is no common power, there is no law: where no law, no justice'. Such notions are applicable only to man in society; in his solitary state they are meaningless, and Hobbes seems to further suggest that in time of war there takes place a reversion to an amoral state, remarking with a nice Machiavellian touch: 'Force and fraud are in war the two cardinal virtues' (*Lev.*, p. 145).

Underlying this position is Hobbes's extreme nominalist view of language and reasoning that we shall have to look at shortly. In a system that attempts in the last analysis to reduce everything to motion, concepts are a matter of names produced by arbitrarily uttered sounds. This fundamental arbitrariness leads Hobbes to the verge of historical relativism:

> *Good* and *evil* are names that signify our appetites and aversions; which in different tempers, customs and doctrines of men, are different: and divers men differ, not only in their judgement on the senses of what is pleasant and unpleasant to the taste, smell, hearing, touch and sight; but also of what is conformable, or disagreeable, to reason, in the actions of common life. (*Lev.*, p. 167)

But such ethical and historical relativism was unacceptable to Hobbes once he had come under the spell of geometrical method. He is convinced that he can offer a more excellent way that will supersede the relativities and uncertainties of traditional ethics. Like Bacon, he is profoundly dissatisfied with the theoretical and idealistic ethical teaching that was common to the classical and Christian traditions. In his humanist phase he had been attracted to the Renaissance method of indirectly inculcating moral virtues through historical examples, but had repudiated this whole approach on his conversion to mathematics. Bacon wanted to reconstruct the humanist method through inductive historical study that would leave history strengthened by adherence to a rigorous method, while ethics would become the empirical study of how men do in fact behave. Hobbes, on the other hand, sought to short-cut all ethical uncertainties by appealing to the finality of pure reason. What is missing from the shining presentations of ethical ideals that we have so far been invited to emulate, he remarks, is

> a true and certain rule of our actions, by which we might know whether what we undertake be just or unjust. For it is to no

purpose to be bidden in everything to do right, before there be a certain rule and measure of right established, which no man hitherto hath established. (*De Corp.*, p. 9)

Hobbes on Man and Society

If we are correct in supposing that the broad lines of Hobbes's view of man and society were established before 1630, when Hobbes became a fanatical convert to mathematical method, and that they stem both from his acute observation of human nature and also from the traditional material of humanist commonplaces such as Aristotle's *Rhetoric*, it follows that his ideas in his first phase must have been such as to lend themselves to recasting in a mathematical mould later. We need to postulate therefore a fundamentally secular and incipiently materialistic view of man even at this stage. Hobbes's fully fledged mechanistic man (as we might call him) of the *Leviathan* is continuous with his earlier outlook.

Hobbes's concept of human nature derives from the assumption that natural life is basically motion: 'life is but a motion of limbs' (*Lev.*, p. 59). The whole of Hobbes's philosophy of man and society is made to appear to follow from this — though one would be hard put to it to find a commentator on Hobbes who believed that it did — all of it — logically follow. Not for nothing has Hobbes's system been called 'the politics of motion' (Spragens). But this is the only premise that Hobbes, given the method that he had espoused, could in fact adopt. As Michael Oakeshott has remarked, Hobbes's doctrine of man and society 'is not the last chapter in a philosophy of materialism, but the reflection of civil association in the mirror of rationalistic philosophy' (p. 26).

To resume: life is motion; man, who is no exception, has the ability to copy nature and construct mechanical devices, such as clocks, that ape his own physical construction. 'For what is the *heart* but a *spring*; and the *nerves* but so many *strings*; and the *joints* but so many *wheels*, giving motion to the whole body, such as was intended by the artificer?' (*Lev.*, p. 59 — original emphasis). The state is simply the projection of mechanistic man on an enormous scale. 'For by art is created that great LEVIATHAN called a COMMONWEALTH, or STATE, in Latin CIVITAS, which is but an artificial man.' (ibid.). In the state, sovereignty is the artificial soul, the heart of the great engine, imparting motion to the whole; the magistrates are the joints; rewards and punishments are the nerves because they provide the stimulus for movement of the limbs and organs; wealth constitutes the strength of the body; concord, health; sedition, sickness; and civil war, death (ibid.).

The analogy of society, or sometimes the whole human race, as a sort of corporate man, is a familiar one in the history of political thought — most familiar in the expression 'the body politic'. It was made much of by thinkers in the tradition of the Christian humanism of Hooker and Butler (reinforced by Romanticist idealism), such as Burke, Coleridge, Arnold and so on. But they were working on totally different premises stemming from a radically different view of man. They saw him as a spiritual being, endowed with creative reason by which he could transcend egotism and the bounds of sense and enter into a fellowship in which he would find his true fulfilment. They operated with a view of language and metaphor radically opposed to that of Hobbes. For them, metaphor was a vehicle of spiritual truth, not a corruption of univocal speech. When Bentham deplored using the analogy of society as an organism that could be healthy or sick, he seemed to be saying the opposite of Hobbes, but in reality he was speaking from a position of mechanistic rationalism like his. Hobbes's ostensibly organic view of society has to be interpreted in the light of his mechanistic view of man.

Hobbes has a Machiavellian insight into fundamental human drives. Man is a restless being, never satisfied with his lot, always seeking to improve his position at the expense of others. The objects of all his striving are a series of receding mirages, for there is no static state of beatitude with which he would be satisfied.

> The felicity of this life consisteth not in the repose of a mind satisfied. For there is no such *finis ultimus*, utmost aim, nor *summum bonum*, greatest good, as is spoken of in the books of the old moral philosophers. Nor can a man any more live, whose desires are at an end, than he, whose senses and imaginations are at a stand. Felicity is a continual progress of the desire, from one object to another. (*Lev.*, p. 122)

What Acton attributed to Machiavelli — the discovery of the dynamics of power that govern history — is equally applicable to Hobbes. His doctrine of human motivation is perhaps narrower than Machiavelli's (whose *necessità* embraced the demands of avarice and pride as well as of survival) but it is both more radical and more systematic. The fundamental human drive is the lust for power, born of fear and generating fear. 'I put for a general inclination of all mankind, a perpetual and restless desire of power after power, that ceaseth only in death'. And just as Machiavelli had argued that the only means of defence was attack, that the safety of the state entailed a commitment to continuous aggression, so Hobbes points out that those who possess power can only secure what they have by acquiring more (*Lev.*, pp. 122f).

D. G. James entitled his valuable discussion of Hobbes 'The Proud Mind' and characterised Hobbes's system as 'the zenith of the pride of the Renaissance' (p. 25). In his confidence in the unaided powers of man's natural reason, Hobbes is a true child of the Renaissance; but in applying those powers to the improvement of society, he is a harbinger of the Enlightenment. Renaissance historical and political thought had been informed by a robust confidence in man's ability to determine his own destiny. Both Machiavelli and Guicciardini — though they acknowledge the mysterious influence of *Fortuna* — assume that history is of man's own making, rather than the unfolding of a predetermined providential scheme. But their grasp of human self-determination is crude and undeveloped since social and economic forces were not understood. In Hobbes, however, as in other theoreticians of a social contract, there is a fuller realisation that society was a natural growth, that institutions were contingent, not necessary in the scheme of things, and alterable by human decision. In addition we find a firmer grasp of the social and economic factors that transcend the individual's impact on history (Peters, p. 197).

The Renaissance had inherited from antiquity the idea of a Golden Age in the past, from which man — precisely civilised man — had steadily degenerated. The notion of the noble savage, the happy heathen, originates with Lucretius and became common coin. The myth of the Golden Age was exposed by Bodin, and though Bacon fell for it, a very different picture of man's origins began to gain currency and held sway until Rousseau. The two philosophers who paint the bleakest picture of man in the state of nature are Hobbes and Vico. This is one more piece of evidence of common ground.

Hobbes's description of man in the state of nature serves his political polemic. Before any social contract, lacking the protection and sanctions of the state, men barely survived, isolated as they were in a hostile environment. What a blessing the creation of Leviathan was! 'Without a common power to keep them all in awe, they are in that condition which is called war; and such a war as is of every man, against every man' (*Lev.*, p. 143). As Hobbes put it in the earlier treatise *De Cive*:

> If now, to this natural proclivity of men, to hurt each other, which they derive from their passions but chiefly from a vain esteem of themselves, you add the right of all to all, wherewith one by right invades, the other by right resists, and whence arise perpetual jealousies and suspicions on all hands . . . it cannot be denied but that the natural state of men, before they entered into society, was a mere war, and that not simply, but a war of all men against all men. (pp. 117f)

(We note here, without further comment at this stage, Hobbes's view that the notions of justice and injustice are not applicable in the state of nature: each has a natural right to ensure his survival by attack or defence as the case may be.)

In this condition of anarchy or 'absolute liberty', as Hobbes pointedly calls it (*Lev.*, p. 310), all the amenities of civilisation are lacking and even survival is barely secured. In a classic passage, he writes:

> In such condition there is no place for industry; because the fruit thereof is uncertain: and consequently no culture of the earth; no navigation, nor use of the commodities that may be imported by sea; no commodious building; no instrument of moving, and removing, such things as require much force; no knowledge of the face of the earth; no account of time; no arts; no letters; no society; and, what is worst of all, continual fear, and danger of violent death; and the life of man, solitary, poor, nasty, brutish and short. (*Lev.*, p. 143)

In the state of nature there is no such thing as personal property or ownership of land: 'no *mine* and *thine* distinct; but only that to be every man's, that he can get, and for so long, as he can keep it' (*Lev.*, p. 145 — original emphasis; cf. p. 264).

Did Hobbes believe that he was describing an actual historical period, as Vico, for one, certainly did? Many commentators seem to assume that the question of the historicity of the state of nature was irrelevant to Hobbes's argument. Peters, for example, remarks that 'Hobbes did not take such a state of nature seriously as an historical hypothesis' (pp. 168f). He was conducting an experiment of the type Galileo had pioneered: 'a resolution of society into its clear and distinct parts so as to reconstruct the whole in order of logical dependence rather than of historical genesis' (pp. 168f).

G. P. Gooch comments helpfully on this question. Noting that, in Hobbes, the necessity for absolute government is said repeatedly to lie in human nature itself as revealed in primitive societies, Gooch points out that neither Hobbes nor his contemporaries knew anything of the actual way of life of primitive communities.

> His terrifying picture of a war of all against all corresponds to no reality. No community lives or could live in the state which he describes. For Hobbes there is no middle term between anarchy and absolutism. He was not aware that custom preceded law, and that the sanction of the one is as potent as of the other. He rightly rejected sentimental rhapsodies on the noble savage and the golden age of innocence and virtue; but he was unaware that the elements of social life are never absent among human beings, and that savages possess a rudimentary morality without any political organisation. (p. 49)

Hobbes himself obviously does not regard it as vital to his position to hold that all societies have emerged from this pre-social state. He anticipates the objection: 'It may peradventure be thought, there was never such a time, nor condition of war as this; and I believe it was never generally so, over all the world: but there are many places where they live so now'. He cites the American Indians and the breakdown of public order (that was always uppermost for Hobbes, timid soul that he confessed himself to be) in times of civil war. Beneath the veneer of civilised life, man's primitive and aggressive instincts were always ready to break out (*Lev.*, p. 144). In a word, Hobbes assumed that he was describing historical realities, but it was not essential to his case that the state of nature should have been universal. The form of his account of the state of nature was historical but its function was that of an explanatory myth. As we shall see, Hobbes came to prefer, on methodological grounds, 'typical' to actual history (cf. Warrender, pp. 237–42).

Hobbes on History

The translation of Thucydides, with its revealing introductory remarks, is the monument of Hobbes's first ('humanist') phase. He ranks Thucydides with other outstanding models of the humanist ideal: Homer for poetry, Aristotle for philosophy and Demosthenes for eloquence. Just as they are supreme in their respective spheres, so in Thucydides, 'the faculty of writing history is at the highest' (*EW*, III, pp. 7ff).

At this time Hobbes accepts the conventional Renaissance rationale of historical study — to inculcate moral truths — and declares that to do this there is no one better equipped than Thucydides, the sacred authors excepted (a purely nominal deference in his case):

> For the principal and proper work of history being to instruct and enable men, by the knowledge of actions past, to bear themselves prudently in the present and providentially [i.e. providently] towards the future: there is not extant any other (merely human) that doth more naturally and fully perform it (ibid.).

Indulging neither in sermonising comment nor speculative probing into men's inward motives, Thucydides achieves a subtle and tacit didacticism that commends him to Hobbes:

> Thucydides is one who, though he never digress to read a lecture, moral or political, upon his own text, nor enter into men's hearts further than the acts themselves evidently guide him: is yet accounted the most politic historiographer that ever writ. (*EW*, III, pp. viif)

As we shall see, Hobbes's espousal of mathematical method left him dissatisfied with this hit-and-miss approach to history. Why waste time with the patient inductivism of the great historians when mathematical method provided a short cut to infallible truth? Why trouble with the humanists' indirect inculcation of ethics, line upon line, precept upon precept, when your infallible science of ethics superseded received ethical norms anyway? Why bother to establish by patient enquiry what actually happened in history when the future well-being of man and the commonwealth lay in the realm of the possible, rather than the actual, when 'typical' history, explanatory myths, would serve equally well? What then becomes of history in Hobbes's mature system? It is relegated to an inferior position alongside all other 'conjectural' pursuits. As D. G. James has pointed out, according to Hobbes the great bulk of human experience falls below the level of reasoning, including sense, memory, image, wisdom, prudence, purely inductive science, history and poetry (p. 32).

History is specifically excluded from the realm of philosophy on the grounds that it does not lend itself to geometrical method: 'such knowledge is but experience, or authority, and not ratiocination' (*De Corp.*, pp. 10f). History is fallible: it can neither tell us with assurance about the past nor form a basis for prediction of the future. Like Guicciardini, Hobbes has a strong sense of the elusiveness of history. 'Sometimes a man desires to know the event of an action . . . supposing like events will follow like actions . . . such conjecture, through the difficulty of observing all circumstances, be very fallacious' (Watkins, p. 38).

As far as Hobbes is concerned, history is not capable of fulfilling its traditional humanist function of providing ethical exempla or its new Renaissance role of delivering the basic data of political science. Could it be, then, that Hobbes entertains a very modern conception of history for its own sake — answering to our insatiable desire to know what actually happened in the past? Hobbes certainly affirms that it is pleasing to recall the past, but his reasons are bound up with his own eccentric morality: 'It is pleasing to represent the past, if it was good, because it was good; and if it was evil, because it is past' (*De Hom.*, p. 51).

The ideal of modern historicism in the tradition of Ranke, to recreate the past as it actually was, is quite foreign to Hobbes. Histories may be pleasing; they may be useful if we are approaching political science from the empirical, inductive end (a method not encouraged by Hobbes) but 'this is so whether they be true or false, provided that they are not impossible. For in the sciences causes are sought not only of those things that were, but also of those things that can be' (*De Hom.*, p. 50). As Strauss points out, the more the ideal character of Hobbes's system became clear to him, the less he had to trouble with history (p. 97). Typical history serves as well as actual history and this is precisely what he offers in his account of the state of nature and the genesis of Leviathan.

We might deduce from the fact that Hobbes lumps together history and poetry as unsatisfactory conjectural sciences, that a certain view of language underlies his position. We can take our cue in this matter from a striking contrast between Hobbes's view of the origins of speech and the theory later put forward by Vico. The disagreement is made all the more significant by the fact that, as we have already noted, Hobbes seems to anticipate Vico's celebrated verum factum principle.

Vico sees language arising spontaneously out of the inarticulate cries and rhythmic utterances of primitive man under the pressure of strong emotion. He postulates a continuum of development from almost animal noises at the lowest level up to the highest achievement of poetic creation. Hobbes, on the other hand, has a profound distaste for the spontaneous, the irrational and the emotional. For him, there is a great gulf fixed between crude animal utterances and rational human discourse:

> Not by their will, but out of the necessity of nature, these calls by which hope, fear, joy and the like are signified, are forced out by the strength of these passions . . . burst forth by the strength of nature from the peculiar fears, joys, desires and other passions. . . (*De Hom.*, pp. 37f)

The words could be either Vico's or Hobbes's, but they would be expressing totally opposed points of view respectively.

For Vico, metaphor and metaphorical expression, i.e. poetry, was the primary form of man's apprehension of reality and a window into truth. For Hobbes, metaphor was at best an aberration, at worst the sign of a sick language. To employ metaphor is to use words in a sense other than the 'intended' one (the assumption being that there is a one to one relation between the sound and its meaning) in a way that can only lead into error. Hobbes deplored the use of metaphors, tropes and other rhetorical figures 'instead of words proper'. 'Metaphors and senseless and ambiguous words are like *ignes fatui*; and reasoning upon them is wandering amongst innumerable absurdities; and their end, contention and sedition, or contempt' (*Lev.*, pp. 75, 81, 85, 86).

Hobbes's fundamental objection to regarding primitive cries as worthy of the designation 'speech' is that they are spontaneous, not brought forth by an effort of will ('not by their will, but out of the necessity of nature'). For him, language is a matter of naming like that of Adam naming the creatures in the Garden of Eden. It is purely a product of will and therefore quite arbitrary. 'A name is a word taken at pleasure to serve as a mark that may raise in our minds a thought like some thought we had before' (*EW*, I, p. 16). Out of names are constructed definitions and by means of definitions rational thought is pursued. Hobbes's much vaunted method consists in reasoning from definitions (*Lev.*, p. 84) by means of adding and subtracting. In a famous metaphor (!) adapted from Bacon, Hobbes asserts: 'Words are wise men's counters, they do but reckon by them; but they are the money of fools' (*Lev.*, p. 78). He thus brings language too into his broadly mathematical and specifically geometrical scheme, for, as he points out, 'in geometry, which is the only science that it hath pleased God hitherto to bestow on mankind, men begin at settling the significations of their words' (*Lev.*, p. 77).

For Vico, to understand another man's metaphor was to gain an entrance into a perhaps distant world of human experience and the possibility of doing this was the justification of historical science. For Hobbes, the metaphorical character of human utterance foreclosed once and for all the possibility that history, conjectural in its method, trivial in its conclusions, could attain the status of a true science.

5 HISTORY AND PHILOSOPHY ON THE EVE OF THE ENLIGHTENMENT

Newton

In the seventeenth century two distinct methods of philosophical and scientific inquiry competed for allegiance. The first, represented by Descartes and Hobbes, took mathematics as its model, deduction as its method, and clear and distinct ideas as its philosophical ideal. The second, represented by Bacon, set out to be rigorously empirical in its approach, to eschew speculation, and to proceed *a posteriori*, by pure induction. The first, the rationalist approach, was profoundly unconducive to historical thinking as well as to poetry and other imaginative arts. The second, the scientific approach, though almost equally antipathetic to free-ranging creative expression, did, however, provide a rationale and a method for 'scientific' history.

In the thought of Newton and Locke, two of the more dominant influences on the outlook of the Enlightenment, these two traditions converge in an unstable but highly productive synthesis. The 'plain historical method' announced by Locke and the method of observation and experiment extolled by Newton, strengthened by a basically rationalist framework, furnished the historians and social philosophers of the Enlightenment with the tools of their trade.

Newton himself combined a critical appropriation of the mathematical rationalism of the Continent with the inductive empiricism of the Royal Society. While the scientific programme devised by Bacon had been crippled by lack of mathematics, Newton turned the labour of observation and experiment into mathematical terms. The first phase of the Renaissance had attempted the Promethean task of grasping the entire content of the physical world and of human life in all its particularity in directly empirical terms. Bacon's endless tables of data represent the highest development of this approach. But they are at the same time a confession of failure, the end of the road. An alternative, streamlined method, employing the resolutive-compositive formula refined at the university of Padua, and anticipated by Nicholas Cusanus, recognised the need radically to simplify the data by turning it into mathematical terms. Leonardo, Kepler and Galileo bequeath this approach to Descartes, in whose hands, however, it becomes the instrument of systematisation rather than the tool of science.

In the light of this tradition, Newton marks a new departure. For him, as E. A. Burtt points out, there is absolutely no *a priori* certainty, such as Kepler, Galileo and supremely Descartes possessed, that the world is inherently mathematical in its constitution, still less that its secrets can be fully unlocked by existing mathematical methods. As far as Newton is concerned, the world is what it is and mathematics is therefore solely a method for the solution of problems presented by sensible experience (pp. 208f).

Newton had been exhilarated by reading Descartes's *Géométrie*, but developed his own approach in conscious opposition to that of Descartes. As Alexandre Koyré has remarked, the *Principia Mathematica* is anti-cartesian to the core (p. 95). Newton's frequent critical remarks on the function of 'hypotheses' in science are directed at the Cartesians and Leibniz. He is not attempting the impossible task of contriving a science independent of what Bacon called *anticipationes naturae*, exploratory theories set up for observational or experimental testing; for Newton, especially in his later phase, 'hypotheses' were synonymous with unfounded and superfluous speculations, such as Descartes's celebrated vortices and Leibniz's monadology (Newton, pp. 6f; Koyré, 'Concept and Experience in Newton's Scientific Thought', *Studies*; Manuel, *Religion*, pp. 70, 75, 98).

The second edition of the *Principia* was edited by Newton's disciple Roger Cotes, who also contributed a preface in which he clearly segregated the Newtonian and the Cartesian methods. The Cartesians (not mentioned by name), while they rightly assume that matter is homogeneous in nature (and not, as the scholastics supposed, composed of specific and occult qualities) and that all the variety of the universe can be explained in terms of simple fundamental principles, go astray when they attempt to construct, with whatever intellectual rigour and ingenuity, fanciful theories on the basis of erroneous principles.

> But when they take a liberty of imagining at pleasure unknown figures and magnitudes, and uncertain situations and motions of the parts, and moreover of supposing occult fluids, freely pervading the pores of bodies, endued with all-performing subtlety and agitated with occult motions, they run out into dreams and chimeras, and neglect the true constitution of things

which certainly is not to be derived from fallacious conjectures when we can scarce reach it by the most certain observations. (Newton, p. 117)

The result is merely a 'romance'.

The Newtonians, by contrast, seek to be faithful to experience alone, assuming 'nothing as a principle that is not proved by phenomena'. 'They frame no hypotheses, nor receive them into philosophy otherwise than as questions whose truth may be disputed'. Their method consists of the twofold procedure of analysis and synthesis (a sort of common tradition in Western philosophy, and central to the approaches of Descartes, Hobbes and Locke too (cf. Schouls)). 'From some select phenomena they deduce by analysis the forces of nature and the more simple laws of forces, and from thence by synthesis show the constitution of the rest'. It is worth noting that too much should not be made of the incongruous expression 'deduce' here; Newton himself was prepared to use 'derive' or 'infer' (Newton, pp. 117f; cf. pp. 182f).

In the *Optics* (1704) Newton expands on his method:

> As in mathematics, so in natural philosophy, the investigation of difficult things by the method of analysis ought ever to precede the method of composition. This analysis consists in making experiments and observations, and in drawing general conclusions from them by induction, and admitting of no objections against the conclusions but such as are taken from experiment, or other certain truths. For hypotheses are not to be regarded in experimental philosophy. And although the arguing from experiments and observations by induction be no demonstration of general conclusions, yet it is the best way of arguing which the nature of things admits of, and may be looked upon as so much the stronger by how much the induction is more general.

In this way, Newton concludes, we proceed from effects to their causes and from particular causes to more general ones, 'till the argument end in the most general'. The second stage, the stage of synthesis or composition, 'consists in assuming the causes discovered and established as principles, and by them explaining the phenomena proceeding from them and proving the explanations' (pp. 178f).

Newton's method provided a model for research in other areas of enquiry, not least in history, where the historians of the eighteenth century would be inspired by the Newtonian vision to undertake vast surveys of empirical data issuing in general laws. The truth about human nature was to be discovered, not by *a priori* definitions and deductions in the manner of Christian scholasticism or even of rationalist systematisers like Descartes and Hobbes, but by observation, experience and even experiment, resulting in the uniform laws of man's individual and social existence (cf. Koyré, 'The Significance of the Newtonian Synthesis', *Studies*).

The Enlightenment's programme for a historical science of man reflected the grandeur of the 'coherence, consistency and continuity' (Wade, *Origins*, p. 534) of the Newtonian universe, and was informed by a uniformitarian conception of human nature, always and everywhere necessarily the same in its fundamental constitution — on the analogy of Newton's God who 'exists necessarily; and by the same necessity He exists *always* and *everywhere*' (Newton, p. 44), and the unchanging Christian dogma defined by St Vincent of Lerins as what had been believed always, everywhere and by all (*semper, ubique at ab omnibus*). But ironically, by its relentless application to the facts of the case which often would not be forced into the procrustean bed of uniformitarianism, the certainties of the Enlightenment's worldview began to be undermined and to suffer the destabilising effects of historical relativism.

Newton's own historical research — 4,000 folios of manuscripts relating to biblical chronology — was uncontaminated by any such anachronistic hestitations. Exhaustiveness, exactitude and precision were its attributes. By the standards of his contemporaries Newton was a critical historian who applied the standards of the new inductive physical science to history. It should not be thought that Newton's rigorous empirical method in the physical sciences gave way, in this area, to undisciplined speculation. As R. W. Southern has commented, 'if we come to him with medieval rather than with modern preconceptions, he never appears more soberly scientific' than in his *Observations* on the prophets ('Aspects', III, p. 178). But in doing so, he turned the past into a pale reflection of the Newtonian universe — cold, colourless, indifferent to human hopes, with absolute space and time grinding on their way. As Frank Manuel has put it in *Isaac Newton, Historian*:

In the end his passion for factual detail shrivelled the past to a

> chronological table and a history of place names. His history was sparse; specific as a businessman's ledger, it allowed for no adornments, no excess. It had the precisionism of the Puritan and his moral absolutism; existence was stripped to a bony framework . . . there were hardly any conscious subjects in Newton's historical world, only objects. An interest in man's creations for their own sake, the aesthetic and the sensuous, is totally absent. (p. 10)

All that was irrational, primitive, extravagant was beyond his ken.

Ironically, Vico sent Newton a complimentary copy of the first *New Science*. It is not known whether Newton received and read it, but as Frank Manuel remarks, in any case 'he would not have remotely comprehended its meaning'.

> When confronted by the more complex manifestations of mankind — polytheist idolatry, luxury and lies, the poetical, the cabalistic, the emotive, the fabulous, the philosophical conceit, the cruel and the lustful — he either pushed them away with repugnance or dropped them into the eighteenth-century catch-alls known as error and deception. (ibid., p. 193)

Even the chronology to which Newton had brought the unrivalled powers of intellect and intuition that his contemporaries regarded as scarcely human, was nothing more than 'a magnificent rationalist delusion' (ibid., p. 49). Newton was, as R. W. Southern remarks, 'the last great scientific mind in European history to accept biblical prophecies as a source for the detailed study of historical facts' ('Aspects', III, p. 179).

While the Enlighteners were more profoundly influenced by Descartes than they cared to acknowledge — the obsession with clear and distinct ideas, the analytical view of language, the penchant for simplistic explanations contributed to the shaping of the Enlightenment — Newton above all was their man. Newton and Descartes became symbolic figures,

> the one, Newton, embodying the ideal of modern, progressive and successful science, conscious of its limitations and firmly based upon experimental and experiential-observational data which it subjected to precise mathematical treatment; the other, Descartes, symbol of a belated, reactionary — and fallacious —

attempt to subject science to metaphysics, disregarding experience, precision and measurement, and replacing them by fantastic, unproved, and unprovable hypotheses. (Koyré, pp. 55f)

Or as Fontenelle, whose long life (1657–1757) bridges the seventeenth century and the Enlightenment, put it in his *Eulogium* for Newton:

One of them, soaring aloft in daring flight, sought to take his stand at the fountain-head of all things in the light of a few clear and fundamental ideas, so that when he came to deal with the phenomena of Nature he would be able to treat them as necessary consequences thereof. The other, less daring, or more modest, in his aims, beginning with phenomena as his starting point proceeded therefrom to unknown principles, resolved to treat them as the logic of the consequences might require. The one starts from a clearly formulated idea to ascertain the cause of what he sees; the other starts from what he sees and goes on to seek out its cause. (Hazard, p. 358)

Descartes and Newton, as the beneficiaries of Galileo, were however at one in the fundamental view of the world that they passed on to the Enlightenment. In terms of 'the Newtonian universe', man was purely peripheral. As E. A. Burtt puts it:

The world that people had thought themselves living in — a world rich in colour and sound, redolent with fragrance, filled with gladness, love and beauty, speaking everywhere of purposive harmony and creative ideals — was crowded now into minute corners in the brains of scattered organic beings. The really important world outside was a world hard, cold, colourless, silent and dead; a world of quantity, a world of mathematically computable motions in mechanical regularity. (pp. 236f)

In such a climate of thought, the study of human life in history could never flourish. That is why, although the Enlightenment made a major contribution to the development of scientific standards of history and Newtonian assumptions profoundly affected the direction taken by literature, especially poetry, as

Marjorie Nicholson has shown in *Newton Demands the Muse*, a deeper historical understanding had to await the Romantic movement's onslaught on the presuppositions of the Newtonian universe. This was the first great battle to which Blake, Coleridge and Carlyle addressed themselves.

Locke

John Locke (1632–1704) is the second of the four great harbingers of the Enlightenment who claim consideration in our account of historical thought at the turn of the seventeenth century. Like the earlier Hobbes, with whom he is often compared and contrasted, Locke was a thinker of whom it can be said that his work remained almost wholly untainted by genuine historical insight. But while Hobbes's system was radically anti-historical in that he believed that his mathematico-deductive method superceded the hit-and-miss efforts of historical researchers, Locke's approach, while having nothing to say directly to historical science, in fact provided the historians of the Enlightenment with many of their characteristic assumptions. The much-vaunted 'historical [i.e. empirical] plain method' of the *Essay Concerning Human Understanding* formed the foundation of the simplistic, uniformitarian, empirical approach of the philosophes.

Locke passed on to the eighteenth century the notions of clear and distinct ideas, precision of language, suspicion of metaphor, and contempt for tradition that he had inherited from Descartes and Hobbes, in potent combination with the principle of the sensory basis of knowledge and the empirical scientific method that he owed ultimately to Bacon. In Locke's psychology it is the conscious operations of the mind that alone count; there is nothing of Vico's sense of the unfathomable depths of the human psyche. All is open and unconcealed in Locke's account of human nature.

Locke's work on *The Reasonableness of Christianity*, which presented an orthodox if somewhat pedestrian faith, suggested the crude deism of Toland's *Christianity not Mysterious*. Locke's influence on historical thought can be summed up in the phrase 'history not mysterious'.

But Locke is too great a thinker to be compressed into the stereotype of the Enlighteners. There is another side to Locke's thought which he bequeathed to the intuitive thinkers of the nineteenth century, principally Coleridge and Newman, through Butler and Burke. Locke is acutely aware of the limits of discursive reason, speaking in the *Essay* of the 'darkness' and 'blindness' of our understanding. Before Bishop Butler he stresses that probability is the guide of life and that we are in a state of probation in this world. Before Coleridge he uses the phrase 'the ocean of Being', and before Newman he all but speaks of the 'illative sense' and of the mind's subliminal and intuitive grasp of a chain of thought. But these are themes — of great significance in the longer term — that do not principally concern us at this stage.

Locke's theory of knowledge is introduced in the *Essay Concerning Human Understanding* as an attack on the notion of innate ideas. This approach leads Locke into one of his rare excursions into the historical field. It was often claimed that innate ideas were proved by universal consent in certain fundamental moral principles. One of Locke's tactics in demolishing innate ideas is to explode the notion of universal consent. To do this, he adduces numerous examples of amoral or immoral behaviour from historical and travel writers. The resulting historical and ethical relativism is in tension with his theory of natural law, but in his early *Essays on the Law of Nature* he had apparently anticipated this problem and worked out a theory of natural law that did not depend on universal consent.

Though the phrase *tabula rasa* does not (as far as I can see) occur in the *Essay*, the idea certainly does. 'Let us suppose the mind to be white paper void of all characters, without any ideas. How comes it to be furnished? . . . To this I answer in one word, from *experience*' (*Essay*, I, p. 77 — original emphasis). But Locke's concept of experience is not pure sensationalism: it comprises reflection as well as sensation; reflection being a kind of internal sensation, the 'notice the mind takes of its own operations, and the manner of them, by reason whereof there come to be *ideas* of these operations in the understanding (*Essay*, I, p. 78 — original emphasis). There is no part of knowledge that does not derive from this source. The highest flights of imagination or of speculation are rooted firmly in the realm of experience.

> All those sublime thoughts, which tower above the clouds and reach as high as heaven itself, take their rise and footing here: in all that great extent wherein the mind wanders, in those remote

speculations it may seem to be elevated with, it stirs not one jot beyond those ideas which sense or reflection have offered for its contemplation. (*Essay*, I, p. 89)

It was precisely the limitations of Lockean epistemology at this point — in its neglect of the powers of creative imagination — that the Romantics found so unacceptable.

It is significant that Locke's account of mental processes is confined to the conscious operations of the mind. Ideas are the product of 'the *perception of the operations of our own minds* within us' (*Essay*, I, p. 78 — original emphasis). 'Consciousness is the perception of what passes in a man's own mind': true, but Locke deduces from this definition that when a man is not conscious (for example, when he is asleep) there is nothing passing in his mind, unless he is dreaming — and he has only dreamed when he recollects that he has. Locke's interesting account of dreams makes it quite clear that he took thought to be explicit cogitation and had no inkling of the subconscious and unconscious depths in which some of the mind's most powerful and significant activity takes place (*Essay*, I, pp. 81f).

Applied to history, this narrow conception of human rationality is going to preclude any grasp of primitive, irrational, instinctive forces at work in human destiny. It as much excludes the insight that produced Machiavelli's *Prince* as it does that which created Vico's *bestioni*. For the Romantics, it was an attempt to survey the human scene with the most crippling of blinkers.

It follows from Locke's understanding of thinking as explicit cogitation that the units of thought are going to be the familiar Cartesian and Hobbesian 'clear and distinct ideas'. Locke, however, takes this nominalist tradition one step further when he advocates using the expression 'determinate' or 'determined' in place of 'clear and distinct'. By this he means that we have an idea and we know exactly what we mean by it (*Essay*, I, p. xxxviii; cf. I, p. 306f). This is the antithesis of, for example, Coleridge's remark that 'we may be said to comprehend what we cannot properly be said to understand', or Polanyi's dictum, 'We know more than we can tell'.

Locke's account of language reflects these presuppositions, though he begins by invoking a traditional theological account of the origins of speech:

> God, having designed man for a sociable creature, made him not only with an inclination and under a necessity to have fellowship with those of his own kind, but furnished him also with language, which was to be the great instrument and common tie of society. *Man*, therefore, had by nature his organs so fashioned as to be *fit to frame articulate sounds*, which we call words. (*Essay*, II, p. 9 — original emphasis)

But this teleological explanation consorts ill with his Hobbesian emphasis on the arbitrariness of language: 'sounds have no natural connexion with our ideas, but all their signification from the arbitrary imposition of men' (*Essay*, II, p. 77; cf. 12ff). Locke's analytical view of language follows from his neglect of implicit, subliminal thinking where metaphors are created. For Locke, as for Hobbes and later Bentham, metaphor was a superfluous accretion of language, at best a worthless ornament, certainly irrelevant to history. For Vico, by contrast, metaphor was the creative source of language and the key to hermeneutics.

For Locke, the incorrigible vagueness of words constitutes their inherent imperfection (*Essay*, II, p. 76). But it is an imperfection that he is determined to minimise. Thus Locke distinguishes between the *civil* and the *philosophical* use of words, the former sufficing for 'common conversation and commerce about the ordinary affairs and conveniences of civil life', the latter serving 'to convey the precise notions of things, and to express in general propositions certain and undoubted truths which the mind may rest upon and be satisfied with in its search after true knowledge' (*Essay*, II, p. 77). Locke is not sanguine that his recommendations as to precision will be adopted:

> To require that men should use their words constantly in the same sense and for none but determined and uniform *ideas*, would be to think that all men should have the same notions and should talk of nothing but what they have clear and distinct *ideas* of. (*Essay*, II, p. 106 — original emphasis)

But this remains the ideal. Locke is still harping on the Baconian theme of the advancement of learning, and believes that nothing will do more to improve knowledge than the alliance of clear and distinct ideas with precise and unambiguous terms; we should '*fix in our minds clear, distinct, and complete* ideas, as far as they are to be had, *and annexe to them proper and constant names*' (*Essay*, II, p. 239 — original emphasis). We should not take words for things, he warns in *The Conduct of the Understanding*, 'nor suppose that names in books signify real entities in nature' until we 'can frame *clear and distinct ideas* of those entities' (Section 29 — my emphasis).

Like his predecessors Descartes and Hobbes, Locke is persuaded that if thought can be reduced to the quasi-mathematical units of determined ideas and precise terms, a deductive science of man becomes a possibility. The earlier thinkers were more confident than Locke about the scope of this science: for them it would embrace both ethics and politics. But Locke is no advocate of a demonstrative science of politics. Political matters are not susceptible of geometrical expression; they are not quantifiable. They depend on prudence and sagacity and operate in the realm of probability not certainty. As Locke noted in his Journal for 1681:

> The well management of public or private affairs depending upon the various and unknown humours, interests and capacities of men we have to do with in the world, and not upon any settled ideas of things physical, polity and prudence are not capable of demonstration. But a man is principally helped in them by the history of matter of fact, and a sagacity of finding out an analogy in their operations and effects.

While the truths of mathematics are certain because they are necessary, the political sphere is uncertain and unpredictable because it operates in the realm of the contingent.

> Whether this course in public or private affairs will succeed well, whether rhubarb will purge or quinquina cure an ague, is only known by experience, and there is but probability grounded upon experience, or analogical reasoning, but no certain knowledge or demonstration. (Laslett, p. 98)

While Locke does not underestimate the difficulties — moral questions are often highly complex and are not capable of being reduced to diagrammatic form — he is confident that, given the fact of a deity and the nature of man as a rational being (both, incidentally, derived from experience in Locke's view), a deductive system of ethics is possible.

The *idea* of a supreme Being, infinite in power, goodness and wisdom, whose workmanship we are and on whom we depend, and the *idea* of ourselves as understanding rational beings, being such as are clear in us, would, I suppose, if duly considered and pursued, afford such foundations of our duty and rules of action as might place *morality amongst the sciences capable of demonstration*: wherein I doubt not but from self-evident propositions, by necessary consequences as incontestable as those in mathematics, the measures of right and wrong might be made out to anyone that will apply himself with the same indifferency and attention to the one as he does to the other of these sciences. (*Essay*, II, p. 154 — original emphasis; cf. pp. 113, 240).

The analytical nature of Locke's epistemology and the deductive method advocated by him in the sphere of ethics tend to create an impression of a rigorous systematiser. This would not have commended him to the philosophes, for whom *esprit de système* was anathema. In this case they were right in their assessment of Locke. He is not logician, metaphysician or system-builder, but essentially a man of affairs of wide reading and massive intelligence bringing acute observation and robust common sense to bear on a wide range of vexed questions. As Peter Laslett has pointed out, to think of the author of the *Two Treatises of Government* as a political philosopher is inappropriate. 'He was, rather, the writer of a work of intuition, insight and imagination, if not of profound originality, who was also a theorist of knowledge'. 'It is pointless', Laslett continues, 'to look upon his work as an integrated body of speculation and generalisation, with a general philosophy at its centre and as its architectural framework' in the style of Spinoza or Hobbes. This fact, Laslett comments, marks Locke off sharply from the other political theorists of his generation as well as from the traditional systematic approach to political thought. The massive treatises of Grotius, Pufendorf, Hooker, Hobbes and others, familiar territory to Locke, were

> all presentations of a single, synthetic system, a view of the world which proceeded from an account of reality to an account of knowledge, and so to an ethic and to politics . . . Natural law was their common assumption and in its terms they endeavoured to discover a closed system, a system which ideally would be complete and entirely consistent. (pp. 99f)

If, however, Locke's thought was not a tightly knit system, derived from first principles, unfolding step by step by logical entailment, as Spinoza's was and Hobbes's purported to be, neither was it a rigorously empirical project grounded in historical research. Locke makes almost no appeal to history. In the essay 'On Study' (1677) Locke regards antiquity and history as obstacles to true knowledge, 'designed only to furnish men with story and talk' rather than instruction in 'the art of living well' or with 'wisdom and prudence'.

In the *Essay* he pays lip-service to the value of historical knowledge:

> I would not be thought here to lessen the credit and use of *history*: it is all the light we have in many cases, and we receive from it a great part of the useful truths we have, with a convincing evidence. I think nothing more valuable than the records of antiquity: I wish we had more of them and more uncorrupted. (*Essay*, II, p. 258 — original emphasis)

But Locke makes it abundantly clear that he was not interested in an historical approach. No one was ever less tempted to fall into the genetic fallacy. For him a fact is what it is in the light of reason, not what it has become by a process of development. Historical distance lends neither enchantment nor insight. Tradition casts no mantle of respectability over error or superstition. Prescription is no warranty of right. 'No *probability* can rise higher than its first original'; '*in traditional truths, each remove weakens the force of the proof*; and the more hands the tradition has successively passed through, the less strength and evidence does it receive from them' (*Essay*, II, p. 258 — original emphasis). Locke is disdainful of those, 'who look on opinions to gain force by growing older;'

> what a thousand years since would not, to a rational man contemporary with the first voucher, have appeared at all probable, is now urged as certain beyond all question, only because several have since, from him, said it one after another. Upon this ground propositions, evidently false or doubtful enough in their first beginning, come by an inverted rule of probability, to pass for authentic truths; and those which found or deserved little credit from the mouths of their first authors are thought to grow

venerable by age and are urged as undeniable. (*Essay*, II, p. 258)

The criticism, while it hits hardest the 'ancient constitution' school whose appeal was to 'time immemorial' (Laslett, p. 89), seems also to anticipate the prescriptivism of Burke and developmental theory of Newman. It is a pre-emptive attack on the assumptions of the Romantic movement. It certainly provided ammunition for the reforming propaganda of the Enlighteners.

It is then entirely consistent — though none the less remarkable in the light of contemporary practice, for that — that in the *Two Treatises of Government* Locke should make no appeal to historical example or traditional precedent. As Peter Laslett has commented:

Nothing in his book could be disproved by the discovery of new evidence about what had happened in England in 1066, or 1215 or 1642, or by a new and more convincing view of how ancient Greek, ancient Roman or medieval English society had actually worked . . . Neither Machiavelli, nor Hobbes, nor Rousseau succeeded in making the discussion of politics so completely independent of historical example, so entirely autonomous an area of discourse. (p. 91)

There are two areas in which Locke does touch on historical issues: in the relativism implied in his attack on universal consent, and in his account of 'the state of nature'. Each of these calls for brief mention.

(i) Locke's attack on innate ideas leads him to explode the myth of universal consent and to arrive at a radical historical relativism. In the introduction to the *Essay*, Locke opposes his 'historical plain method' to the babel of conflicting opinions that a knowledge of the world presents us with:

those persuasions which are to be found amongst men, so various, different, and wholly contradictory; and yet asserted somewhere or other with such assurance and confidence that he that shall take a view of the opinions of mankind, observe their opposition, and at the same time consider the fondness and devotion wherewith they are embraced, the resolution and eagerness wherewith they are maintained, may perhaps have reason to

> suspect that either there is no such thing as truth at all, or that mankind hath no sufficient means to attain a certain knowledge of it. (*Essay*, I, p. 6)

Locke is here evidently putting his work forward as an answer to the doubts circulating at the time as a result of the work of the Pyrrhonists and sceptics. Truth is attainable, but it is not to be sought in history or in general consent.

The same bewildering and demoralising picture is presented by the moral (or immoral) practices of mankind. As Locke remarks in his early *Essays on the Law of Nature* (reiterated in the *Essay Concerning Human Understanding*),

> there is almost no vice, no infringement of natural law, no moral wrong, which anyone who consults the history of the world and observes the affairs of men will not readily perceive to have been not only privately committed somewhere on earth, but also approved by public authority and custom. Nor, [he adds] has there been anything so shameful in its nature that it has not been either sanctified somewhere by religion, or put in the place of virtue and abundantly rewarded with praise'. (p. 167, cf. pp. 141, 167–77; *Essay*, I, 30ff)

Locke's response is not to abandon all hope of establishing an objective moral standard, a natural law, but instead to found it upon the natural light of reason in enlightened minds, thus making natural law independent of general consent. His ethical relativism is an aspect of his historical relativism; it is purely descriptive not prescriptive.

(ii) Locke's concept of the law of nature also shapes his view of the state of nature. In writing on this matter he was never more conscious of the shadow of Thomas Hobbes looking over his shoulder. Locke's thought was imbued with deeply assimilated though unacknowledged Hobbesian ideas and turns of phrase. Here, however, he is explicitly rebutting Hobbes's account of the state of nature.

In the state of nature men are free and equal; their inalienable right and prime duty is preservation. Whereas for Hobbes it was a condition of war, of all against all, and the individual was concerned only to preserve his own life, for Locke, by contrast, it is a state in which all are responsible for all and each has the duty of preserving all mankind committed to him. Motivated by benevolence (an attribute absent from Hobbes's thought but developed later in Hume's), and guided by natural law, the individual has the power to apply sanctions. Where there is no common authority, 'every *Man hath a Right to punish the Offender, and be Executioner of the Law of Nature*' (*Gov.* p. 313 — original emphasis). The state of nature is not confined to primitive societies, but exists wherever men have not yet freely and voluntarily entered into a social contract to resign their rights and power of punishment to a common authority, thereby constituting political or civil society. The corollary is that every absolute monarchy belongs to the state of nature and that the individual's executive power to enforce the natural law gives the right of rebellion against tyrants (*Gov.*, pp. 368ff; cf. Yolton).

The historicity of the state of nature is assumed and defended but is not essential to Locke's argument (cf. Aarsleff). Just as Hobbes's individualistic concept of the state of nature could be supported by appeal to human nature rather than history, Locke's corporate understanding of it is supported by the evidence of contemporary societies.

> 'Tis often asked as a mighty Objection, *Where are* or ever were, there any *Men in such a State of Nature?* To which it may suffice as an answer at present; That since all *Princes* and Rulers of *Independent* [i.e. absolute] Governments all through the World, are in a State of Nature, 'tis plain the World never was, nor ever will be, without Numbers of Men in that State. (*Gov.*, p. 317 — original emphasis)

But Locke also has another answer, one that reveals both his assurance that this state is an historical one and at the same time the essential irrelevance of history to his thesis:

> It is not at all to be wondered, that *History* gives us but a very little account of Men, *that lived together in the State of Nature*. The inconveniences of that condition, and the love, and want of Society no sooner brought any number of them together, but they presently united and incorporated, if they designed to continue together. And if we may not suppose *Men* ever to have been *in the State of Nature*, because we hear not much of them in such

a State, we may as well suppose the Armies of *Salmanasser*, or *Xerxes* were never Children, because we hear little of them till they were Men, and imbodied in Armies.

The reason is not far to seek.

Government is everywhere antecedent to Records, and Letters seldom come in amongst a People, till a long continuation of Civil Society has, by other more necessary Arts provided for their Safety, Ease, and Plenty. And then they begin to look after the History of their *Founders*, and search into their *original*, when they have out-lived the memory of it. For 'tis with *Commonwealths* as with particular Persons, they are commonly *ignorant* of their own Births and Infancies. (*Gov.*, p. 378 — original emphasis)

Locke is not simply a precursor of the Enlightenment. There are a number of themes to be found in his work that serve to qualify the bare analytical character of his epistemology and theory of language. The seeds of destruction are present within the system. Locke sometimes seems to go to the brink of 'the vast ocean of *Being*' (*Essay*, I, p. 8 — original emphasis) but will not launch himself upon it. He has probability without intuition; a strong sense of the limits of discursive reason but nothing to say about the possibilities of creative imagination; he stresses the fiduciary character of political society, but overlooks the fiduciary nature of language. His immediate beneficiaries, the Enlighteners of the eighteenth century, invoked the rationalistic Locke; his remoter heirs, Coleridge and Newman, adopted the neglected themes that had been kept alive by Butler and Burke.

Leibniz

Leibniz (1646–1716) has a foot in both camps — he is a speculative thinker of enormous power and scope who spawned numerous sketches for deductive systems of the universe; on the other hand, he is immersed in empirical research, an indefatigable archivist as historian of Hanover, and an experimental scientist (Ross, Ch. 1). Voltaire called him the most universal scholar in Europe. Meinecke gave him an honoured place among the forerunners of historicism, remarking, 'There can scarcely be any modern historical and empirical science that does not in some way or other have Leibniz as its forerunner' (*Historism*, p. 25). We are not concerned here with Leibniz's actual historical work, the subject of a virtually unobtainable book by Louis Daville, (*Leibniz historien*, 1909), but with the way in which he began to bring about an effective channelling of speculative reason into channels that lent themselves to historical modes of thought — notably in his concepts of individuality, continuity and progress. We might call this his historicising of reason.

As a great rationalist systematiser, Leibniz belongs firmly in the tradition of Descartes and Spinoza. Like Descartes, he dreams of establishing all knowledge on a mathematical basis, of constructing a calculus — a symbolic logic — of universal knowledge (pp. 10f). He believes that every fact is entailed in every other fact and that, given his two fundamental principles of contradiction and sufficient reason, he can demonstrate all rational truth.

> The great foundation of mathematics is the *principle of contradiction or of identity*, that is to say, that a statement cannot be true and false at the same time and that thus *A is A, and cannot be not A*. And this single principle is enough to prove the whole of arithmetic and the whole of geometry, that is to say all mathematical principles. But in order to proceed from mathematics to physics another principle is necessary . . . that is, the *principle of sufficient reason*, that nothing happens without there being a reason why it should be thus rather than otherwise . . . Now by this principle alone . . . I prove the existence of the Divinity, and all the rest of metaphysics or natural theology, and even in some manner those physical principles which are independent of mathematics, that is to say, the principles of dynamics or of force. (pp. 206f — original emphasis)

It is the rationalist character of Leibniz's thought — combined with his theory of the pre-established harmony ordained by God at creation — that has led some commentators to claim that Leibniz's assumptions negate the notion of history. Thus Lewis Spitz writes: 'If history is predetermined, if its course unfolds always for the best within the limits of possibility and develops progressively toward the infinite good, then its meaning lies well beyond the realm of *a posteriori* investigation' (p. 343).

Leibniz made some attempt to safeguard his philosophy from precisely this interpretation (he was after all writing as a defender of Christian theism) by distinguishing between absolute necessity (whose contrary implies a logical contradiction) and hypothetical necessity (whereby creatures fulfil their own natures in the contingent realm of second causes) (pp. 23ff). Spitz's criticism would apply equally to the problems of the compatibility of Thomism or Calvinism, where a similar distinction between absolute and contingent necessity is employed, with history. He does, however, concede that Leibniz cannot be confined within rationalist categories and that he anticipates several aspects of historical thought. It is these elements in Leibniz that we shall touch on now.

(a) Underlying Leibniz's system is a view of perception that departs from Locke's predilection for conscious, explicit thinking. For Leibniz, the latter is a separate category which he calls apperception (p. 180); it is merely the tip of the iceberg: below the surface of consciousness we are being continually bombarded with an infinite number of tacit perceptions which, in Leibniz's favourite metaphor, are like the roaring of the waves on the seashore (pp. 43, 201, 155f; cf. Wade, *Origins*, pp. 452f). The Cartesian emphasis on explicit thinking was integral to an outlook hostile to history. Leibniz was one of the first to acknowledge (if not to exploit: this has been done in modern times, notably by Michael Polanyi) the tacit functions of the mind as it thinks below the threshold of explicit consciousness. This is precisely where the capacity for historical empathy takes its rise.

(b) One central aspect of Leibniz's historicising of reason is what he calls the principle of continuity. He has an overmastering sense of the whole. There are no radical disjunctions in his universe, no abrupt transitions, no sudden interventions of a *deus ex machina*. This is tied up with Leibniz's view of tacit perception: the distant roar of the recesses of the universe speaks of our indissoluble unity with all that surrounds us. Leibniz speaks of these 'minute perceptions',

> those images of the qualities of the senses, clear in the mass but confused in the parts, those impressions which surrounding bodies make on us, which include the infinite, that link which connects every being with all the rest of the universe.

He therefore affirms that '*Every individual substance involves in its perfect notion the whole universe*, and everything existing in it, past, present and future,' (original emphasis) and that 'all created individual substances are diverse expressions of the same universe' and that 'every created individual substance exercises physical action on, and is acted on by all others' (pp. 156ff, 90).

Aspects of A. N. Whitehead's process philosophy are evidently restatements of this vision of Leibniz. Whitehead's notion of the unity and interrelatedness of the universe is expressed in his concept of 'prehension'. Everything — every 'event' or 'occasion' — exists in relation to and ultimately influences every other. It may seem to be isolated, but in reality, 'its influence streams away from it with finite velocity throughout the utmost recesses of space and time' (Whitehead, *Adventures*, p. 186). Perhaps Whitehead's words, though couched in post-Einsteinian terminology, will help to illuminate the unfamiliar idiom of Leibnizian speculation.

(c) Another fundamental element in Leibniz's historicising of reason is his stress on individuality. His universe is made up of an innumerable population of monads, atomic entities, each one different and with its own pre-established destiny to fulfil. 'Every monad must be different from every other. For there are never in nature two beings which are precisely alike' (Leibniz, p. 180). This strong sense of individuality and diversity in the world marked a break with the uniformitarianism of Locke and the steamrollering rationalism of the Cartesians. Leibniz dismisses them together, along with Newtonian absolute space and time:

> By virtue of insensible variations, two individual things can never be perfectly alike . . . This at once puts out of court the blank tablets of the soul, a soul without thought, a substance without action, the void in space, atoms and even particles not actually divided in matter, absolute rest, complete uniformity in one part of time, place, or matter [etc.] and a thousand other fictions of the philosophers. (p. 158)

It was E. Cassirer's view that Leibniz's doctrine of individuality constituted a shift in the centre of gravity of European philosophy. In contrast to uniformitarian rationalism with its levelling and equalising tendency, Leibniz believed that truth, harmony and reality lay in the highest development of all individual energies.

In Leibniz's philosophy an inalienable prerogative is first gained for the individual entity. The individual no longer functions merely as a special case, as an example; it now expresses something essential in itself and valuable through itself . . . every individual substance is not only a fragment of the universe, it is the universe itself, seen from a particular viewpoint. And only the totality of these unique points of view gives us the truth of reality. (*Enlightenment*, p. 32f)

It is not difficult to see the relevance of Leibniz's concept of the individual to the growth of a modern historical consciousness.

(d) A further ingredient of the Leibnizian worldview was a sense of dynamic movement towards perfection. In contrast with Newton's universe, in which cold, lifeless bodies hurried relentlessly through infinite space and absolute time in obedience to mechanical laws, Leibniz's vision was of vital forces unfolding their potential until they attained moral and aesthetic perfection. 'There is nothing waste, nothing sterile, nothing dead in the universe,' Leibniz declares in the *Monadology* (1714) (p. 190). He gives a dynamic thrust to the principle of plenitude that informs medieval thought:

Each portion of matter is not only infinitely divisible, as the ancients recognised, but is also actually subdivided without limit, each part into further parts, of which each one has some motion of its own: otherwise it would be impossible for each portion of matter to express the whole universe. Whence it is evident that there is a world of created beings . . . in the least part of matter. (p. 190)

The universe is like a rockpool, teeming with life and every tiny drop of it, as the microscope had revealed, a world of its own, alive with movement.

Quoting Leibniz's dictum that 'the nature of the monad consists in being fruitful and in giving birth to an ever new variety', Cassirer has commented:

The Leibnizian 'monad' is no arithmetical, no merely numerical unit, but a dynamic one. The true correlate of this unit is not particularity but infinity. Every monad is a living centre of energy, and it is the infinite abundance and diversity of monads which constitute the unity of the world. (*Enlightenment*, p. 29)

The inner dynamism of the monads, when translated into human and social terms, produces a high doctrine of progress. 'We realise that there is a perpetual and a most free progress of the whole universe towards a consummation of the universal beauty and perfection of the works of God, so that it is always advancing towards a greater development' (p. 144). Disasters and sufferings must be interpreted as temporary setbacks, and as indirectly productive of good. And Leibniz's system provides him with an answer to those who, reasonably, ask why, if all is progressing to perfection, the earth has not long ago become a paradise:

> Although many substances have already come to great perfection, yet owing to the infinite divisibility of what is continuous, there always remain in the abyss of things parts that are asleep, and these need to be awakened and to be driven forward into something greater and better — in a word, to a better state of development. Hence this progress never comes to an end. (p. 144, cf. p. 203)

It is difficult to estimate what influence Leibniz's esoteric doctrines had on the Enlightenment's belief in material and humanitarian progress, but he undoubtedly contributed one element to that recovery of nerve that, as Peter Gay has suggested, constitutes the fundamental attitude of the eighteenth century. Another dictum of Whitehead's seems to sum up this side of Leibniz's thought: 'There is one all-embracing fact which is the advancing history of the one universe' (*Adventures*, p. 177).

(e) Finally, in his conception of historical science Leibniz gave theoretical justification to the work of the great annalistic historians of the Continent, Mabillon, Tillemont, Muratori; and at the same time inspired a future generation of Enlightened historians to attempt a history of civilisation. Leibniz had a truly Baconian grasp of the scope of empirical study in the spheres of both natural and human history. It should include 'les phénomènes admirables du Ciel et de la terre, l'histoire de la Nature et de la Technique, les migrations des peuples, les changements des langues et des empires, l'état présent du monde' (Wade, *Origins*, pp. 447f).

The annalistic historians, while not attaining an ultimate critical synthesis, were strong on the collation of documents and their work was informed by the logic of serial continuity. According to Hayden White, this mirrored central themes of Leibniz's thought;

most notably his celebrated principle of continuity ('nature makes no leaps').

> The annalistic form of historiography was consistent with his notions of continuity, of transition by infinitesimal degrees, of the harmony of the whole in the face of the dispersion in time and space of the elements or parts. Leibniz, perhaps alone among all the major figures of his time, had adequate grounds for believing that annalistic historiography was a philosophically justified mode of historical representation. (*Metahistory*, p. 61)

For Voltaire, who would attempt to put Leibniz's programme for an encyclopedic history of civilisation into effect, Leibniz, 'historien, indefatigable dans ses recherches', was a model.

Bayle

No one would dispute that Pierre Bayle (1647–1706) commands a place of unrivalled pre-eminence in historical thought on the eve of the Enlightenment. But his exact significance has long been a subject of scholarly controversy. In the first place, Bayle has succeeded in baffling his readers as to his personal religious beliefs — if he had any. He has generally been taken as a complete sceptic whose method of systematic doubt and of opposing conflicting evidence and points of view was corrosive of all dogma. The various shades of opinion on this matter have been surveyed by I. O. Wade, who comes down on the side of Elizabeth Labrousse, who has virtually said the last word on the study of Bayle for the time being. Labrousse emphasises Bayle's Huguenot background and his loyal membership of the Protestant church in Rotterdam (Wade, *Origins*; Labrousse, *Bayle*). However, it is still uncertain whether Bayle should be classed as a fideist, who, despairing of reason, casts himself into the arms of faith, or as an early example of modern liberalism, minimalist in belief, standing lightly to the divisions of the Christian tradition, open to theological revision in the light of new knowledge.

Related to this is the question of the extent of his scepticism. Certainly it was applied remorselessly to the claims of reason. Bayle challenged the scope and the findings of speculative reason in the systematisers of the seventeenth century, undermining all the certainties of their rational universe. Whereas Descartes had applied the method of systematic doubt to sense-knowledge and tradition, Bayle applied it to the Cartesian confidence in reason itself. His sceptical approach also embraced the biblical documents and the doctrines of the Christian church, as we have already observed. But some have interpreted Bayle as going further and adopting a position of complete Pyrrhonism even in the field of empirical fact, content to oppose one piece of historical evidence to another, without coming to a conclusion. Others (notably Devolvé) have seen Bayle as the first positivist, with a confidence in the ability of criticism to establish factual conclusions in the sphere not only of history but of ethics, politics, science, etc. But one would certainly have to qualify this, distinguishing Bayle from the incipient positivism of some *philosophes* and the full-blown positivism of the nineteenth century, by stressing that his sceptical, critical method could never come to rest in any form of (secular) dogma.

Bayle is an outsider; he does not belong to the mainstream. He is neither an érudit — his criticism is too advanced for that — nor a *philosophe* — for he is not a secularist. He stands in the tradition of Protestant, 'political, freethinking. Elizabeth Labrousse has indicated Bayle's true provenance when she places him not between Montaigne and Voltaire, but between Calvin and Rousseau (*Bayle*, p. 609f).

Bayle's achievement is summed up in the title of his life's work, the *Dictionnaire historique et critique*. This work, originally intended simply as an exposé of the errors of other compilers, was both historical — an attack on ignorance, a reconstruction of the truth — and critical — a demolition of the pretensions of reason and the distortions of bias. Bayle himself said:

> J'ai divisé ma composition en deux partis: l'une est purement historique, un narré succinct des faits: l'autre est un grand Commentaire, un mélange des preuves et de discussions ou je fais entrer la censure de plusieurs fautes, et quelquefois même une tirade de reflexions philosophiques. (Devolvé, p. 232)

While it is broadly true to say that Bayle devoted the text to historical reconstruction and confined his critical dialectics to the notes, it would be misleading to distinguish too rigidly between his two aims. We can break down the various aspects of Bayle's work more closely as follows:

(i) Primary among the attributes of Bayle's approach is his passion for the particular and the factual, his love of the concrete, the contingent and the give-away detail. For him, as Wade has remarked, all facts are equally interesting. Bayle accepts for himself the title of *minutissimarum rerum minutissimus scrutator*, most minute explorer of most minute things. This is both his strength and his weakness, for as Cassirer has pointed out, Bayle has no developed principle for taking possession of the empirical world and mastering it intellectually: for him historical knowledge is still a mere concatenation of unrelated facts, and he luxuriates in this (*Enlightenment*, pp. 202ff; Wade, *Voltaire*, p. 467).

(ii) Following from this is Bayle's critical method of research which makes him a pioneer of the critical philosophy of history, of the epistemology of history (Cassirer, *Enlightenment*). Bayle's answer to the question, 'How can we know the truth about the past?' is unremitting critical documentary research. For him, facts are not our starting point, as they are for, say Bacon, but our *terminus ad quem*. With Bacon, facts were not problematic, but with Bayle, as Cassirer says, 'the pure concept of the factual is here grasped as a profound problem'. The documentary pursuit of truth was for Bayle a passionate quest and all the weary travail a labour of love. His hermeneutic rested on both scientific skill in tracking down evidence and on critical insight in interpreting its original setting:

> ils veulent tout vérifier; ils vont toujours à la source; ils examinent quel a été le but de l'auteur; ils ne s'arrêtent pas au passage dont ils ont besoin, ils considèrent avec attention ce qui le précède, ce qui le suit'. (Labrousse, *Bayle*, p. 4; cf. Wade, *Voltaire*, pp. 456f)

(iii) Bayle was confident that historical truth could be established. While for Descartes systematic doubt seemed to reveal the gulf between mathematical, rational certainties on the one hand, and historical, contingent uncertainties on the other, for Bayle the principle of critical doubt needed to be applied within the historical sphere itself, sifting the true from the false, refining the evidence until one arrived at a core of historical fact. As Labrousse has remarked: 'On pourrait dire que Bayle conçoit la méthode historique comme une transposition de la méthode Cartesienne — ou plus précisément de sa première règle — à un nouveau domaine' ('La Méthode Critique', p. 465). Not that Bayle believed that this was easy to achieve: he dismissed the ancient historians for their 'mille contradictions partout, mille faits incompatibles, mille fausse dates', and medieval history for its distortion by religious controversy — not to mention its barbarous Latin (Labrousse, *Bayle*, pp. 20f). Bayle's massive scholarship would have been futile unless he had believed that historical truth was attainable. As C. B. Brush has pointed out, there is a significant distinction between 'le pyrrhonisme historique', which is sceptical of the value of all historical enquiry, and 'le doute méthodique historique', which is Bayle's chosen method (Brush, p. 253; cf. Labrousse, 'La Méthode Critique'; Devolvé, p. 425).

(iv) As far as the content of Bayle's massive output is concerned, there are two themes that seem to rise like mountain peaks above the foothills of his research. They are the concepts of the history of civilisation and of the history of philosophy. Bayle is reaching towards the notion of a history of the spirit of the nations that would include 'l'histoire de l'esprit humain, de ses sottises, et de ses extravagances et l'histoire des variétés infinies qui se trouvent dans les lois, et dans les usages des nations' (*Oevres diverses*, I, p. 579b; Wade, *Voltaire*, p.459). This was of course the ambitious project that found fruition in the work of Montesquieu and Voltaire. Within this context it was primarily the history of thought that interested Bayle. His work constitutes an exposition of and critical dialogue with the whole tradition of Western philosophy from the pre-Socratics to the seventeenth century. Only occasionally — and most strikingly in the article on Spinoza — did Bayle depart from unbiased commentary to display a flash of hostility or of passionate commitment. As a storehouse of all previous philosophical positions, Bayle's *Dictionnaire* was plundered by the *philosophes:* Voltaire depended on it. This aspect of Bayle's achievement has earned him the accolade of the first of modern historians of ideas (Wade, *Origins*, p. 583).

(v) Bayle's scrupulous objectivity had a polemical purpose; he did not need to take sides in the arguments that he records; his quarrel was with the whole of history; he puts the human race itself in the dock, exposing its crimes and follies.

> L'histoire est le miroir de la vie humaine, or la condition de la vie humaine est que le nombre des méchants et des impies, tout de même que celui des fols, soit infini, l'histoire n'est autre chose que le portrait de la misère de l'homme. (*Oevres diverse*, III, p. 548; Wade, *Voltaire*, p. 459)

Paul Hazard (p.131), echoed by C. B. Brush (p. 330), labels the *Dictionnaire* a documented indictment of the human race,

> the most damning indictment that was ever drawn up by man to the shame and confusion of his fellows. Well-nigh every name calls up the recollection of some delusion, error, misdemeanour or crime. All those kings whose misrule brought misery to their people; all those popes who debased the Catholic religion to the level of their own ambitions, their own passions; philosophers with their futile, foolish systems; all those cities, towns and countries whose names call back the memory of wars and plunder and massacres.

This dominant theme of Bayle's work is a further bond between him and the Enlightenment. The scourge of human cruelty and superstition, he was a source of inspiration to the *philosophes*' reforming spirit; he contributed to Voltaire's 'Ecrasez l'infâme'.

(vi) Finally, we must briefly consider the question (helpfully discussed by Elizabeth Labrousse in the first part, 'La Verité de Fait', of her second volume and in the article 'La methode critique de Pierre Bayle et l'histoire') as to Bayle's stature as an historian. The only work in which Bayle sets out to do the job of a pure historian is the *Discours historique sur la vie de Gustave Adolphe* (*Oevres diverses*, IV) and this was — perhaps significantly — left unfinished. Here Bayle appears to be out of his element. He adopts a pompous style and an imperious tone. He has to forego the delicious pleasure of footnotes and references, notes to notes and references to references, in whose depths could lurk some of his most subversive remarks. The material is confined to explicit documentation: he has no eye for the involuntary tell-tale scraps of evidence that a modern historian would seize on. Like Bacon in his *Henry VII*, he is shuffling his documents and interpreting them. His history is predominantly political, with princes, generals, bishops and favourites as the prime movers. The significance of the mass of humanity is overlooked, along with all social and economic aspects of history. The result, as Labrousse argues, is that the effects are out of proportion to the causes. All in all, Bayle was, she concludes, less an historian than a critic of historians — and, we might add, a critical philosopher of history (*Bayle*, pp. 29ff). The encomium 'the Galileo of history' which Cassirer awards to Bayle, is not for his historical research as such, but because, by boldly challenging the authority of the Bible (as then uncritically interpreted) and ecclesiastical tradition, he had emancipated historical study from authority and made it an independent science.

6 VICO: THE HARVEST OF PRE-ENLIGHTENMENT HISTORY

Vico's Place in the Philosophy of History

The best introduction to Vico is to read the *Autobiography* — we may not completely understand him (who does?), but we may be gripped by a fascination for this elusive, obscure and yet titanic thinker that will lead to a deeper exploration of his world. It tells the story of a 'heroic spirit', toiling away in comparative obscurity for a quarter of a century at his self-imposed task of forging a 'new science' of humanity — a science that, he believed, would open up unlimited horizons for the understanding of man in society in a way that would demand comparison with what Bacon had done for the study of the physical world. At the same time we cannot fail to be impressed by the power and scope of his intellectual vision, and the breathtaking audacity with which he stands accepted ideas on their heads to effect a revolution in the study of history and the science of man.

The outward circumstances of Vico's life make a sorry tale. Passed over for the academic preferment that he deserved; reduced to soliciting hagiographical hack work to supplement his meagre stipend; failing to get his massive treatises published and unable to foot the bill himself; looking in vain for recognition and encouragement from the great scholars of the day, Jean le Clerc and Montesquieu; the last year of his life spent slumped in dejected silence in a dark corner of the house; and — the final indignity — his dead body left unburied for a week in the Naples heat because of a squabble about precedence at the funeral. A 'timid, obsequious, poverty- and anxiety-ridden scholar', as Isaiah Berlin calls him, his work had been achieved, as he said himself, 'in the midst of the conversation of his friends and the chatter and clatter of his children'.

But Vico saw in his academic failures the hand of providence, enabling him to devote himself to his life's work, *The New Science*. As the book began to take shape he felt himself 'clothed upon with a new man'. Filled with 'a certain heroic spirit' he was 'no longer troubled by any fear of death' — nor, he adds, by the thought of the triumphs of his rivals. He at least knew, even if no one else recognised it at the time, that he had made a momentous discovery and, as Isaiah Berlin puts it, opened the door to a world of which he alone was master. What was this discovery, this new world?

When they come to speak of Vico's achievement even the most sober scholars tend to become ecstatic. The very principle of historical relativism that Vico was the first to enunciate in a comprehensive and coherent form has taught us to expect no new thing under the sun, to be sceptical of claims to originality, and to look for hidden connections and forgotten antecedents where we think we detect bold new departures in the history of thought. But this sort of world-weary and cynical relativism cannot accommodate Vico himself. His originality is undisputed. Precursors he certainly had — his thought reveals a tissue of contributory influences — and others such as Herder reached similar conclusions at a later date. But the imaginative vision, the bold theorising and the architectonic power are Vico's alone. As far as the content of his work is concerned, he gave birth to a new understanding of man in history. As far as his distinctive method is concerned, it was nothing less than a new way of apprehending reality — the way of imaginative indwelling and reconstruction, of what nineteenth-century historicism called *Verstehen*.

Long before Marx, Freud and Jung, Vico recognises the deep irrational urges, the corporate drives and the social structures that motivate men and determine their actions. Well in advance of modern anthropology, he perceives the true significance of primitive myth-making and rituals. Before the birth of German philosophical idealism, Vico grasps the truth of the inescapable subjectivity of knowledge, the principle that mind has the making of reality. With the trumpets of the Enlightenment sounding in his ears, he turns his back on rationalist uniformitarianism and enunciates a principle of historical relativism. Anticipating the historicist tradition that runs from Herder through Dilthey to Collingwood, Vico offers an account of the organic development of societies, clarifies the distinction between the sciences and the humanities, and affirms that there is a way to the understanding of primitive and alien worlds of thought through a supreme and agonising effort of imaginative indwelling. As Isaiah Berlin has said, each of Vico's fundamental principles is a major advance in thought, 'any one of which by itself is sufficient to make the fortune of a philosopher' (*VH*, p. xix).

Vico's life and thought exhibit that paradox, familiar in the record of human endeavour, of neglect, adversity and discouragement, on the one hand, and of brilliant creativity and lasting achievement on the other. Isaiah Berlin brings together the two themes of these introductory remarks when he reflects that 'it is scarcely credible that Vico could have achieved all this in the intellectual solitude and squalor of the conventional, timid and narrow society which he accepted completely and in which he lived out his long, oppressed, unhonoured life' (*VH*, p. 57). Vico seems to have been 'born out of due time'. A child of the seventeenth century — he was born in 1668 and was awarded his chair of rhetoric in 1699 — he crossed swords with the dominant philosophy of the eighteenth-century Enlightenment, but his insights did not receive proper recognition until the age of revolution, spanning the period 1789 to 1919.

Vico is clearly a man of the seventeenth century in his ambition to offer a new science or method of study after the manner of Descartes, Galileo and Bacon. The title of his great work explicitly echoes Bacon's *Novum Organum* and Galileo's *Dialoghi delle Nuove Scienze*. But he lags woefully behind his peers in his way of organising his material. In this respect he is recognisably the heir of the polymaths, antiquarians and compilers of ill-assorted information who dominated scholarship in the period between the Renaissance and the Enlightenment and whose methods — though not their learning — Vico's work would serve to discredit. As Frank Manuel has put it: 'In form and style his turgid and obscure work belongs to the seventeenth-century erudite system-makers and decadent humanists; in content, however, it breathes with a spark of new life' (*ECCG*, p. 150).

Even in his own time Vico was isolated. A devout catholic working in Naples, he was out of tune with contemporary catholic scholarship. The questions that interested him had been formulated a generation or two earlier by protestant scholars and had reached Vico through their published works. The authors who most influenced the direction of his thought — Plato, Lucretius, Tacitus, Spinoza, Bacon, Grotius — were either pagan or Protestant — or, in the case of Spinoza, something worse. Catholic historical scholarship had been influenced by the Cartesian scientific spirit which Vico regarded as the kiss of death for historical understanding. As Arnaldo Momigliano has written:

The whole of his information was superficially anachronistic and intrinsically suspect to catholic eyes . . . With the trust in reason which came from Descartes and the trust in methodical historical criticism which came from Mabillon, the best French and Italian minds were reasserting in a modified form a catholic view of the world. Speculations on the early stages of mankind, on the early migrations of folks and myths, were replaced by archeological explorations, researches in medieval libraries, exact studies in physics and mathematics. (*Essays*, p. 254)

Vico inherited the scientific history that had evolved from the antiquarian movement under the influence of Cartesian rationalism, weighed it in the balance and found it wanting. He closed that chapter of historical study and opened a new one, that of philosophical romanticism or historicism. As Isaiah Berlin remarks, Vico's thought contains 'the whole doctrine of historicism in embryo' (*VH*, p. 41). Vico's 'transforming vision' was worked out in reaction to Cartesianism. It is the concept of a science of mind whose method is the study of its development in history and whose presupposition is that ideas evolve, that knowledge is not 'a static network of eternal, universal, clear truths, either Platonic or Cartesian', but a social process that can be traced through the evolution of the symbols and expressions of a given culture (Berlin, *AC*, p. 113). It is informed throughout by a recognition that the intuitive, the poetic, the mythopoeic — in other words, all that Descartes regarded as irrational — were the springs of creativity in language, religion and the building of a society. Descartes's clear and distinct ideas were sterile and irrelevant as far as historical understanding was concerned.

The consequences of Vico's recognition of the primacy of the intuitive, poetic and mythopoeic over the derivative modes of discursive reason were nothing short of revolutionary. 'Its first effect', claims A. R. Caponigri, 'is the re-examination of the total structure of the human spirit as it has been conceived by Western thought since Plato' (*Time and Idea*, p. 83). It is therefore hardly surprising that Vico was incomprehensible to the men of the Enlightenment. In both the content and the method of his work, what Vico had to offer the eighteenth century was not what it wanted to hear. 'In the study of primitives, who in response to fears and desires established religions, created languages and poetry, built civilisations, Vico captured the spirit of a world that was alien, even repulsive to the rational man of the Enlightenment'. But

Vico was not merely asking them to turn their attention to uncongenial matters: he was demanding that they learn to think in a new way. He was claiming that historical understanding is a form of cognition, a primary mode of perceiving the truth about reality and one vastly superior to mathematics and the exact sciences. As Frank Manuel remarks, 'that presumption in itself would have jolted an eighteenth-century gentleman dabbling in the sciences'! (*ECCG*, pp. 154, 150).

Vico's work suffered neglect in the age of reason, but came into its own when the very fears, forces and irrational drives that Vico had revealed as underlying human society exploded in revolution. Both romantics and reactionaries were willing to learn from him then. As Momigliano has written: 'Vico's hour came when the French Revolution showed that an entire generation of "bestioni" was in existence. Scholars were persuaded to look back, either with nostalgia or in horror, at the unreasonable beginning of human history' (*Essays*, p. 271; cf. Hutton).

Vico is the father of modern philosophy of history, both in its critical form, concerned with how we understand the past and interpret its legacy, and in its speculative form, in which we attempt to read an overall pattern — linear, cyclical, or some variation or combination of these — in the story of the past and draw what conclusions we may for the present and the future. But Vico's influence skips nearly a century before in Arnold and Coleridge in England and Cousin and Michelet in France, the line of descent is picked up and handed on. In Germany, Herder, Wolf and Niebuhr did their work independently, and it was only in retrospect that Vico was recognised as their precursor and as marking the transition from positive history, in which history was assimilated to the sciences, to historical understanding in which history became an aspect of the Romantic imaginative vision of the world.

Vico and Descartes

Vico was a renegade Cartesian. As one of the greatest Cartesians of Italy, he had once stood for the epistemological ideal of clear and distinct ideas and held geometry to be the model science. The bedrock of knowledge was self-evident truth, reached by a process of logical analysis which provided a basis for deduction leading to more complex propositions. Disciplines that did not lend themselves to this method were relegated to a position of inferiority.

History was obviously a prime casuality. Concerned with contingencies, dependent on testimony, probable in its conclusions, history was at the furthest remove from the Cartesian ideal of geometrical necessary truths characterised by clarity and distinctness.

In 1709 Vico was still going along with this, swallowing Descartes's jibe that the sum total of what classical scholars can hope to discover is less than what was known to Cicero's servant girl (Berlin, *AC*, p. 113). But it was a treason to his calling. As a professor of rhetoric, Vico was necessarily concerned with 'topical' rather than 'critical' work — that is to say, with constructive and synthetic as opposed to analytical thought. As Flint pointed out in his book on Vico (nearly a century old but still of value): 'His opposition to the method of Descartes was in fact avowedly on the ground that that method was injurious to eloquence; it was in part the opposition of a professor of eloquence to a mathematician' (*Vico*, pp. 66f). Steeped in the researches and reconstructions of sixteenth-century jurisprudence, Vico was professionally committed to recognising the importance of the principles of authority, probability and experience, for which the individualistic and atomistic approach of Descartes had no room. The rationalist ideal that the contemporary climate of learning imposed upon Vico clashed with the mental habits and assumptions of a lifetime's academic work. Out of that intense conflict an insight was born that enabled Vico to depose Descartes from his methodological pedestal and to reinstate the disciplines — history in particular — that had suffered most at his hands. This was Vico's celebrated principle verum ipsum factum, we can know only what we have made.

The first intimation of Vico's rebellion against the dominance of Cartesianism and the first hint of what has become known as the Vichean theory of knowledge occurs in the academic oration of 1708 *On the Study Methods of our Time*. What Vico has to say is cast in the conventional mould of the *Querelle des Anciennes et Modernes*: the moderns have indeed made great improvements in the physical sciences, but have unduly depreciated those studies that are concerned with human nature and are therefore by definition marked by contingency and probability — language, poetry, eloquence, history, jurisprudence, politics. Viewed in retrospect, Vico here seems to announce his commitment to the reconstruction of humane studies, to the project of a science of humanity which, as A. R. Caponigri has claimed, 'constitutes the widest frame of reference of Vico's thought' and 'the definitive commitment of his intellectual effort'. 'It is only with reference to this project that the unity and continuity and the actual direction of his thought can be established' (*Time and Idea*, p. 55).

Two years later, in 1710, Vico returned to the attack in *The Ancient Wisdom of the Italians*. Now greatly emboldened, Vico attempted to demolish the entire structure of Cartesianism. Descartes had laid down the cogito ergo sum as a self-evident truth, shining in its clarity and distinctness, the foundation principle of his reconstruction of knowledge. To this Vico opposes another supposedly self-evident truth: we can know only what we have made: 'the criterion and rule of the true is to have made it' (*Ancient Wisdom*, p. 55).

The Vichean dictum verum factum convertantur (the true and the made are convertible) is a two-edged sword. First, it refutes Descartes: mathematics is indeed the purest form of knowledge, verum itself, not because it opens the door to the world of objective reality, but because it is a human projection, a man-made world of arbitrary symbols that tell us nothing that we really want to know. Secondly, at the same time, it provides grounds for a science of humanity, for the understanding of man's existence in time through an empathetic reading of all that he has created. While God alone can fully comprehend the physical universe, for he has made it — *creatio ex nihilo* — man possesses within himself the key to history for it reflects 'the modifications of the human mind'.

The full ramifications of the verum factum principle were not yet clear to Vico; the above summary has anticipated somewhat. What he had done in *The Ancient Wisdom of the Italians* was to relativise Descartes and his favoured sciences. But he had also sown the seeds of the historical method that was to develop into the *Nuova Scienza*. At the time, he seemed to have scored only a tactical victory. If mathematics was a science, it was a hollow and futile one. The realm of humane studies, even if not a science (merely certum, not verum) was infinitely more rewarding. Vico had justified to himself the labours on which he was already engaged. He had enunciated the epistemological foundations of those studies in the principle of verum factum. This was what mattered. It was secondary, though of burning importance to Vico himself, that he later came to see that the verum factum principle also gave him unassailable grounds for claiming that he had founded a new *science* (verum, not merely certum), thus ranking him with Galileo, Bacon and Newton — not to mention Descartes himself.

From now on Vico's work seemed to take the form of a series of direct antitheses to all that Descartes represented. While Cartesianism concerned itself with the universal and the abstract, Vico became more and more fascinated by the individual and the particular. While Cartesianism 'shrank in horror from the tangled forest of history' (Croce), Vico plunged eagerly into those periods where 'the historical flavour is strongest', the primitive, the impenetrable. And while Cartesianism with its uniformitarian assumptions interpreted all periods and cultures in the light of an enlightened European outlook, Vico attempted 'to investigate in all their profound divergencies and contradictions the modes of feeling and thought proper to various times' (Croce, *Vico*, p. 45).

As *The New Science* took shape, it became apparent that Vico had succeeded in developing a comprehensive and coherent alternative to the Cartesian worldview — an alternative concept of reason, of culture, of history and of science.

> To posit as the founders of civilisation not sages but brutes; to posit as the primitive and therefore basic forms of apprehension, not reason but instinct, feeling, intuition, manipulatory inventiveness (that is, the apprehension not of the universal but of the particular); and to posit as the primitive and basic modes of generalisation not the universals of science and philosophy but those of poetry . . . was to emancipate oneself at last from Descartes and to give a new dignity to those philological and historical disciplines which he had despised as resting on inferior cognitive faculties. (*Auto*, p 43)

But Vico did not leave Descartes behind. The renegade Cartesian felt a presence looking over his shoulder. At the beginning of his *Autobiography* — described by the translators as 'the first application of the genetic method by an original thinker to his own writings' — Vico felt bound to dissociate himself from Descartes's procedure in his own autobiographical account of the genesis of his ideas, the *Discourse on Method*. 'We shall not here feign', wrote Vico, 'what René Descartes craftily feigned as to the method of his studies simply in order to exalt his own philosophy and mathematics and degrade all the other studies included in divine and human learning.' The Vico who had wrestled for a quarter of a century with the problems of *The New Science* could not accept that the postulates of Descartes's own revolutionary method had come to him in the course of a single day at the age of twenty-three! (*Auto*, p. 7; Descartes, *Discourse*, p. 35).

Vico's Intellectual Debts

How had Vico occupied those twenty years and more, what had he read? As far as original research in the primary sources is concerned, Vico did not carry a great weight of learning. Those, like Arnaldo Momigliano, who are professionally engaged in researching the same field, tend to speak of Vico as having reached his brilliant theory by a process of inspired, rather than informed, guesswork. This could not have been otherwise, for the painstaking empirical reconstruction of antiquity had to wait for the labours of F. A. Wolf and B. G. Niebuhr. But if Vico's theory was not a new interpretation of research data, what was it?

Vico speaks of himself as self-taught — *autodidaskalos* — and mentions with affection his 'four authors': Plato, Tacitus, Bacon and Grotius, whose insights had contributed to the formation of the 'new science'. It seemed awkward enough at the time to acknowledge a debt to thinkers, two of whom were pagan and two protestant. But Vico chose not to reveal a debt to others whose influence was just as great, but whose reputation was even more unsavoury: Lucretius, Machiavelli, Hobbes and Spinoza. To this list should be added Pufendorf, the theorist of natural law, and Bodin the author of the *Methodus*. Vico's science was a creative and critical synthesis of the insights he derived from his wide and eclectic reading.

Plato

From the transcendental ethos of Plato's dialogues, as much as from any particular platonic doctrine, such as the Forms, Vico drew inspiration for his science of a *storia ideale eterna*, 'an ideal eternal history, traversed in time by the history of every nation in its rise, development, maturity, decline and fall' (*NS*, 349).

Tacitus

If Plato provided the thesis, Tacitus suggested the antithesis: the detailed, specific, particularist aspect of *The New Science*, its earthing in empirical reality. Tacitus stands for a clear-sighted vision of how men act, and of the irrational passions, social forces and power-structures that motivate them — the very factors that natural law philosophers tended to leave out of the reckoning. As Peter Gay has written of Tacitus:

> All the cutting, epigrammatic edge, all his psychological finesse, all his tight-lipped spleen are concentrated on a single task: to get behind surfaces, to strike through the mask of fair appearance and grasp the hidden reality . . . Tacitus' epigrams are like the thrust of a knife, clean and wounding. (I, pp. 157f)

Epicurus, Lucretius, Machiavelli and Hobbes also contributed to this dimension of Vico's thought; but he acknowledges only Tacitus.

Besides his ruthless realism, Tacitus also provided a model of a more philosophical approach to history than that of the mere chroniclers, classical, medieval or humanist. His *Germania* struck an anthropological note and may have suggested to Vico new approaches to primitive societies. Gibbon would later record his admiration for Tacitus as a 'philosophical historian', the first historian to apply philosophical methods to the study of facts. This is of course precisely the ideal that Vico himself was striving for, a marriage of the empirical and the theoretical, of philology and philosophy.

Momigliano has remarked that in practice Vico made little use of Plato and Tacitus; 'they remained pieces of classical scenery, the one contemplating man as he should be, the other as he is' (*Essays*, p. 258). Nevertheless, they remained archetypes, models of the complementary approaches that Vico wanted to fuse together.

Lucretius

Vico's lurid picture of the violent lives of the *bestioni* was probably coloured by subconscious impressions received in his youthful reading of Lucretius' vision of the rise of man from savagery. But Vico transposes Lucretius' sunny Epicurean images into a much more sombre mood. Lucretius' big-boned men, wandering amidst a bountiful nature, enjoying both sunshine and showers, and procreating themselves as 'Venus coupled the bodies of lovers in the greenwood', became Vico's Cyclopean figures, both hunter and hunted, cowering at thunder and lightning, the capricious threatenings of a hostile universe, and abandoning their offspring to the elements (Lucretius, Book V).

Spinoza

Like Descartes, Spinoza is seldom mentioned, but he is never far from Vico's thoughts. And, again like Descartes, he contributed to the development of *The New Science* mainly by provoking a reaction. He is alluded to in the opening remarks of the 1725 edition where Vico rejects the immanental Spinozistic concept of a self-contained nature (*natura naturans*) — his dominant notion of providence ordering the slow development of human society demands a God who is distinct from the world (in Spinozistic terms, *natura naturata*). But, as Momigliano points out, it was Spinoza who ultimately provided the model for the geometrical structure (*mos geometricus*) of the 1730 edition of *The New Science* (*Essays*, pp. 253f).

Bodin

Bodin's *Methodus* of 1566 has recently been claimed as a source of certain features of *The New Science*. It is true that Vico would have found a number of congenial suggestions in Bodin: use of myths as instruments of historical research, theories about the origins of society, philological speculations and a critique of the Golden Age and of the Four Empires of the prophecies of Daniel. But Vico's mind did not work by borrowing wholesale from the work of others; it is more likely that elements of Bodin were incorporated into Vico's great synthesis by being translated into the language that Vico had made his own (Cotroneo).

Grotius

In the early seventeenth-century jurist Hugo Grotius, Vico found a fusion of the two elements that he strove to wield together: the universal and the particular, the Platonic and the Tacitean, *verités de raison* and *verités de fait* (Leibniz), *cogitare* and *videre* (Bacon), philosophy and philology. In Grotius, the science of universal truths and research into particular historical facts had been united in a system of universal law. The *De jure belli et pacis*, asserted Vico, 'with certain passages excised,' deserves to be called 'peerless' ('On the Heroic Mind', p. 244).

Hobbes

In Hobbes, Vico found confirmation of what he had already learned from Tacitus — a pessimistic view of man in his natural state — and from Machiavelli — the realities of the dynamics of power. But is worth noting the possibility that he may have found in Hobbes an astonishing anticipation of his central principle that man's historical existence is necessarily open to our understanding because it is the product of mind: in his reflections on geometrical method, Hobbes asserts that 'civil philosophy is demonstrable because we make the commonwealth ourselves' (*EW*, VII, p. 184; Rubinoff, p. 98).

Bacon

Finally, and perhaps most dominantly, there was the influence of Bacon, the founder of a new science himself, the great exemplar to whom Vico looked up with awe — but who was also the giant with feet of clay whom he learned to criticise and attempted to supplant. Bacon ranked with Lucretius and Tacitus as one of Vico's non-anachronistic historians. The *De augmentis scientiarum* is 'worth its weight in gold, and, apart from a few passages, ever to be looked up to and borne in mind' ('On the Heroic Mind', p. 242).

Had not Bacon spoken of the spontaneous origins of human speech (neither a direct gift of God nor a pure invention of the rational faculties), of inarticulate gestures preceding utterance, of the significance of ideograms and hieroglyphs, and so on? But, on the other hand, had he not capitulated to the hoary superstition of the matchless wisdom of the ancients, regarding the fables of Homer and Hesiod as relics of a wiser and more blessed age, designed to convey physical and moral truths in allegorical form? And had not Bacon also failed to bring the whole social dimension within the orbit of his brave new world of empirical science? He had overlooked the truth, so central to Vico's philosophy, that God alone, as its creator, could fully know the physical universe, while the proper sphere of human enquiry was the life of man revealed in the history that he had made (verum ipsum factum). While Bacon 'discovers a new cosmos of sciences', writes Vico in *On the Study Methods of our Time*, 'the great Chancellor proves to be rather the pioneer of a completely new universe than a prospector of this world of ours.'

His vast demands so exceed the utmost extent of man's effort that he seems to have indicated how we fall short of an absolutely complete system of sciences rather than how we may remedy our cultural gaps. This was so I believe, because those who occupy the heights of power yearn for the immense and the infinite. Thus Bacon acted in the intellectual field like the potentates of mighty empires who, having gained supremacy in human affairs, squander immense wealth in attempts against the order of nature herself, by paving the sea with stones, mastering mountains with sail and other vain exploits forbidden by nature. No doubt all that man is given to know is, like man himself, limited and imperfect. (p. 4)

Vico is reminding Bacon that 'the proper study of mankind is man' — not on the shallow deistic basis of Pope's famous couplet, but on the grounds of his own profound philosophical conception, verum ipsum factum. Vico's comments on Bacon lend support to the view that, whatever Vico owed to him, his method is actually more Kantian than Baconian, in that it seems to anticipate Kant's principle that 'reason has insight only into that which it produces after a plan of its own' (Rubinoff, p. 99).

Renaissance Humanism

Time and again the humanists bring us up sharp with their extraordinary prophetic anticipations of later historical thinking, particularly Vico's.

In his oration *De Hominis Dignitate*, Pico della Mirandola seems to challenge the received view — inherited from antiquity, unchallenged until post-Enlightenment thought — of the uniformity of human nature. Pico portrays man in dynamic, almost existential, terms in place of the familiar language of substance or nature. Of all the creatures, he asserts, man alone has no determining nature beyond his own freedom. Confined by no unchanging essence of humanity, he creates himself by his deeds (Garin, p. 105).

The language of modern hermeneutics and of R. G. Collingwood's idealist philosophy of history with its talk of thinking men's thoughts after them, seems to be anticipated in E. Barbaro's announcement at the beginning of his lectures on Aristotle that his aim was not merely to comment on a dead text but to make Aristotle come to life and take part in human converse (*ut cum ipso vivo et praesente loqui videamur*) (Garin, p. 14).

Other humanists, as we have already noted in the case of Valla, are responsible for insights that we have to wait until Vico to see developed systematically. Salutati, for example, recognises the true character of law as the reflection of human spiritual solidarity. 'Laws', he claims, 'exist unshakeably in the relations of human minds to each other' (Garin, p. 33). And Vico's doctrine that the poets were the first legislators as well as the first historians of mankind inevitably springs to mind when we come across this apostrophe to poetry by Pontano:

> When the poets imagine their pictures and then express them sweetly, miraculously and magnificently, they teach at the same time other men to speak . . . In this sense every mode of expression is derived from history. For poets were the first sages and expressed themselves in songs and other rhythms . . . Hail to thee, O poetry, most fertile mother of all knowledge . . . Thou didst lead men forth from their forests and caves. Through thee we arrive at knowledge; through thee we can revive and recall in front of our eyes things of the past; through thee we know God. . . (Garin, p. 74)

These examples do not of course establish a direct debt to fifteenth and sixteenth-century Italian humanism in particular cases, but they do raise the question as to whether Vico's indebtedness to his predecessors, which we have been taught to look for in seventeenth-century jurisprudence and the methodological treatises of Descartes and Bacon, does not in fact extend more widely and deeply to the very springs of Renaissance humanism in his own country (cf. Struever, pp. 65, 71, 132).

To enumerate in this way the acknowledged, and some of the unacknowledged sources of Vico's system, by no means accounts for his distinctive theory and is not intended to. A more ill-assorted cloud of witnesses could hardly be encountered in the history of thought. But a deep and luminous intelligence had forged out of their diverse contributions a brilliant and original synthesis. For, as Isaiah Berlin remarks, whatever Vico may have owed to his favourite thinkers, 'none of this coalesced, none of it would have come to life in the new synthesis, the conception of philosophy as the consciousness of the cumulative experience of entire societies, without the central principle which is Vico's ultimate claim to immortality' — the doctrine of imaginative reconstruction of past human life (*AC*, p. 114).

Vico's Critique of Traditions

Like his mentors Descartes and Bacon, Vico begins with a process of demolition. Just as Descartes had set out to divest himself of all acquired opinions as a preliminary to the task of reconstruction, and Bacon had exposed the various 'idols' of wrong thinking to clear the way for the *Novum Organum* of his empirical method, so Vico attacks what he calls the 'conceit of nations' and the 'conceit of scholars' for the errors of anthropomorphism and anachronism. His targets are the scholastic thinkers, antiquarians and system-builders of the seventeenth century, and the natural-law philosophers like Grotius and Pufendorf to whom he owed much — all, in fact, including Bacon himself, who accepted the myth of 'the matchless wisdom of the ancients'.

The 'conceit of nations' is the illusion, fostered by national pride, that all peoples have of their own superiority. They will have it that their history goes back to the beginning of the world, that they were the first to invent the comforts of civilisation, and so on. The 'conceit of scholars' is closely analogous: academics like to convince themselves and others that what they know is as old as the world and to cite the authority of the ancients for their views. Even Descartes felt it necessary to claim, for views that were actually subversive of all tradition, that 'they have been known from all time, and even received as true and indubitable by all men' (Frankel, p. 24). Hence belief in the matchless wisdom of the ancients, far from being a well-attested empirical theory about the state of learning and culture in antiquity, is merely a ploy to cast a mantle of respectability over academic reputation-building (*NS*, 125ff).

Both errors rest on the human failings of anthropomorphism and anachronism. Man inevitably attempts to bring the unknown into line with the known. He projects the present onto the past, and mind onto nature. This perception has great heuristic importance for Vico. 'Because of the indefinite nature of the human mind, wherever it is lost in ignorance man makes himself the measure of all things' (*NS*, 120). And again: 'When men are ignorant of the natural causes producing things, and cannot explain them by analogy with similar things, they attribute their own nature to them. The vulgar, for example, say that the magnet loves the iron' (*NS*, 180). But this is not a vice that is confined to ignorant savages. The same principle is operating when scholars interpret ancient cultures 'on the basis of their own enlightened, cultivated and magnificent times' (*NS*, 123). Vico's criticism of scholarly methods or assumptions struck at several key areas of historical investigation.

The Origins of Speech

In place of the notion of language as the direct gift of God at creation, a sort of *bonum superadditum*, Vico traces its origins to the inarticulate utterances that gave vent to deep feelings (*NS*, 401ff). Here Vico was probably indebted to Lucretius, who had designated the view that gifted individuals had invented names for objects which had then caught on, as madness. (Lucretius could not know the Genesis story of Adam naming the creatures. Vico did, but his theory was tactfully confined to pagan history.) As Lucretius says:

> What after all, is so surprising in the notion that the human race, possessed of a vigorous voice and tongue, should indicate objects by various vocal utterances expressive of various feelings? Even dumb cattle and wild beasts utter distinct and various sounds when they are gripped by fear or pain or when joy wells up within them. (p. 203)

Poetry

Received scholarly opinion saw prose as the original spoken word and poetry as a later and derivative development — serving as an ingenious disguise for popularising profound truths, or simply as a harmless amusement. But for Vico, poetry came before prose, arising spontaneously out of the inarticulate cries and rythmic utterances of early man. Thinking poetically was the primary activity of the human mind; prose was artificial and derivative. Poetry revealed the springs of creativity and the compositions of the primitive poets have never been excelled. 'It was deficiency of human reasoning power that gave rise to poetry so sublime that the philosophies which came afterwards, the arts of poetry and of criticism, have produced none equal or better' (*NS*, 384). 'The first nations', asserted Vico, summing up his radical reappraisal of the matter, 'thought in poetic characters, spoke in fables and wrote in hieroglyphs' (*NS*, 429). Cartesianism and the intellectual climate influenced by Descartes was hostile to metaphor. But Vico argues that far from being misleading and contemptible, metaphor is a window into reality, a basic category of human rationality, and at a given stage of development, the only way in which men could look at their world (Berlin, *VH*, p. 103). This discovery, commented Vico, that 'the first Gentile peoples . . . were poets who spoke in poetic characters . . . is the master key of this science'; it had cost him 'the persistent research of almost all' his working life (*NS*, 34).

Homer

The two great Homeric epics presented Vico with an apparent challenge to his theory. They were not only supposedly the oldest literary creations, outside the sacred canon, but were also the most accomplished. Vico did not hesitate to carry through his theory. Anticipating intuitively the later empirical findings of Wolf, Vico claimed that the Homeric books were not the creation of a single genius, but had been composed and compiled by various hands through successive ages and handed on in oral form. The Greek peoples 'were themselves Homer' for 'our Homer truly lived on the lips and in the memories of the peoples of Greece throughout the whole period of the Trojan War down to the time of Numa, a period of 460 years' (*NS*, 804, 875f).

Myth

A succession of writers from Plato to Bacon had interpreted the Greek fables as symbolic representations of esoteric philosophical doctrines. Running parellel to this tradition was the euhemerist school of myth-interpretation which attributed the origins of pagan religion to the apotheosis of a king or hero, rather than to free-ranging imaginative response to the mystery of the universe. Here Vico was striking at the prevailing scholarly methods of his day, for as Frank Manuel points out,

> If euhemerism is broadened to include those who recognised in most pagan myths the elaboration of ancient political and other historic events of great moment, then the concept would encompass the great majority of mythographers and chronologists who flourished in the first half of the eighteenth century. (*ECCG*, pp. 103f)

For Vico, myth never dealt with the minor personal or political events of Mediterranean kingdoms, but with momentous occurences in the gradual socialisation of mankind: the origin and genesis of pagan religion, the establishment of families, the invention of speech and writing, the institution of marriage and burial rites [and so on]. (ibid., pp. 161f)

Religion

In place of euhemerist interpretations of the origins of religion, Vico offers the following account. When, a century or two after the Flood, the first thunder and lightning appeared, the most robust of the race of giants, 'who were dispersed through the forests on the mountain heights where the strongest beasts have their dens', were compelled to look up in amazement.

> And because in such a case the nature of the human mind leads it to attribute its own nature to the effect . . . they pictured the sky to themselves as a great animated body . . . And thus they began to exercise that natural curiosity which is the daughter of ignorance and the mother of knowledge, and which, opening the mind of man, gives birth to wonder' (*NS*, 377ff).

Thus the primitive religions were born:

> The first theological poets created the first divine fable, the greatest they ever created: that of Jove, king and father of men and Gods, in the act of hurling the lightening bolt; an image so popular, disturbing and instructive that its creators themselves believed in it and feared, revered and worshipped it in frightful religions. (ibid.)

Wonder led to worship and worship to faith: religious belief was the product of primitive experience not the rational achievement of 'the matchless wisdom of the ancients'. 'Thus, through the thick clouds of those first tempests, intermittently lit by those flashes, they made out this great truth: that divine providence watches over the welfare of all mankind' (*NS*, 385).

Roman History

Vico exposed the anachronistic assumptions of much work on early Roman history. When the historian came across words like 'people', 'kingdom', 'liberty', he tended to interpret them in eighteenth-century terms and not according to their cultural context. For Vico, on the other hand, 'each age lives, speaks, acts, thinks, governs, legislates, dreams in its own language and idea-system; it has a distinct metaphysic, a cosmography, a logic, an economy and a politics; above all, it has a psyche' (Manuel, *ECCG*, p. 151). Interpretation of individual concepts must presuppose all this (Pompa, *Vico*, p. 12).

Laws

One aspect of the myth of the matchless wisdom of the ancients that Vico set out to demolish was the belief that the laws and constitutions of ancient states had been decreed by outstanding lawgivers, not evolved by a process of trial and error out of the clash of interests in an untamed society. 'The wisdom of the ancients was the vulgar wisdom of the lawgivers who founded the human race, not the esoteric wisdom of great and rare philosophers' (*NS*, 384). The natural-law philosophers, Grotius, Selden and Pufendorf, believed, according to Vico, 'that natural equity in its perfect form had been understood by the Gentile nations from their first beginnings' (*NS*, 329). They assumed, with Descartes, that laws devised systematically by a single mind were superior to laws that had grown up piecemeal. The natural-law philosophers, Vico points out, had overlooked the fact that it had taken some two thousand years for philosophers to appear in any of these societies (*NS*, 329).

Society

The origins of the state looked very different to Vico. After the Flood, he conjectured, Noah's descendants, having renounced the religion of their forefathers which alone had been able to hold society together, 'dissolved their marriages and broke up their families by promiscuous intercourse and began roving wild through the great forest of the earth.'

> By fleeing from the wild beasts with which the great forest must have abounded, and by pursuing women, who in that state must have been wild, indocile and shy [why?], they became separated from each other in their search for food and water. Mothers abandoned their children, who in time must have come to grow up without ever hearing a human voice, much less learning any human custom, and thus descended to a state truly bestial and savage. Mothers, like beasts, must merely have nursed their babies; let them wallow naked in their own filth, and abandoned them for good as soon as they were weaned. (*NS*, 369)

This period of antecedent chaos and savagery gave way to a three-stage development of society. The dawning awareness of superhuman powers of nature gave birth to religions of fear in which men were shamed into retreating into caves, out of the sight of gods and men, to mate, and a primitive reverence inspired the practice of burying the dead. This was the first age, 'the age of the gods', in which the family structure gradually formed and superseded the fortuitous and promiscuous coupling of savages. Vico thus connected the origins of society with the origins of religion.

The age of the heroes supervened, an alliance of fathers in a sort of feudal aristocracy, in which the common people were oppressed. According to the almost Freudian primal myth imagined by Vico, the oppressed sons rose against their fathers and ushered in the third age, 'the age of men', of 'free, popular republics'. But this was not the end, for through a combination of effeteness and corruption, the societies of the third age broke down into barbarism, and the whole cycle began again (*corsi e ricorsi*).

With this picture of the origins of society, Vico effectively discredited the writers of the natural-law school, who, as Frank Manuel puts it, had made 'aborigines enter into civil contracts and establish religious ceremonies on the basis of a perception of orderliness in the world' (*ECCG*, p. 157). In place of the 'natural law of the philosophers', Vico expounded what he called the 'natural law of the nations': the way men actually lived and acted, not the way philosophers thought they ought to behave.

Vico's 'Historicism'

Some aspects of Vico's thought belong to the ethos of pre-Enlightenment history; others mark a new departure and the formation of a distinctive tradition of the philosophy of history — the movement known as 'Historicism'. His stress on detailed empirical research — though this was not his own strong point — belongs to the general spirit of the historical movement. 'The useful historians', he claims, 'are not those who give general descriptions of facts and explain them by reference to general conditions, but those who go into the greatest detail and reveal the particular cause of each event' (cf. Berlin, *AC*, p. 118n). This genetic and inductive method Vico learned from Bacon: we know a thing only if we know why it is as it is, how it came to be. Knowledge is 'through causes' (*per caussas*). 'Every theory must start from the point where the matter of which it treats first began to take shape' (*NS*, 314, 347f, 350, 374). The historian *qua* historian is concerned not with final causes — what is it for? — in the manner of the Aristotelianising scholastics, but with second causes — how did it come about?

Much more pronounced, and indeed impressive, is the way that, looked at in retrospect, Vico seems to anticipate the approach to history that became characteristic of the philosophical romanticism of the late eighteenth and early nineteenth centuries in Germany, France and England, though we must not fall into the trap of setting Vico in an age not his own. B. A. Haddock's warnings of the danger of 'precursoritis' are well taken ('Vico and Anachronism'; 'Vico, the Problem of Interpretation'). (The title of this chapter is intended to guard against this tendency: Vico is certainly a pre-Enlightenment thinker.) A number of points of comparison will come before us shortly. First of all, however, we should notice one striking omission from the list of Vico's 'historicist' tenets. For it would not be true to say that he possesses a fully fledged doctrine of development. A certain notion of development he certainly does have. The theme of corsi e ricorsi combines, as Momigliano has pointed out, the humanist idea of decline with the Christian idea of the fall. But it is perhaps the least original of Vico's doctrines, going back as it does through Anabaptist and Renaissance spiritualist speculations, through the thought of Joachim of Fiore, to the Montanists and beyond that to classical myths of cosmic decay and renewal. But it would be anachronistic to expect to find in Vico the mature historicist doctrine of organic development which was worked out in opposition to the high Enlightenment doctrine of mechanical progress as found, for example, in the writings of Condorcet.

Though development was not an issue for Vico, there can be no doubt that he prepared the ground in which later theories could germinate. As Isaiah Berlin says: 'Vico goes far beyond Bodin and Montaigne and Montesquieu: they (and Voltaire) may have believed in different social *esprits*, but not in successive stages of historical evolution, each phase of which has its own modes of vision, forms of expression'. Vico attacked the Cartesian concept of knowledge on which later views of progress were based — 'the idea of the cumulative growth of knowledge, a single corpus, governed by single, universal criteria, so that what one generation of scientists has established, another generation need not repeat'

(Berlin, *AC*, pp. 104f). Vico rejects the notion of progress and points towards the idea of development.

We turn now to the positive principles of Vico's 'historicism'.

Historical Imagination

As Frank Manuel has written, Vico outraged his contemporaries with a picture of primitive beings whose nature seemed to have nothing in common with the sophisticated eighteenth-century Neapolitans who paid court to the great cardinals and to the Spanish rulers. As Manuel aptly remarks, they seemed to belong to a different species (*ECCG*, p. 165).

Vico speaks powerfully and movingly of the remoteness of early human history.

> To discover the way in which this first human thinking arose in the gentle world, we encountered exasperating difficulties which have cost us the research of a good twenty years. We had to descend from these human and refined natures of ours to those quite wild and savage natures which we cannot at all imagine and can comprehend only with great effort. (*NS*, 338)

And again:

> It is . . . beyond our power to enter into the vast imagination of those first men whose minds were not in the least abstract, refined, or spiritualized, because they were entirely immersed in the senses, buffeted by the passions, buried in the body. (*NS*, 378)

His language exceeds whatever any late twentieth-century purveyor of historical scepticism might want to claim.

Nevertheless, Vico affirms categorically that it *is* possible 'to descend from these human and refined natures of ours to those quite wild and savage natures'. Though we 'can scarcely understand, still less imagine, how those first men thought who founded gentile humanity' (*NS*, 378), historical insight is vouchsafed to those who are prepared to make an agonising effort. With his concept of fantasia, Vico 'uncovered a species of knowing not previously clearly discriminated, the embryo that later grew into the ambitious and luxuriant plant of German historicist *Verstehen* — empathetic insight, intuitive sympathy, historical *Einfühlung*, and the like'

(Berlin, *AC*, p. 116).

The first utterance of this great principle of historical understanding is made by Vico with visionary power:

> In the night of thick darkness enveloping the earliest antiquity, so remote from ourselves, there shines the eternal and never-failing light of a truth beyond all question: that the world of civil society has certainly been made by men and that its principles are therefore to be found within the modifications of our own human mind. (*NS*, 331, cf. 349, 374)

Vico's idealist principle is echoed by Dilthey when he claims: 'The fact that the investigator of history is the same as the one who makes it is the first condition which makes scientific history possible' (p. 67).

The analogy between the individual and society was already common coin in the eighteenth century. Pascal had pictured scientific advance as being like the growth of an individual who could assimilate one lesson and go on to the next: he did not have to keep relearning. But in Vico's usage, this metaphor is much more than an analogy. There is a real ontological connection between the individual mind and the historical process, for history is precisely the product of mind. The three stages of society correspond to the three phases of individual mental development, which begin with crude feeling and pass through a transitional stage to a sort of Cartesian clarity: 'Men at first feel without perceiving, then they perceive with a troubled and agitated spirit; finally, they reflect with a clear mind' (*NS*, 218). Early man was a creature of feeling, lacking in discriminatory reflection; his society and its expressions in religion, law, communication and so on, corresponded to this.

Vico's law of reflux, *corsi e ricorsi*, is epistemological as well as historical, and although this aspect of his thought is not worked out as fully or consistently as the other, the pattern is clear. As Croce writes:

> Where reflection is at a low ebb and imagination flourishes, the passions also flourish, habits are violent, governments aristocratic or feudal, families subject to strict paternal rule, laws severe, legal procedure symbolical, language couched in metaphor and writing in hieroglyphics. Where, on the other hand, reflection predominates, poetry becomes either separate from or

charged with philosophy, manners and customs lose their violence, the passions are brought into subjection, the people take government into their own hands, all members of the family are alike citizens of the state, law is mitigated by equity and its procedure simplified, language loses its metaphorical clothing and writing becomes alphabetical. (*Vico*, pp. 103f)

In this summary and paraphrase of Vico's system, Croce has simplified the scheme into two contrasting types, ironing out the transitional stage between. But in Vico's thought, the threefold pattern is prominent. The three ages of history correspond to three forms of human thinking and self-expression, comprehending perception, customs, law, language, government, and reasoning. For example, the first age, the age of the gods, was ruled by sense or feeling, and 'natural law' was sanctioned by fear — fear of the gods. In the second age, the age of heroes, imagination characterises human thinking and natural law is enforced by earthly rulers. In the third age, the age of men, reason holds sway and natural law is sanctioned by individual conscience.

Vico himself loses track of these complex patterns of correspondences, but the principle is clear. Vico affirms the apparently contradictory propositions, first, that the past is virtually impenetrable, and secondly, that it yields to the agonising efforts of creative imagination. Only a crude idealist metaphysic arcs the two poles of Vico's historical imagination.

Relativism and Human Nature

'Vico is not essentially a relativist', remarks Isaiah Berlin. This is true if it means that Vico's relativism is not unqualified or that it is not the thoroughgoing sort of modern relativism that would have us resign ourselves to the closed world of the past. But I would prefer to indicate Vico's position, not by playing down the relativism that is undoubtedly there, but by showing it is complemented in his historical perspective by other considerations.

The key to Vico's relativism is his sense of the unique and self-contained character of every culture, a concept that calls out for Montesquieu's expression, 'the spirit of the age'. Peoples have acquired diverse natures and cultural characteristics through being exposed to different climates which have in turn influenced customs and even languages (*NS*, 445). This gives them a set of what Collingwood was to call 'absolute presuppositions', but what

Vico terms *sensus communis*, based on 'judgement without reflection' (*NS*, 142). Each culture thus has its own 'pervasive pattern' (Isaiah Berlin) with which all its expressions and institutions are stamped. As Vico puts it, in perhaps his strongest statement of historical relativism, combining the concept of becoming with that of conditioning: 'The nature of institutions, is nothing but their coming into being (*nascimento*) at certain times and in certain guises. Whenever the time and guise are thus and so, such and not otherwise are the institutions that come into being' (*NS*, 147). In the hands of Herder, the German and Italian idealists and their Anglo-Saxon disciples, this relativist insight became the principle, expressed by Croce, that 'no human age was in the wrong, for each had its own strength and beauty' (*Theory and Practice*, p. 269).

It is, however, not only individual cultures that have a distinctive 'common sense' at the level of judgement without reflection. The entire human race has an essential nature, a sensus communis of its own. Vico rejected the transmission theory of civilisation, and argued that the parallel development of civilised practices in various parts of the world resulted from a basic human nature. Sometimes (possibly in a conscious attempt to avoid the language of substance), Vico spoke of this human nature in terms of a uniform *voci mentali* or mental language:

> There must in the nature of human institutions be a mental language common to all nations, which uniformly grasps the substance of things feasible in human social life and expresses it with as many diverse modifications as these same things may have diverse aspects. (*NS*, 161)

The proverbs, or 'maxims of vulgar wisdom' in which basically the same meaning is expressed in as many different idioms as there are nations ancient or modern, is cited as an example (ibid.). But Vico has in mind, as Isaiah Berlin puts it (*VH*, p. 109), the basic symbols or notions, common to all nations, that embody the great natural, non-arbitrary, institutional human regularities — the analogous responses of human groups, remote in time and space, to similar conditions, springing from similar needs: belief in God or gods (there are, Vico points out, many Joves, Zoroasters and Hercules) and in providence (leading to the practice of marriage and burial, basic family life, an so on). As Vico puts it elsewhere in *The New Science*, we are required to postulate an 'identity of intelligible substance in the diversity of their [i.e. the nations'] modes of development' (*NS*, 1096).

Vico's philosophy of history is intensely paradoxical — a fact which puts him in the company of the romantics like Blake, Coleridge and Kierkegaard, and, of course, the German idealists, rather than his contemporaries, the post-Cartesian harbingers of Enlightenment. The two poles of his thought seem to be flatly contradictory: the past is enveloped in thick darkness; the minds of primitive men were unlike our own, alien and incomprehensible. But, on the other hand, we can know what it felt like to be a savage, cowering beneath the crash of thunder; his world is not ultimately closed to us. There could be no reconciliation of these two poles of Vico's thought at the Cartesian level of clear and distinct ideas: only by a supreme effort of imaginative insight could the gap between the present and past be bridged, and this was only possible because there was a fundamental metaphysical unity of the human race and an innate affinity between mind and the history that was the creation of mind.

Vico's significance for modern philosophy of history is seen, first of all, in the fact that it is almost impossible not to resort to anachronistic terminology, such as 'spirit of the age' or 'absolute presuppositions' to describe his thought; and secondly, in the fact that he manages to combine and hold together the conflicting ideas of 'the pastness of the past' on the one hand, and 'imaginative empathy' on the other, both historical relativism and the uniformity of fundamental human nature — poles of thought that have split apart in modern philosophy of history and become representative of rival camps.

Vico's Theology of History

It is deceptively easy to see Vico purely as some kind of proto-Hegelian philosopher of the immanent world-process, an exponent of the secular dimension of the Enlightenment, a Roman Catholic only in name and out of sympathy with the Roman Catholic thought of his time. In two hefty volumes on the philosophy of the Enlightenment, Jonathan Israel interprets Vico in that sense, lumping him together with Spinoza and Hobbes (though I do not agree with his interpretation of Hobbes either) (Israel, *Radical Enlightenment*; id. *Enlightenment Contested*; Avis, *In Search of Authority*). But to categorise Vico in this way would be to overlook an essential dimension of the *New Science*. A theological – an apologetic – theme runs strongly through the work, making him very definitely a Christian philosopher of history, one who (in Milton's words) sought to 'assert Eternal Providence,/ And justify the ways of God to men' (Milton, p. 114: *Paradise Lost*, Book I, lines 25-26). Two main aspects of Vico's apologetic concern can be identified.

(a) Vico's radical dualism of sacred and profane history has an apologetic motive, that is to say in the defence of the Christian faith. In the early eighteenth century the Christian theological concept of the history of salvation (creation and fall – the Patriarchs – the Exodus – the history of Israel – the prophets – the incarnation, ministry, death and resurrection of Jesus Christ – the sending of the Holy Spirit and the mission of the Church to the present day) was being distorted by speculations that postulated cross-currents of influence between the biblical writers on the one hand and pagan philosophers and law-givers on the other. This tactic had its origin in time-honoured Christian apologetic, going back to the second century AD, when Christian writers had attempted to account for Greek philosophy by claiming that Plato *et al.* had borrowed from the wisdom of Moses. One variation on this theme explained pagan religions as the degenerate relics of the preaching of the true faith by the Patriarchs (Abraham, Isaac and Jacob) to all nations in the first age of the world. The massive and ingenious *Demonstratio Evangelica* (1672) of the Gallican bishop Peter Daniel Huet, in which it was claimed that the whole of pagan theology originated as corruptions of Mosaic monotheism, was the swansong of this apologetic gambit. Already the idea was being turned on its head by deists and freethinkers (unwittingly aided and abetted by Protestant Christian thinkers like Francis Bacon who propagated the notion of 'the matchless wisdom of the ancients'). The mirror-image of Huet's theory was the claim that the philosophies, histories and literatures of non-biblical, non-Christian cultures were independent of, older than and superior to the Hebrew theology, history and literature of the Christian Old Testament. Vico, however, believed that the logic of this reversal of Huet's argument discredited the Bible's authority and made the Church's claims about divine revelation and divine providence in history superfluous.

Vico's answer was twofold. First, he revived the dualistic view of history that goes back to St Augustine's *The City of God* in the early fifth century, which allowed him (Vico) to treat pagan and Jewish history on different terms (Augustine). Secondly, Vico turned the notion of 'the matchless wisdom of the ancients' on its head. As Momigliano puts it (Momigliano, *Essays*, p. 256), Vico 'put all morality and rationality on the side of sacred history and saw in profane history the development of irrational instincts, truculent imagination, violent injustice – which providence knew how to guide to its own ends'. Momigliano continues:

> In emphasising the poetic, irrational, even beastly elements of primitive fantasy, Vico refuted by one stroke the claims of those who preferred Chinese or Egyptian chronology to Biblical chronology, the claims of those who interpreted pagan myths as symbols of Jewish and Christian doctrines, and finally the claims of those who believed early pagan nations to have been ruled by natural law. (ibid., p. 261)

However, the rigid dualism of sacred and profane history that allowed Vico to gain this tactical victory also prevented him from applying his methods to the Bible. The Scriptures were bracketed off. Vico is not among the ranks of the early scientific biblical scholars, though his ideas had the potential to shed intense light on the Bible. The fact that it was precisely the application of Vico's concepts of poetry, myth and historical development by the pioneers of biblical criticism that brought about a revolution in our understanding of the biblical literature, in a way that is now normative, is one of the great ironies of Vico's contribution to modern thought. It is a further irony that Vico's philosophy of history ('one of the most serious and profound attempts to reassert a Christian – or perhaps Hebrew – dualistic vision of the world', as Momigliano calls it [*Essays*, p. 273]) should have been produced on the very eve of the high Enlightenment which stood for the breakdown of all such dualisms of sacred and secular, for the abolition of 'hands-off' areas of enquiry, and for the unification of knowledge.

(b) Taken in isolation, in abstraction from the overall argument of the *New Science*, Vico's dualism is sacred and profane history can give a misleading impression. It certainly seems paradoxical to stress Vico's apologetic motive and then go on to show how he gives an apparently naturalistic motive for those key features of human existence that the Bible ascribes to divine intervention: the origin of language, the growth of conscience, the institution of marriage and the creation of society. But Vico's perspective is twofold: historical and theological. He offers not only an immanental account of human society but also a transcendental one. It may be true, historically speaking, to say that primitive men and women received their first religious impressions as a result of a thunderbolt striking the earth. But it is equally true to say, theologically speaking, that God was making Godself known in this event, in a revelatory way, according to primitive people's capacity to understand. Vico combines these two ideas when he suggests that the concept of God was 'created' by humans 'out of the flash of the thunderbolts in which this true light of God shone forth for them, that he governs mankind' (*NS*, 1098). The immanent and transcendent accounts of the origin of religion are not opposed in Vico, but are complementary perspectives. Those interpreters of Vico, such as Jonathan Israel, who take him to be a secular thinker, are misled by Vico's use of such terms as 'created' in the above statement. He does not mean this in the Feuerbachian sense that the divine is a projection of human needs and longings, that we create our gods and make them in our own image, but writ large (Feuerbach; Avis, *Faith in the Fires of Criticism*). Vico is writing in a 'so to speak' and 'as it were' manner. From the point of view of human experience of the world, especially of its numinous phenomena, it seems that the idea of God emerged from within – but that is only one aspect of, one angle on the reality, one limited perspective.

In the same way, the slow evolution of the idea of natural law, to regulate the social life of humankind, and the concept of divine providence, are two complementary ways of explaining the same phenomenon, according to the point of view you are adopting (*NS*, 629). The institution of marriage, the felt obligation to follow virtue, and the practice of burying the dead with respect – an intimation of immortality – are three universal forms through which the providence of God governs, leads and preserves mankind.

Vico's Providence is not merely a grand name for an internal logic of the world-process – we have noted that he rejected Spinoza's concept of *natura naturans* – but has a transcendent source (Spinoza). It is precisely as a transcendent power that Providence works immanently and in a hidden way within the historical process, 'making use of the customs of men, which are as free of all force as the spontaneous expressions of their own nature'. Providence is an inherent logic of development within history that trumps the conscious intentions of its agents. Vico's appalling vision of the irrational, violent and superstitious foundations of human society did not arise, as one might suspect, from a dark and desperate cynicism about the human prospect. The picture is suffused with the light of a benevolent Providence working patiently and ceaselessly for the well-being of human kind. Vico was convinced that 'this world has evidently issued from a mind often diverse, at times quite contrary, and always superior to the particular ends that men have proposed to themselves; which narrow ends, made means to serve wider ends, it has always employed to preserve human life upon the earth.' For example, in the state of savagery, 'men who meant to gratify their bestial lust and abandon their offspring' founded instead, and in spite of themselves, 'the chastity of marriage' which provided the basis for the development of the family as a social institution.

In just such a way, every particular vice is turned by Providence to contribute to the good of humankind. Out of ferocity it creates the military caste and thus provides for the strength and safety of the commonwealth. It directs avarice into the channels of trade and commerce. It converts ambition into political power and thence into sound government. And so, says Vico, 'out of these three great vices [ferocity, avarice and ambition], which could certainly destroy all mankind on the face of the earth, it [Providence] makes civil happiness.' 'Out of the passions of men each bent on his private advantage,' Vico continues, 'for the sake of which they would live like wild beasts in the wilderness, it has made the civil institutions by which they may live in human society' (*NS*, 132-3). Though he appears to offer a purely naturalistic explanation of the salient features of human life in society, what Vico has in fact done is to reinterpret the Christian doctrine of the providence of God, guiding, directing, protecting and overruling in history, to create 'a rational civil theology of divine providence' which constituted an persuasive alternative to the 'physico-theology', tinged with deism, of the Christian physicists who inadvertently removed the presence of the creator and provider from the historical process (Reventlow).

In setting out this stereoscopic vision of history, natural and theological, each complementary to the other, Vico was not advocating a version of the medieval notion of the 'double truth', that something could be true in theology while false in philosophy. He did not have to choose between the natural and the theological explanations; they were both true in their own spheres. He was in fact working with a sophisticated polarity of transcendence and immanence which his idealist metaphysic enabled him to hold together. He anticipated in a remarkable way the Hegelian notion of 'the cunning of reason', working within the historical process and shaping it to fulfil purposes that humans are not aware of at the time. This insight provides one more link between Vico and mature historicism. For Vico, however, what was at work in history was not an impersonal 'reason', but a benevolent Creator, both revealed and hidden, the God of Christian theology.

POSTSCRIPT

The decision to include Vico in a volume that terminates before the Enlightenment proper, will reveal to the discerning reader a particular view of Vico's place in the evolution of modern historical thought. We should not be blinded by the brilliance of his insights — startlingly modern though they seem. It is essential to root him firmly in the seventeenth century. Vico lends himself to the 'precursoritis' that has tended to afflict recent study of the history of ideas. Nevertheless, it is undeniable that he is the dominant figure of this book and its *terminus ad quem*. Although we are often admonished that the historian is not in the business of awarding prizes for modernity, we cannot attempt to unfold the development of a movement of thought so central to the formation of our modern worldview as the historical movement without discerning pattern and progress. I have striven to be accurate but not to be clinically neutral. I confess to having caught some of my excitement about Vico, and the principles of historical philosophy of which he is the acknowledged founder, from Sir Isaiah Berlin's infectious enthusiasm (in *Vico and Herder* and the papers collected in *Against the Current*).

We do not give our time and energy to intensive study of past thinkers unless we are convinced that they have something to offer us — some valuable insight (Vico?) or daunting challenge (Hobbes?) — and that their words and lives can still communicate with us from 'the dark backward and abysm of time'. The fact that we feel that a *rapport* has been established is decisive evidence against the dismal purveyors of the total historical relativism of the closed-world-of-past school. Nothing that is said nowadays about the inaccesible and alien assumptions on which men of the remote past lived their lives can exceed the vehemence of Vico's assertions — born of bitter experience — about the darkness and impenetrability of history. But for Vico, that is not the end of the matter: it merely creates the conditions for his passionate belief that by backbreaking toil and an agonising effort of imagination we can indeed reach out across the span of history and enter into the thoughts and feelings of men long dead.

Herbert Butterfield remarked in *The Whig Interpretation of History* that 'the primary assumption of all attempts to understand the men of the past must be the belief that we can in some degree enter into minds that are unlike our own' (p. 16). This is not the truism that it seems to be at first glance. Their minds *are* unlike our own: that is a significant admission and it is vital that we make it. The possibilities of historical understanding do not arise from some postulated naïve uniformitarianism. It is precisely the understanding of man in his uniqueness, his particularity, his relativity that interests us. Nothing less would qualify as history. What then are the grounds on which the possibility of historical understanding is based?

To get the problem into proportion, we do well to bear in mind that we attempt — with varying degrees of success, no doubt — to enter into 'minds that are unlike our own' every day of our lives. The mind of every individual we meet is unique to himself: a circumscribed, self-contained world of experience with which we try to make contact in ordinary social intercourse. Sometimes we find other people completely baffling and have to admit defeat, but usually some meeting of minds is possible.

The real difficulty arises when the communication in question is intercultural as well as interpersonal, and it is intensified when that culture is remote from us in time as well as in geography. But whenever we read a work of autobiographical literature — whether it be Augustine or Montaigne or Rousseau, we are crossing this barrier. Through imaginative empathy we are enabled to indwell the lives and thoughts of other men and women. If historical scepticism is valid it is valid for literature too.

The reference to 'imaginative empathy' indicates the impossibility of justifying the claim to a real communication transcending history within the limits of the rationalistic notions of knowledge that figure largely in the systems covered in this work. It is not by the formal, explicit and fully specifiable methods of discursive reason that we can hold a living communion with other minds, but only on the basis of an alternative epistemology that stresses tacit communication, personal involvement in the process of knowing, and the transcendent power of insight. This is of course why Vico had to break decisively with Cartesian rationalism before he could establish a viable basis for historical understanding.

Vico is the founder of the great European tradition of 'historicism' (to be distinguished from Popper's use of this term, as in the *The Poverty of Historicism*, where it is equivalent to historical necessity) whose central principle is a belief in the power of historical imagination to reconstruct the experience of the past. Similar ideas to Vico's were taught by the German pre-Romantic Herder half a century later, and by Dilthey at the end of the nineteenth century, who spoke of the historian reliving in his own mind the spiritual experience of the past that he finds enshrined in documents and other historical data. Dilthey's notion of the historian living in his object, or rather making his object live in him (as Collingwood puts it) has obvious affinities with Michael Polanyi's doctrine of indwelling as a mode of 'personal knowledge' — Polanyi being the most recent exponent of the epistemological tradition here under discussion.

There is, however, an obvious objection to Dilthey's historiological theory. For history is not concerned with having experiences but with attaining knowledge. Dilthey's concept requires translation, therefore, from terms of feeling into terms of thought or cognition. Accordingly, Collingwood prefers to speak of the historian re-enacting past thought, rather than past experience, in his own mind.

By describing historical method as the re-enactment in the mind of the historian of the thoughts of past men, Collingwood drew attention to the need to penetrate beyond the mere sequence of outward events to their inner logic. He must not only ask what happened, but also why it happened as it did. Collingwood was asserting the importance of imaginative, intuitive thinking in historical science in a way that invites comparison with the reconstruction of the methods of the physical sciences by Whitehead, Popper and Polanyi for example.

Needless to say, Collingwood did not mean to imply that some sort of mystical intuition could ever replace the patient accumulation of evidence or the sifting of testimony — any more than Polanyi or Popper would propose that the scientific procedure of observation and experiment should be superceded by 'personal knowledge' or inspired conjecture as a short cut to truth. Nevertheless, a few words in qualification of Collingwood's views would perhaps be in order.

The cruder forms of the historiological theory associated with Collingwood's name do indeed tend to confuse two separate and complementary aspects of historical method (cf. Gardiner, pp. 120–33). Stressing the vital role of imaginative conjecture in illuminating the 'inside' logic of an event could have the effect of eclipsing the indispensable need for procedures of research by which one would actually set about confirming or refuting that hypothesis. The whole sphere of historical data belongs to the 'outward' aspect of an event. The impersonally determined structures of the world of space and time constitute the stage of history. It would therefore be disastrous to treat historical events as simply expressions of mental experience, for personal action is subject to all the constraints of cause-and-effect in a physical universe that continues on its way regardless of the human drama being played out on its stage. Besides this, we have to take account of the social constraints affecting the individual. The social determinants of his beliefs, values and actions, together with the refracting and distorting effect of social structures on the ways in which he tries to express or assert himself, mean that the result in the 'outer' world of the 'inward' thoughts on which Collingwood places such emphasis are often very different from those intended. It is ironical that the theory of historicism, developed initially by Vico and those who followed him in explicit reaction to Cartesian rationalism, should manifest in its extreme form the symptoms of a rigid Cartesian dualism of subject and object, mind and matter, history and nature.

We come, finally, to the work of the contemporary philosopher, Hans-Georg Gadamer, in developing a hermeneutic in the historicist tradition that justifies the claim that history can 'speak' across the centuries. Gadamer makes no attempt to play down the paradox of continuity and discontinuity in history. The function of hermeneutics (i.e. of interpreting a given text) takes place precisely within the tension thus created.

> Every encounter with tradition that takes place within historical consciousness, [he writes] involves the experience of the tension between the text and the present. The hermeneutical task consists not in covering up this tension by attempting a naïve assimilation but in consciously bringing it out.

For Gadamer, as for Collingwood (p. 60), the problem of the temporal distance between past events and experiences, on the one hand, and the position of the historian, on the other — or as it is sometimes put, between the mental horizon of the text and the mental horizon of the interpreter — is not a ground for radical scepticism about the possibility of knowing the truth about the past: on the contrary, it is a positive asset. Temporal distance has the effect of filtering the assumptions and pre-judgements that the historian inevitably brings to his study of the past. This filter of temporal distance

> not only lets those prejudices that are of a particular and limited nature die away, but causes those that bring about genuine understanding to emerge as such. It is only this temporal distance that can solve the really crucial question of hermeneutics, namely of distinguishing the true prejudices, by which we understand, from the false ones, by which we misunderstand.

As the hermeneutically trained mind becomes critically conscious of the assumptions and pre-judgements that it brings to study of the past, it is enabled to transcend its own horizon with the result that a fusion of horizons (*Horizontverschmelzung*) between the past and the present, the text and the interpreter, takes place. Gadamer thus holds out the possibility of a real communication across the span of history (pp. 271ff, 266).

These concluding reflections perhaps indicate the contemporary relevance of Vico's response to the heritage of pre-Enlightenment history. In the period we have covered, the broad lines of an argument that has continued up to the present were laid down. The protagonists gradually clarified into three schools of thought: the rationalist, led by Descartes and Hobbes, with its *a priori* approach, modelled on mathematics, that was prepared to exclude from its purview anything that could not be reduced to clear and distinct ideas; the empiricist, founded by Bacon, with Newton its chief glory, concerned with measurement, with quantity, with observable regularities; the historicist or proto-Romanticist, represented solely in this period by Vico, with its notions of imaginative empathy, and gradual development from primitive but creative origins.

In the eighteenth century the rationalists and empiricists forged an alliance (or rather, the rational and empirical methods were found to be compatible) and in the hands of the *philosophes* they carried the day — but not without unwittingly undermining the uniformitarian assumptions on which they were based and making it possible for historicist theory to re-emerge, albeit fragmentarily, in the thought of the pre-Romantics.

Following as it did in the wake of the scientific movement, it was perhaps inevitable that historical science in the eighteenth century should come to be understood by analogy with Newtonian physical science with its characteristic apparatus of observation, induction and generalisation. But as long as the task of history was conceived of in these terms, the recovery of the real past was impossible. Physical science is concerned with general laws of universal reference and with the predictable behaviour of inanimate objects in relation to involuntary forces. History, on the other hand, deals largely with what is particular, unique, individual, personal and irreversible. For the past is the product not only of the impersonal pressures of climate, geography and natural resources, but also of the thought, the consciousness, of individuals (that is to say, all who have ever lived) who were not merely acted upon by their environment, but who themselves both reacted upon it and upon each other. What therefore distinguishes history from the physical sciences is, as Collingwood has taught us, that it is concerned with human consciousness in the only form in which we can come to know it, that is, in the past. That is why what we decide about the nature of historical science has an immediate bearing on the character of all the human sciences — which is perhaps sufficient justification for this book and its successors!

BIBLIOGRAPHY

PRIMARY TEXTS

Abbreviation: PC = Penguin Classics edition, Harmondsworth

Abelard, P., *The Letters of Abelard and Heloise*, trans. B. Radice, PC, 1974
Aubrey, J., *Brief Lives*, Harmondsworth, 1972
Augustine, *Confessions*, trans. R. S. Pine-Coffin, PC, 1961
——, *The City of God*, trans. H. Bettenson, PC, 1972
Bacon, F., 'Sacred Meditations' in *Works* VII, (eds) J. Spedding, R. L. Ellis, D. D. Heath, London, 1861
——, (*PW*) *The Philosophical Works of Francis Bacon*, (ed.) J. M. Robertson, London, 1905
——, *PFB, The Philosophy of Francis Bacon*, Liverpool, 1964
——, (*AL*) *Of the Advancement of Learning*, London, (Everyman), 1915
Bayle, P., *Oeuvres diverses*, 4 vols, (ed.) E. Labrousse, Hildesheim, 1964
——, *Historical and Critical Dictionary*, (ed. and trans.) R. H. Popkin, Indianapolis, 1965
Bede, *The Ecclesiastical History of the English Nation*, London, (Everyman), 1910
Bodin, J., *Method for the Easy Comprehension of History*, trans. B. Reynolds, New York, 1945
Descartes, R., *Discourse on Method and the Meditations*, trans. F. E. Sutcliffe, PC, 1968
Dilthey, W., *Meaning in History*, (ed.) H. P. Rickman, London, 1961
Eusebius, *The History of the Church*, trans. G. A. Williamson, PC, 1965
Guicciardini, F., (*Ric.*) [*Ricordi*], *Maxims and Reflections*, New York, 1965 (cited by paragraphs)
——, (*Con.*) *Considerations on the 'Discourses' of Machiavelli* in C. and M. Grayson, *F. Guicciardini: Selected Writings*, London, 1965

———, *The History of Italy*, trans. S. Alexander, New York, 1969
Hobbes, T., (*EW*) *English Works*, 11 vols, (ed.) W. Molesworth, London, 1843
———, (*De Corp.*) [*De Corpore*] *English Works*, I, (ed.) W. Molesworth, London, 1843
———, (*Lev.*) *Leviathan*, (ed.) J. Plamenatz, London, 1962
———, (*De Hom.*) [*De Homine*] in *Man and Citizen*, (ed.) B. Gert, Sussex, 1972
———, (*De Cive*) in *Man and Citizen*, (ed.) B. Gert, Sussex, 1972
Leibniz, G. W., *Philosophical Writings*, (ed.) G. H. R. Parkinson, London, (Everyman), 1973
Locke, J., *The Conduct of the Understanding*, Oxford, 1901
———, *Essays on the Law of Nature*, (ed.) W. von Leyden, Oxford, 1954
———, *An Essay Concerning Human Understanding*, 2 vols, London, (Everyman), 1961
———, (*Gov.*) *Two Treatise of Government*, New York, 1965
Lucretius, *The Nature of the Universe*, trans. R. Latham, PC, 1951
Machiavelli, N., *The Prince*, trans. G. Bull, PC, 1961
———, (*Disc.*) *Discourses on the First Decade of Titus Livius*, in *The Chief Works and Others*, I, trans. A. Gilbert, Durham, N. Carolina, 1965
Malebranche, N., *De la recherche de la vérité, Oeuvres completes*, II, Paris, 1963
Marco Polo, *The Travels*, trans. R. Latham, PC, 1958
Montaigne, M. de, *Essays*, trans. J. M. Cohen, PC, 1958
Newton, I. *Newton's Philosophy of Nature*, (ed.) H. S. Thayer, New York, 1953
Pascal, B., *Pensées*, trans. A. J. Krailsheimer, PC, 1966
Petrarch, [on Mount Ventoux], in E. Cassirer, *et al.*, (eds), *The Renaissance Philosophy of Man*, Chicago, 1948
Pico Della Mirandola, 'On the Dignity of Man' in E. Cassirer *et al.* (eds), *The Rennaissance Philosophy of Man*, Chicago, 1948
Rousseau, J. -J., *The Confessions*, trans. J. M. Cohen, PC, 1953
Tacitus, P. C., *The Agricola and the Germania*, trans. H. Mattingly and S. A. Handford, PC, 1970
———, *The Annals of Imperial Rome*, trans. M. Grant, PC, 1971
Vico, G. B., (*Auto.*), Autobiography, trans. M. H. Fisch and T. G. Bergin, Ithaca, 1944
———, (*NS*) *The New Science*, trans. T. G. Bergin and M. H. Fisch, New York, 1961 (cited by paragraphs)

———, *On the Study Methods of Our Time*, trans. E. Gianturco, Indianapolis, 1965

———, 'On the Heroic Mind' in G. Tagliacozzo, M. Mooney, D. P. Verene (eds), *Vico and Contemporary Thought*, London, 1980

———, *On the Ancient Wisdom of the Italians*, in L. Pompa (ed. and trans.), *Vico, Selected Writings*, Cambridge, 1982

SECONDARY STUDIES

Abbreviations of Journals and Symposia

Hist.Th.	*History and Theory*
JEGP	*Journal of English and German Philology*
JHI	*Journal of the History of Ideas*
J.Hist.Phil.	*Journal of the History of Philosophy*
Med.Hum.	*Medievalia et Humanistica* (new series)
Mod.Phil.	*Modern Philology*
PMLA	*Proceedings of the Modern Language Association of America*
Pol.St.	*Political Studies*
VCT	G. Tagliacozzo, M. Mooney, D. P. Verene (eds), *Vico and Contemporary Thought*, London, 1980
VIS	G. Tagliscozzo, H. V. White (eds), *Giambattista Vico: An International Symposium*, Baltimore, 1969
VSH	G. Tagliacozzo, D. P. Verene (eds), *Giambattista Vico's Science of Humanity*, Baltimore, 1976
VPP	G. Tagliacozzo (ed.), *Vico: Past and Present*, Atlantic Highlands, NJ, 1981

Aarsleff, H., 'The State of Nature and the Nature of Man in Locke', in J. W. Yolton (ed.), *John Locke: Problems and Perspectives*, Cambridge, 1969

Acton, J. E. E., *Lectures on Modern History*, London, 1960

Baker, H., *The Race of Time: Three Lectures on Renaissance Historiography*, Toronto, 1967

Baron, H., *The Crisis of the Early Italian Renaissance*, 2 vols, (2nd edn) Princeton, 1966

———, *From Petrarch to Leonardo Bruni: Studies in Humanist and Political Literature*, Chicago, 1968

———, 'Petrarch: His Inner Struggles and the Humanistic Discovery of Man's Nature' in J. G. Rowe and W. H. Stockdale (eds), *Florilegium Historiale: Essays Presented to W. K. Ferguson*, Toronto, 1971

Battistini, A., 'Contemporary Trends in Vichean Studies' in *VPP*

Becker, C. L., *The Heavenly City of the Eighteenth-Century Philosophers*, New Haven, 1932

Belaval, Y., 'Vico and Anti-Cartesianism' in *VIS*

Berlin, I., (*VH*) *Vico and Herder*, London, 1976

———, (*AC*) *Against the Current*, Oxford, 1981

Bietenholz, P. G., *History and Biography in the Work of Erasmus of Rotterdam*, Geneva, 1966

Bishop, M., 'Petrarch' in J. H. Plumb (ed.), *The Horizon Book of the Renaissance*, New York, 1961

Bolgar, R. R., *The Classical Heritage and Its Beneficiaries*, Cambridge, 1954

Brandt, W. J., *The Shape of Medieval History: Studies in Modes of Perception*, New Haven, 1966

Brown, J. L., *The Methodum ad Facilem Historiarum Cognitionem of Jean Bodin; A Critical Study* [1939] New York, 1969

Brush, C. B., *Montaigne and Bayle*, The Hague, 1966

Burckhardt, J., *The Civilization of the Renaissance in Italy*, London, 1965

Burke, P., 'A Survey of the Popularity of Ancient Historians, 1450–1700', *Hist.Th.*, 5 (1966), 135–52

———, *The Renaissance Sense of the Past*, London, 1969

———, *Montaigne*, Oxford, 1981

Burtt, E. A., *The Metaphysical Foundations of Modern Physical Science*, (2nd edn) London, 1932

Bury, J. B., *The Idea of Progress*, London, 1928

Butterfield, H., *The Whig Interpretation of History*, [1931] Harmondsworth, 1973

———, *Origins of Modern Science*, London, 1949

———, *The Statecraft of Machiavelli*, London, 1955

———, *The Origins of History*, London, 1981

Caponigri, A. R., *Time and Idea: The Theory of History in G. B. Vico*, Chicago, 1953

Caramella, S., 'Vico, Tacitus and Reason of State in *VIS*

Cassirer, E., 'Giovanni Pico della Mirandola', *JHI*, 3 (1942), 123–44; 319–46

———, *The Philosophy of the Enlightenment*, Princeton, 1951

——, *The Individual and the Cosmos in Renaissance Philosophy*, Philadelphia, 1972
Chabod, F., *Machiavelli and the Renaissance*, London, 1958
Clark, S., 'Francis Bacon: The Study of History and the Science of Man', unpublished PhD Dissertation, Cambridge University, 1970
——, 'Bacon's *Henry VII*: A Case Study in the Science of Man', *Hist.Th.*, 13 (1974), 97–118
Collingwood, R. G., *The Idea of History*, Oxford, 1946, 1961
Collis, P. A., 'The Preface of the *Acta Sanctorum*' *Catholic Historical Review*, 6 (1920–21), 294–307
Cotroneo, G., 'A Renaissance Source of the *Scienza Nuova*: Jean Bodin's *Methodus*' in *VIS*
Croce, B., *The Philosophy of G. B. Vico*, London, 1913
——, *History: Its Theory and Practice*, New York, 1960
Daville, L., *Leibniz historien*, Paris, 1909
Dean, L. F., 'Sir Francis Bacon's Theory of Civil History Writing', *English Literary History*, 8 (1941), 161–83
Delvaille, J., *Essai sur l'histoire de l'idée de progress jusqu'à la fin de XVIII Siècle*, Paris, 1910
Devolvé, J., *Religion, Critique et Philosophie Positive chez Pierre Bayle*, [1906], New York, 1971
Douglas, D. C., *English Scholars 1660–1730*, London, 1951
Farrington, B., *The Philosophy of Francis Bacon: An Essay on its Development from 1603 to 1609 with Translations of Fundamental Texts*, Liverpool, 1964
Fasso, G., 'The Problem of Law and the Historical Origin of the *New Science*' in *VSH*
Ferguson, A. B., 'By Little and Little: The Early Tudor Humanists on the Development of Man' in J. G. Rowe and W. H. Stockdale (eds), *Florilegium Historiale: Essays Presented to W. K. Ferguson*, Toronto, 1971
——, *Clio Unbound: Perception of the Social and Cultural Past in Renaissance England*, Durham, N. Carolina, 1979
Ferguson, W., *The Renaissance in Historical Thought*, Boston, Mass., 1948
Feuter, E., *Histoire de l'historiographie moderne*, Paris, 1914
Flint, R., *Vico*, Edinburgh and London, 1884
——, *History of the Philosophy of History: I: Historical Philosophy in France* [etc.], Edinburgh, 1893
Fox, L. (ed.), *English Historical Scholarship in the Sixteenth and*

Seventeenth Centuries, London, 1956
Frame, D. M., *Montaigne's Discovery of Man*, New York, 1955
Frankel, C., *The Faith of Reason: The Idea of Progress in the French Enlightenment*, New York, 1969
Franklin, J. H., *Jean Bodin and the Sixteenth-century Revolution in the Methodology of Law and History*, New York, 1963
Fussner, F. S., *The Historical Revolution in English Historical Writing and Thought, 1580–1640*, New York, 1962
Gadamer, H-G., *Truth and Method*, London, 1975
Gardiner, P., *The Nature of Historical Explanation*, Oxford, 1952
Garin, E., *Italian Humanism*, Oxford, 1965
Gay, P., *The Enlightenment: An Interpretation*, 2 vols, I: *The Rise of Modern Pagaism*; II: *The Science of Freedom*, London, 1966, 1970
Gilbert, F., 'The Humanist Concept of the Prince and *The Prince* of Machiavelli', *J.Mod.Hist.*, *11* (1939), 449–83
——, (MG) *Machiavelli and Guicciardini*, Princeton, 1965
——, 'Machiavelli's "Istorie Fiorentine": An Essay in Interpretation' in M. P. Gilmore (ed.), *Studies on Machiavelli*, Florence, 1972
Gilbert, N. W., *Renaissance Concepts of Method*, New York, 1960
Gilmore, M. P., *The Argument from Roman Law in Political Thought, 1200–1600*, Harvard, 1941
——, *Humanists and Jurists*, Cambridge, Mass., 1963
Gilson, E., *History of Christian Philosophy in the Middle Ages*, London, 1955
Gooch, G. P., *Political Thought in England from Bacon to Halifax*, London, 1914
Green, L., *Chronicle into History*, Cambridge, 1972
Greenleaf, W. H., *Order, Empiricism and Politics: Two Traditions of English Political Thought, 1500–1700*, London, 1964
Guibbory, A., 'Francis Bacon's View of History: the Cycles of Error and the Progress of Truth', *JEGP*, *74* (1975), 336–50
Haddock, B. A., 'Vico: The Problem of Interpretation' in *VCT*
——, 'Vico and Anachronism', *Pol.St.*, *24* (1976), 483–7
——, *An Introduction to Historical Thought*, London, 1980
Hampshire, S., *Spinoza*, Harmondsworth, 1951
Hannaford, I., 'Machiavelli's Concept of *Virtù*', *Pol.St.*, *20* (1972), 185–9
Haskins, C. H., *The Renaissance of the Twelfth Century*, Cambridge, 1927

Hay, D., *Polydore Vergil: Renaissance Historian and Man of Letters*, Oxford, 1952
——, *Annalists and Historians: Western Historiography from the Eighth to the Eighteenth Centuries*, London, 1977
Hazard, P., *The European Mind, 1680–1715*, Harmondsworth, 1964
Hill, C., *Intellectual Origins of the English Revolution*, London, 1972
Huppert, G., 'The Renaissance Background of Historicism', *Hist.Th.*,5 (1966), 48–60
——, *The Idea of Perfect History: Historical Erudition and Historical Philosophy in Renaissance France*, Urbana, 1970
Hutton, P. H., 'Vico's Theory of History and the French Revolutionary Tradition', *JHI*, 37 (1976), 241–56
James, D. G., *The Life of Reason*, London, 1949
Janik, L. G., 'Lorenzo Valla: The Primacy of Rhetoric and the De-[sic] moralization of History', *Hist.Th.*, 12 (1973), 389–404
Jones, R. F., 'Science and English Prose Style in the Third Quarter of the Seventeenth Century', *PMLA*, 45 (1930), 977–1009
——, 'Science and Language in England of the Mid-Seventeenth Century', *JEGP*, 31 (1932), 315–31
——, *Ancients and Moderns: A Study of the Rise of the Scientific Movement in Seventeenth Century England*, (2nd edn), Berkeley and Los Angeles, 1965
Keeling, S. V., *Descartes*, Oxford, 1968
Keller, A. C., 'Historical and Geographical Perspective in the *Essays* of Montaigne', *Mod.Phil.*, 54 (1957), 145–57
Kelley, D. R., *Foundations of Modern Historical Scholarship: Language, Law and History in the French Renaissance*, New York, 1970
——, 'The Development and Context of Bodin's Method' in H. Denzer (ed.), *Jean Bodin: Verhandlüngen der internationalen Bodin Tagung in München*, München, 1973
——, 'Clio and the Lawyers: Forms of Historical Consciousness in Medieval Jurisprudence', *Med.Hum.*, 5 (1974), 25–49
——, 'Vico's Road: From Philology to Jurisprudence and Back' in *VSH*
——, '*Vera Philosophia*: the Philosophical Significance of Renaissance Jurisprudence', *J.Hist.Phil.*, 14 (1976), 267–79
Kendrick, T. D., *British Antiquity*, London, 1950
Knowles, D., *Great Historical Enterprises*, London, 1963

——, 'The Humanism of the Twelfth Century' in *The Historian and Character*, Cambridge, 1963
——, 'Jean Mabillon' in *The Historian and Character*, Cambridge, 1963
Koyré, A., *Newtonian Studies*, London, 1965
Kristeller, P. O., *Eight Philosophers of the Italian Renaissance*, Stanford, California, 1964
Labrousse, E., 'La Méthode critique de Pierre Bayle et l'histoire', *Revue Internationale de Philosophie, 11* (1957), 450–65
——, *Pierre Bayle:* II: *Heterodoxie et rigorisme*, The Hague, 1964
Laslett, P., Introduction to Locke, *Two Treatises of Government*, New York, 1965
Levin, H., *The Myth of the Golden Age in the Renaissance*, Bloomington, Indiana, 1969
Levine, J. M., 'Ancients, Moderns and History: The Continuity of English Historical Writing in the Later Seventeenth Century' in P. J. Korshin (ed.), *Studies in Change and Revolution: Aspects of English Intellectual History 1640–1800*, London, 1972
Levy, F. J., *Tudor Historical Thought*, San Marino, 1967
Levy-Bruhl, L., 'The Cartesian Spirit and History' in R. Klibansky and H. J. Paton (eds), *Philosophy and History* (The E. Cassirer Festschrift), New York, 1963
Lovejoy, A. O., *The Great Chain of Being*, Cambridge, Mass., 1953
Manuel, F., *ECCG, The Eighteenth Century Confronts the Gods*, Cambridge, Mass., 1959
——, *Isaac Newton: Historian*, Cambridge, Mass., 1963
——, *The Religion of Isaac Newton*, Oxford, 1974
Maritain, J., *Three Reformers*, London, 1928
Markus, R. A., *Saeculum: History and Society in the Theology of St Augustine*, Cambridge, 1970
Mas, E. De, 'Vico's Four Authors' in *VIS*
——, 'On the New Method of a New Science, A Study of Giambattista Vico', *JHI, 32* (1971), 85–94
Mattingly, G., 'Machiavelli' in J. H. Plumb (ed.), *The Horizon Book of the Renaissance*, New York, 1961
Meinecke, F., *Machiavellism*, London, 1957
——, *Historism: The Rise of a New Historical Outlook*, London, 1972
Momigliano, A., *Studies in Historiography*, New York, 1966
——, *Essays in Ancient and Modern History*, Oxford, 1977

Morris, C., *The Discovery of the Individual 1050–1200*, London, 1972
Morrison, J. C., 'Philosophy and History in Bacon', *JHI*, 38 (1977), 586–606
——. 'Vico's Doctrine of the Natural Law of the Gentes', *J.Hist.Phil.*, 16 (1978), 47160
——, 'Vico's Principle of *Verum* is *Factum* and the Problem of Historicism', *JHI*, 39 (1978), 579–95
——, 'Vico and Spinoza', *JHI*, 41 (1980), 49–68
——, 'Vico and Machiavelli' in *VPP*
Nadel, G. H., 'Philosophy of History before Historicism', *Hist. Th.*, 5 (1966), 275–87
Naudeau, O., *La Pensée de Montaigne*, Geneva, 1972
Nicolson, M. H., *Newton Demands the Muse*, Princeton, 1946
Oakeshott, M., *Hobbes on Civil Association*, Oxford, 1975
Passmore, J. A., 'The Malleability of Man in Eighteenth-century Thought' in E. R. Wasserman (ed.), *Aspects of the Eighteenth Century*, Baltimore, 1965
Peters, R., *Hobbes*, Harmondsworth, 1956
Phillips, M., *Francesco Guicciardini: The Historian's Craft*, Toronto, 1977
Pocock, J. G. A., *The Ancient Constitution and the Feudal Law*, Cambridge, 1957
——, *The Machiavellian Moment: Florentine Political Thought and the Atlantic Republican Tradition*, Princeton, 1975
Polanyi, M., *The Tacit Dimension*, London, 1967
——, *Personal Knowledge*, London, 1958
Pompa, L., *Vico: A Study of the 'New Science'*, Cambridge, 1975
——, 'Vico and the Presuppositions of Historical Knowledge' in *VSH*
Popkin, R. H., 'Pierre Bayle's Place in Seventeenth-century Scepticism' in P. Dibon (ed.), *Pierre Bayle: Le philosophe de Rotterdam*, Amsterdam, 1959
——, *The History of Scepticism from Erasmus to Descartes*, Assen, 1960
Popper, K., *The Poverty of Historicism*, London, 1957
——, *Conjectures and Refutations*, London, 1963
Preston, J. H., 'Was there an Historical Revolution?' *JHI*, 37 (1976), 353–64
Quinones, R. J., *The Renaissance Discovery of Time*, Cambridge, Mass., 1972

Quinton, A., *Francis Bacon*, Oxford, 1980
Righter, A., 'Francis Bacon' in H. S. Davies and G. Watson (eds), *The English Mind*, Cambridge, 1964
Rome, B. K., *The Philosophy of Malebranche*, Chicago, 1963
Ross, G. M., *Leibniz*, Oxford, 1984
Rossi, P., *Francis Bacon: From Magic to Science*, Chicago, 1968
Rubanowice, R. J., 'Ernst Troeltsch's History of the Philosophy of History', *J.Hist.Phil.*, *14* (1976), 79–95
Rubinoff, L., 'Vico and the Verification of Historical Interpretation' in *VCT*
Schouls, P. A., *The Imposition of Method: A Study of Descartes and Locke*, Oxford, 1980
Seigel, J. E., *Rhetoric and Philosophy in Renaissance Humanism . . . Petrarch to Valla*, Princeton, 1968
Skinner, Q., *Machiavelli*, Oxford, 1981
Smalley, B., *The Historian in the Middle Ages*, London, 1974
Southern, R. W., *Medieval Humanism*, Oxford, 1970
——, 'Aspects of the European Tradition of Historical Writing: I: The Classical Tradition from Einhard to Geoffrey of Monmouth; II: Hugh of St Victor and the Idea of Historical Development; III: History as Prophecy; IV: The Sense of the Past', *Transactions of the Royal Historical Society*, 5th series, *20* (1970), 173–96; *21* (1971), 159–79; *22* (1972), 159–80; *23* (1973), 243–63
Spitz, L., 'The Significance of Leibniz for Historiography', *JHI*, *13* (1952), 333–48
Spragens, T. A., *The Politics of Motion: the World of Thomas Hobbes*, London, 1973
Strauss, L., *The Political Philosophy of Thomas Hobbes*, [1936] Chicago, 1952
Streuver, N., *The Language of History in the Renaissance: Rhetoric and Historical Consciousness in Florentine Humanism*, Princeton, 1970
Tillyard, E. M. W., *The Elizabethan World Picture*, Harmondsworth, 1963
Trevor-Roper, H. R., Review of Christopher Hill, *Intellectual Origins of the English Revolution*, *Hist.Th.*, *5* (1966), 61–82
——, *Queen Elizabeth's First Historian: William Camden and the Beginnings of English 'Civil History'*, London, 1971
Ullman, W., *The Individual and Society in the Middle Ages*, London, 1967

———, *Medieval Foundations of Renaissance Humanism*, London, 1977
Verene, D. P., *Vico's Science of Imagination*, Ithaca, 1981
Wade, I. O., *Voltaire's Intellectual Development*, Princeton, 1969
———, *The Intellectual Origins of the French Enlightenment*, Princeton, 1971
Warrender, H., *The Political Philosophy of Hobbes*, Oxford, 1957
Watkins, J. W. N., *Hobbes' System of Ideas*, London, 1965
Watson, G., 'Joseph Butler' in H. S. Davies and G. Watson (eds), *The English Mind*, Cambridge, 1964
Weisinger, H., 'Ideas of History during the Renaissance', *JHI*, 6 (1945), 415–35
Westfall, R. S., 'The Changing World of the Newtonian Industry', *JHI*, 37 (1976), 175–84
White, H. V., 'The Irrational and the Problem of Historical Knowledge in the Enlightenment' in H .E. Pagliara (ed.), *Irrationalism in the Eighteenth Century*, Cleveland, 1972
———, *Metahistory: The Historical Imagination in Nineteenth-Century Europe*, Baltimore, 1973
Whitehead, A. N., *Adventures of Ideas*, Harmondsworth, 1942
Whitfield, J. H., *Machiavelli*, Oxford, 1947
Wilcox, D. J., *The Development of Florentine Humanist Historiography in the Fifteenth Century*, Cambridge, Mass., 1969
Willey, B., *The Seventeenth-century Background*, Harmondsworth, 1962
Wood, N., 'Machiavelli's Concept of *Virtù*', *Pol.St.*, 15 (1967), 159–72
Yolton, J. W., 'Locke and the Law of Nature', *Philosophical Review*, 67 (1958), 477–98
Zilsel, E., 'The Genesis of the Concept of Scientific Progress', *JHI*, 6 (1945), 325–49

Additions to Bibliography

Primary Texts

Feuerbach, Ludwig, *The Essence of Christianity*, trans, George Eliot (New York: Harper, 1957)

Milton, John, *The English Poems of John Milton*, ed. H. C. Beeching (*The World's Classics*, London: Oxford University Press, 1913)

Spinoza, Benedict de, *Ethics and On the Improvement of the Understanding*, ed. James Gutmann (New York: Hafner, 1949)

Secondary Studies

Avis, Paul, Faith in the Fires of Criticism: Christianity in Modern Thought (London: Darton, Longman & Todd, 1995)

——, In Search of Authority: Anglican Theological Method from the Reformation to the Enlightenment (London and New York: Bloomsbury T&T Clark, 2014)

Israel, Jonathan, Radical Enlightenment: Philosophy and the Making of Modernity (Oxford: Oxford University Press, 2001)

——, Enlightenment Contested: Philosophy, Modernity, and the Emancipation of Man 1670-1752 (Oxford: Oxford University Press, 2006)

Reventlow, Henning Graf, The Authority of the Bible and the Rise of the Modern World, trans. John Bowden (London: SCM Press, 1984)

SUBJECT INDEX

anachronism 7, 10, 146
antiquarianism, antiquarians 24ff, 146
astrology 6, 55

Bible 1, 4, 7, 9, 15f, 39f, 72, 100, 108, 127, 131
biography, autobiography 3f, 12, 27, 57
Bollandists 27f

chronicle, chroniclers 8f, 11, 20ff
clear and distinct ideas 82f, 104, 110, 112, 135f, 157
cyclical theories 55, 70f, 151, 154

development 15, 82, 116, 135, 152

empiricism 85, 88, 91, 94, 104, 110, 116, 120, 125, 128, 141, 151, 162
Enlightenment 38, 43, 81f, 88, 97, 104–31 *passim*, 133ff, 152, 157
epistemology 63f, 112, 122
eschatology 31, 33, 39, 51, 72

Fortune 22, 30, 34f, 45, 47, 50, 97

Golden Age 23, 55, 69f, 73, 97, 142

hagiography *see* biography
Historicism 8, 34, 101, 133, 135, 151ff, 162
humanism *see* Renaissance humanism
human nature 30f, 36f, 47, 86, 95f, 107, 144, 155ff

individual, individualism 1ff, 10, 123

jurisprudence *see* law

language 67f, 85, 87, 94, 96, 102f, 110, 113, 143, 146
law 7, 17ff, 21f, 82f, 92ff, 99, 137, 142, 145, 150
  canon 4, 21
  common 17
  customary 21
  natural 111, 115, 118f
  Roman 4, 17, 21

matchless wisdom of the ancients 18, 74f, 143, 146
Maurists 27ff
method 87, 90ff, 106, 110, 137, 145
  historical 6f, 22, 26, 41ff, 49, 61, 65, 79
myth 53, 74ff, 83, 117, 133, 135, 142, 148f

natural law *see* law, natural

periodisation 9, 56
philology 15f, 19, 25, 42, 53, 139, 141
philosophes 86, 110, 127, 129, 162
plenitude, principle of 124
poetry 24, 67, 76ff, 135, 145, 147f
positivism 32, 127
progress 38, 55, 72f, 80, 125
prophecy, prophetic movements 4, 8, 25, 27, 152
Protestantism *see* Reformation
providence 8f, 20, 22f, 25, 45

realism 30ff, 34, 44, 53
Reformation 20, 38, 53, 68
relativism 5f, 15, 23, 45, 54, 57
  historical 10, 16, 93f, 111, 117, 155f, 158
  ethical 40, 86, 93f, 111
Renaissance humanism 1f, 5f, 32f, 57f, 81, 144f
rhetoric 7, 9, 11f, 14ff, 30, 42, 53, 65, 77, 134, 137
Romantic movement 1f, 13, 21, 24, 54, 64, 83, 96, 110, 112, 136, 152, 162

scholasticism, scholastic method 4f, 7, 52, 105, 146, 152
science 81, 88
  human 64, 163
  natural 64, 163
secularism 4f, 30, 45, 61f

181

social contract 97, 119, 151
state of nature 92ff, 97ff, 101, 118f

uniformitarianism 37, 47, 54, 82, 110, 123, 133, 139, 144, 159, 162
utopianism *see* eschatology

INDEX OF NAMES

Abelard, P. 1
Acton, J. E. E. D. 35, 46, 96
Albert the Great 5
Alberti, L. B. 34
Alciati, A. 18, 42
Amyot, J. 4
Aquinas, T. 5, 17, 40, 122
Aristotle (Aristotelianism) 5ff, 17, 24, 32, 87, 95, 100, 144
Arnold, T. 96, 136
Aubrey, J. 86
Augustine of Hippo 1, 3f, 12f, 28, 40, 57, 159

Bacon, F. 14, 22, 24, 30, 44, 61–80, 81, 86, 88, 94, 97, 103f, 110, 128, 130, 132, 134, 139f, 142ff, 148, 151, 162
Barbaro, E. 144
Bartolus of Saxoferrato 17
Bayle, P. 2, 19, 60, 126–31
Bede 7
Bellarmine, R. 20
Bentham, J. 67, 96, 113
Blake, W. 64, 110, 157
Bodin, J. 18ff, 23ff, 52–7, 68f, 97, 142, 152
Bolland, J. 27f
Bonhoeffer, D. 40
Bruni, L. 11
Budé, G. 15f
Burke, E. 21, 96, 111, 120
Butler, J. 96, 111, 120

Caesar, J. 7
Calvin, J. 122, 127
Camden, W. 25
Carlyle, T. 1, 24, 75, 110
Charlemagne 4, 7
Charles V 33
Charles VIII 31
Charron, P. 24
Cicero 5, 10ff, 16f, 137
Coleridge, S. T. 13, 67, 96, 110ff, 120, 136, 157
Condorcet 152
Copernicus, N. 86
Cosimo the Old 39

Cortesi 12
Cotes, R. 105
Cousin, V. 136
Cromwell, O. 40
Cusanus, N. 15, 57, 84, 104

Damian, P. 3
Dante Alighieri 3, 31
Dati, A. 37
de Thou, J. A. 25
Democritus 70
Demosthenes 100
Descartes, R. 18, 54, 63, 80, 81ff, 87f, 104ff, 108, 110, 114, 121, 127f, 134f, 136–40, 146f, 150, 152, 157, 162
Diderot, D.19
Dilthey, W. 133, 154, 160
Dionysius, pseudo- 15
Dodsworth, R. 28
Dugdale, W. 28

Elizabeth I 25
Epicurus 141
Erasmus, D. 15ff, 18
Euclid 89f
Eusebius 7

Facio, B. 14
Fichte, J. G. 1
Ficino, Marsilio 14
Fontenelle, B. de 109
Foxe, J. 20
Francis of Assisi 38
Freud, S. 133, 151

Galilei, G. 84, 86, 90f, 104f, 109, 131, 134, 139
Gibbon, E. 20, 141
Grotius, J. 115, 140, 142, 150
Guicciardini, F. 12, 30, 38f, 42, 46–51, 54, 58, 97, 101
Gustavus Adolphus 130

Hannibal 36
Harvey, W. 86, 90
Hearne, W. 25
Hegel, G. W. F. 56

Henry VII 79f
Herder, J. G. 133, 136, 156, 160
Hermann of Cologne 3
Hickes, G. 25
Hippocrates 70
Hobbes, T. 23f, 63, 67, 78, 81f, 86–103, 104, 106, 110, 113f, 116ff, 141, 143, 158, 162
Holinshed, R. 22
Homer 100, 148
Hooker, R. 96, 115
Hume, D. 2, 119

James I 25
Joachim of Fiore 27, 152
Jung, C. G. 133

Kant, I. 64, 144
Kepler, J. 84, 104
Kierkegaard, S. 157

La Popelinière, L. V. 19
Le Clerk, J. 132
Leibniz, G. W. 105, 120–6, 142
Leland, J. 25
Leonardo da Vinci 84, 104
Le Roy, L. 19
Livy 12, 43'
Locke, J. 19, 47, 54, 67, 81f, 88, 104, 106, 110–20, 123
Lorenzo the Magnificent 34
Lucretius 14, 97, 141ff, 147
Luther, M. 1, 20, 39f, 68

Mabillon, J. 28, 125, 135
Machiavelli, N. 12, 14, 22ff, 30–51, 53f, 79, 86, 88, 96f, 112, 117, 141, 143
Malebranche, N. 81f, 85f
Marx, K. 133
Michelet, J. 136
Mill, J. S. 66
Montaigne, M. de 1, 57–60, 127, 152, 159
Montesquieu, C. L. J. de S. 19, 52, 55, 129, 132, 152, 155
Montfaucon, B. de 28
Muratori, L. O. 125

Niebuhr, B. G. 26, 136, 140
Niebuhr, R. 40
Newman, J. H. 111, 120
Newton, I. 19, 87f, 104–110, 123f 139, 162

North, T. 4

Odo of Cluny 3
Origen 17
Otloh of St Emmeram 3

Pappenbroch, D. 27
Pascal, B. 60, 80, 154
Pasquier, E. 18f
Petrarch, F. 2f, 12ff, 39, 57
Pico della Mirandola 6, 144
Plato (Platonism) 5, 70, 87, 140ff, 148
Plutarch 4
Poggio Brachiolini 43
Polo, M. 6
Pontano, G. 145
Pope, A. 144
Pufendorf, S. 115, 150

Ralegh, W. 22f, 25
Ranke, L. von 1, 26, 76, 101
Ronmauld 3
Rosweyde, H. 27
Rousseau, J.-J. 60, 97, 117, 127, 159

Sallust 12, 43
Salutati, C. 10, 145
Scaliger, J. 19
Scott, W. 26
Selden, J. 150
Seneca 10
Sextus Empiricus 24
Shakespeare, W. 22
Sidney, P. 24, 78
Spinoza, B. 63, 84, 88, 116, 121, 129, 142

Tacitus 12, 53, 59, 79, 140ff
Temple, W. 40
Thucydides 89, 100
Tillemont, L. S. de N. 125
Toland, J. 110
Troeltsch, E. 81

Valla, L. 6, 14ff, 65, 144
Vergil, P. 22, 25
Vico, G. B. 15, 18f, 53ff, 68, 74, 77, 83, 88, 97f, 102f, 108, 110, 112f, 132–163
Vincent of Lerins 107
Voltaire 19f, 42f, 81, 120, 126f, 129f, 152

Wanley, H. 25
William of Malmesbury 3, 8

Wolf, F. A. 136, 140, 148
Wordsworth, W. 83

For Product Safety Concerns and Information please contact our EU
representative GPSR@taylorandfrancis.com
Taylor & Francis Verlag GmbH, Kaufingerstraße 24, 80331 München, Germany

www.ingramcontent.com/pod-product-compliance
Lightning Source LLC
Chambersburg PA
CBHW070300230426
43664CB00014B/2593